FOR ORGANS, PIANOS & ELECTRONIC KEYBOARDS

E-Z PLAY® TODAY

187

ULT...
CHRISTMAS

• 75 SEASONAL FAVORITES •

ISBN 0-634-03266-6

HAL•LEONARD®
CORPORATION
7777 W. BLUEMOUND RD. P.O. BOX 13819 MILWAUKEE, WI 53213

E-Z Play® Today Music Notation © 1975 by HAL LEONARD CORPORATION

E-Z PLAY and EASY ELECTRONIC KEYBOARD MUSIC are registered trademarks of HAL LEONARD CORPORATION.

Visit Hal Leonard Online at
www.halleonard.com

FOR ORGANS, PIANOS & ELECTRONIC KEYBOARDS

EZPLAY TODAY

187

ULTIMATE

CHRISTMAS

• 75 SEASONAL FAVORITES •

Angels We Have Heard on High

Registration 3
Rhythm: None

Traditional French Carol
Translated by James Chadwick

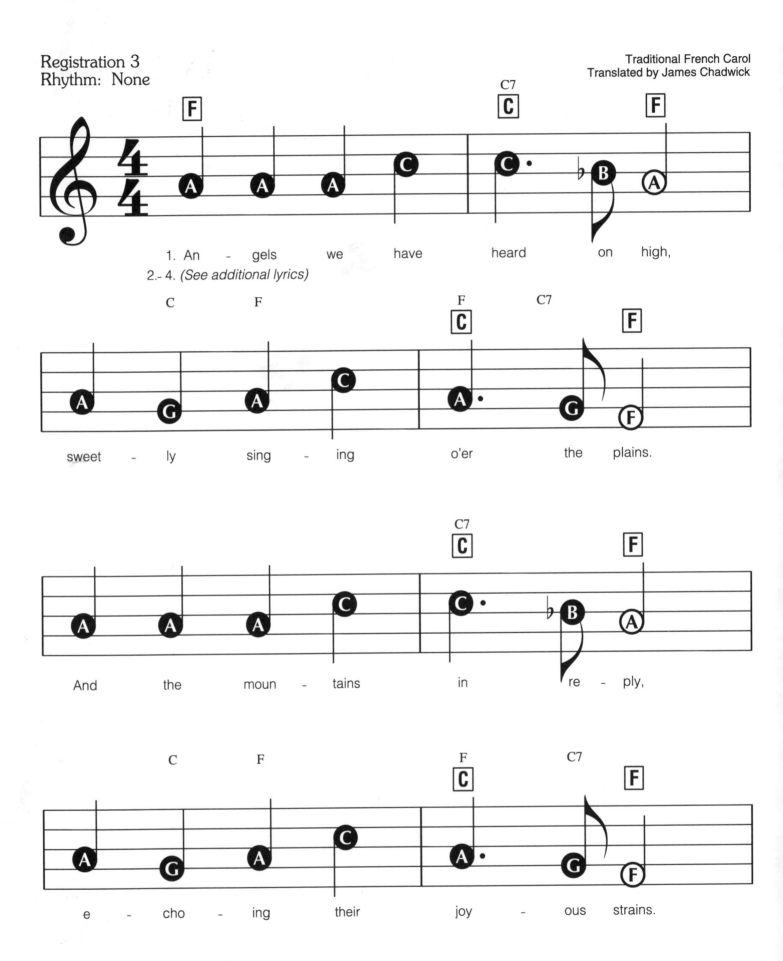

1. An - gels we have heard on high,
2.- 4. (See additional lyrics)

sweet - ly sing - ing o'er the plains.

And the moun - tains in re - ply,

e - cho - ing their joy - ous strains.

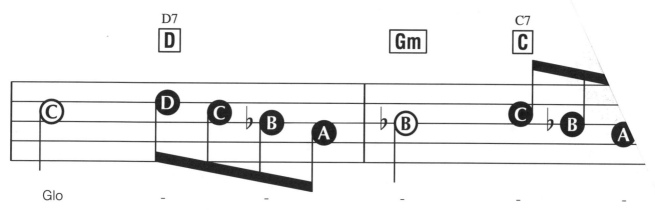

Glo - - - - -

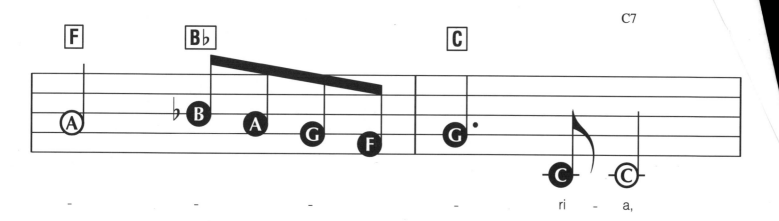

- - - - ri - a,

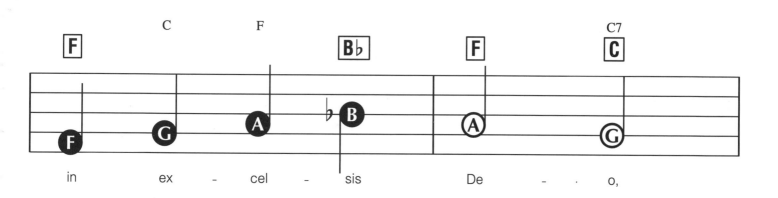

in ex - cel - sis De - o,

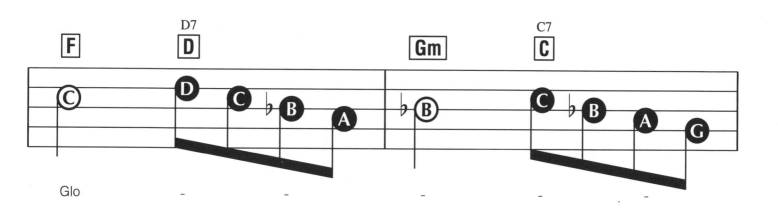

Glo - - - -

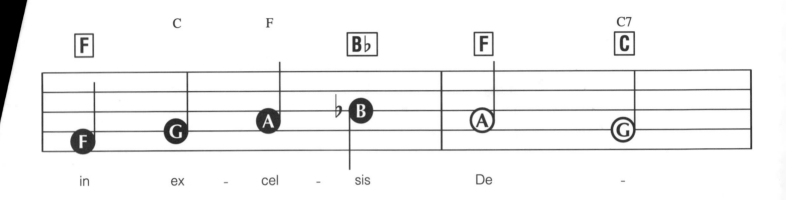

\-   \-   \-   \-   ri - a,

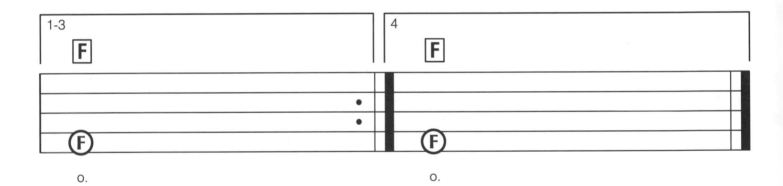

in   ex - cel - sis   De   \-

o.   o.

Additional Lyrics

2. Shepherds, why this jubilee?
   Why your joyous strains prolong?
   Say what may the tidings be,
   which inspire your heavenly song?

   Gloria, in excelsis Deo,
   Gloria, in excelsis Deo.

3. Come to Bethlehem and see,
   Him whose birth the angels sing.
   Come, adore on bended knee,
   Christ the Lord, the newborn King!

   Gloria, in excelsis Deo,
   Gloria, in excelsis Deo.

4. See within a manger laid Jesus,
   Lord of heaven and earth!
   Mary, Joseph, lend your aid,
   with us sing our Savior's birth.

   Gloria, in excelsis Deo,
   Gloria, in excelsis Deo.

Carol of the Bells

Registration 1
Rhythm: Waltz

Ukrainian Christmas Carol

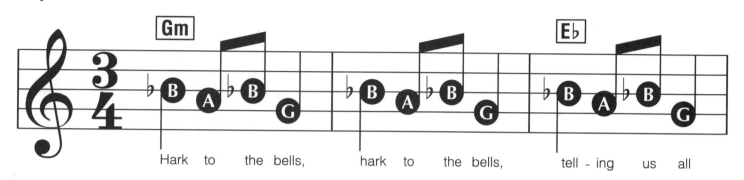

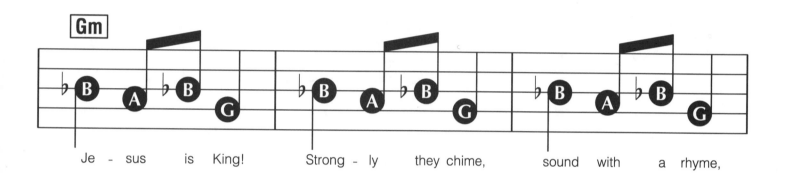

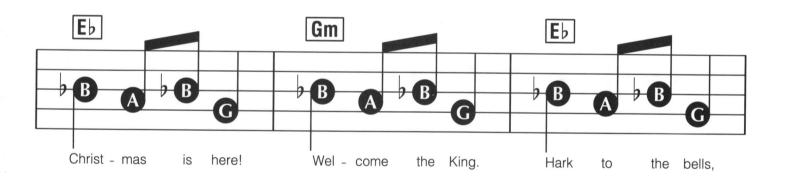

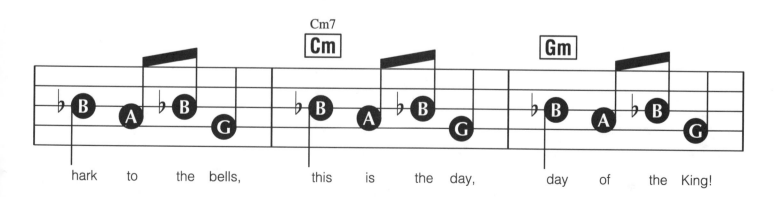

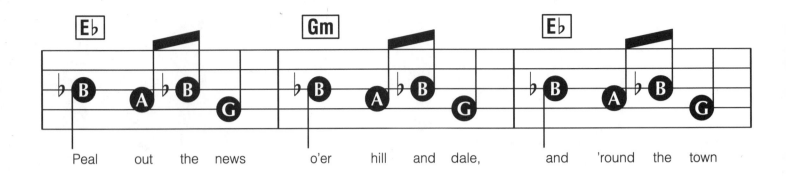

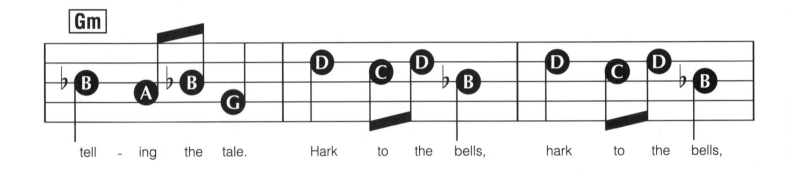

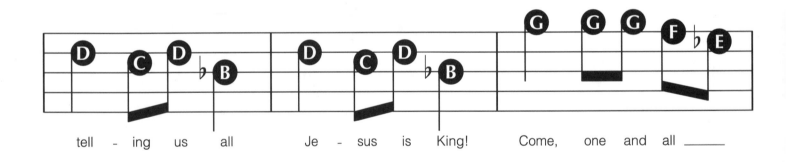

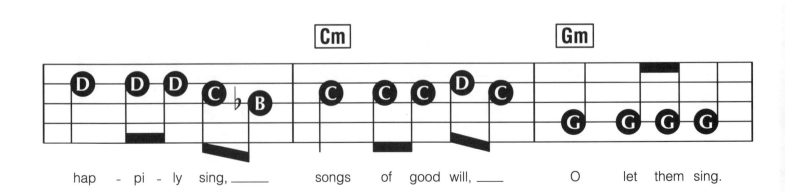

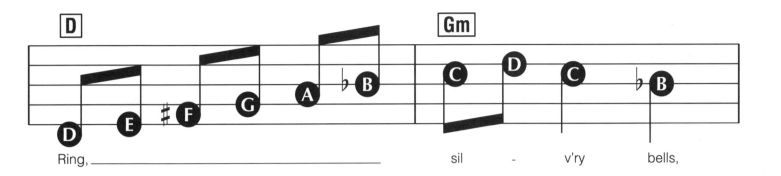

Ring, _____ sil - v'ry bells,

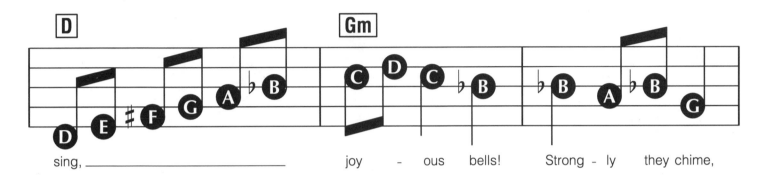

sing, _____ joy - ous bells! Strong - ly they chime,

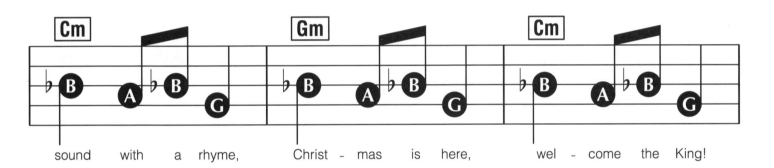

sound with a rhyme, Christ - mas is here, wel - come the King!

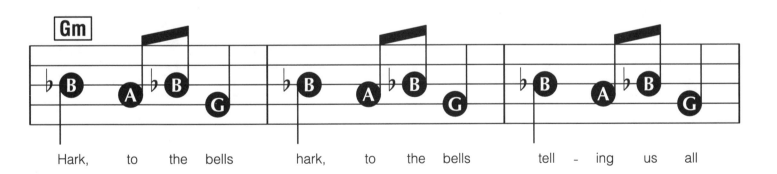

Hark, to the bells hark, to the bells tell - ing us all

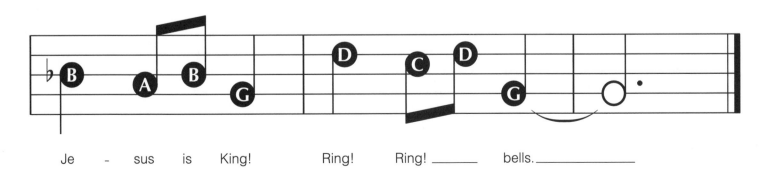

Je - sus is King! Ring! Ring! _____ bells. _____

Away in a Manger

Registration 1
Rhythm: Waltz

Traditional
Words by John T. McFarland (v.3)
Music by William J. Kirkpatrick

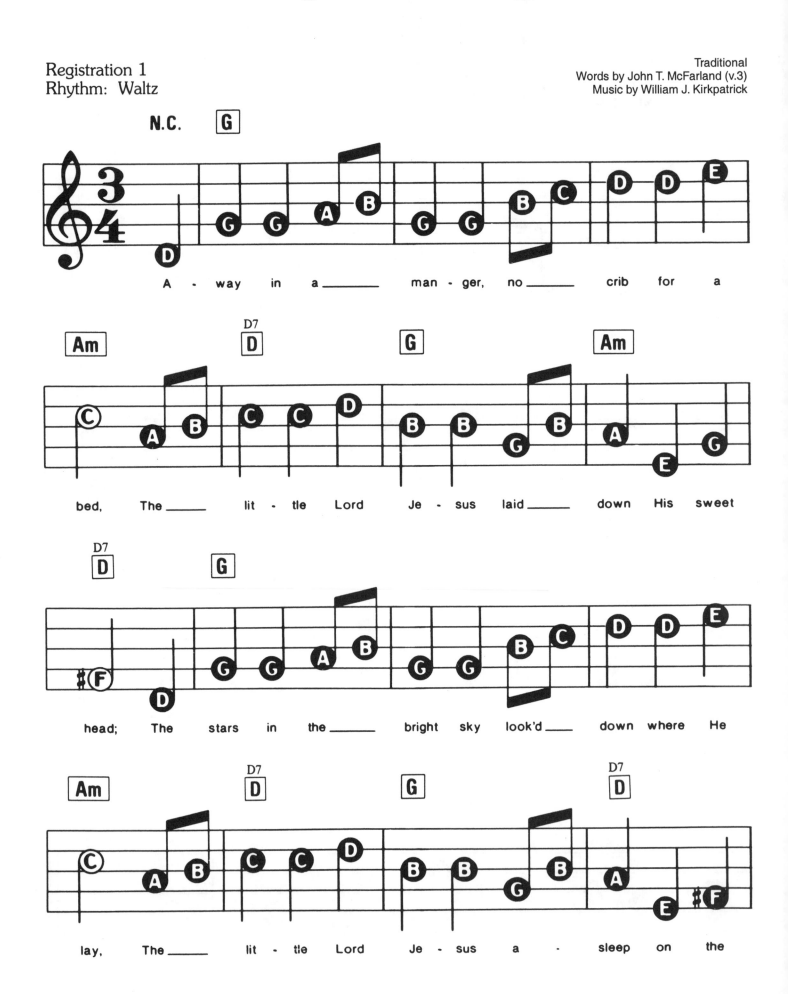

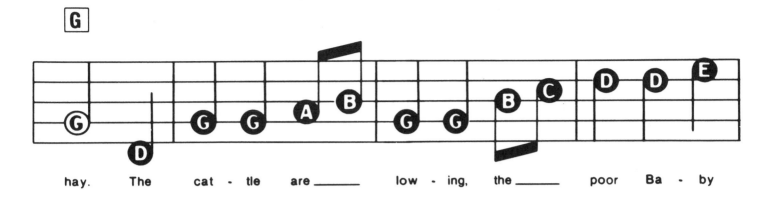

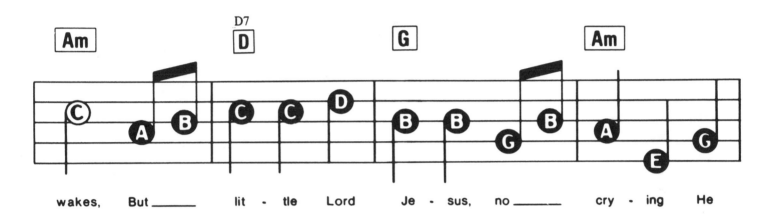

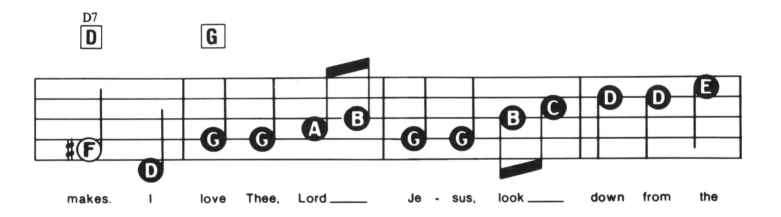

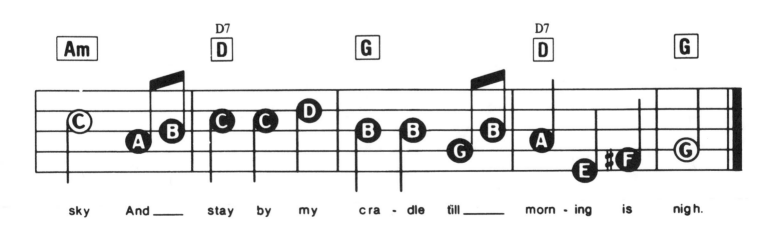

Away in a Manger

Registration 1
Rhythm: Waltz

Traditional
Words by John T. McFarland (v.3)
Music by James R. Murray

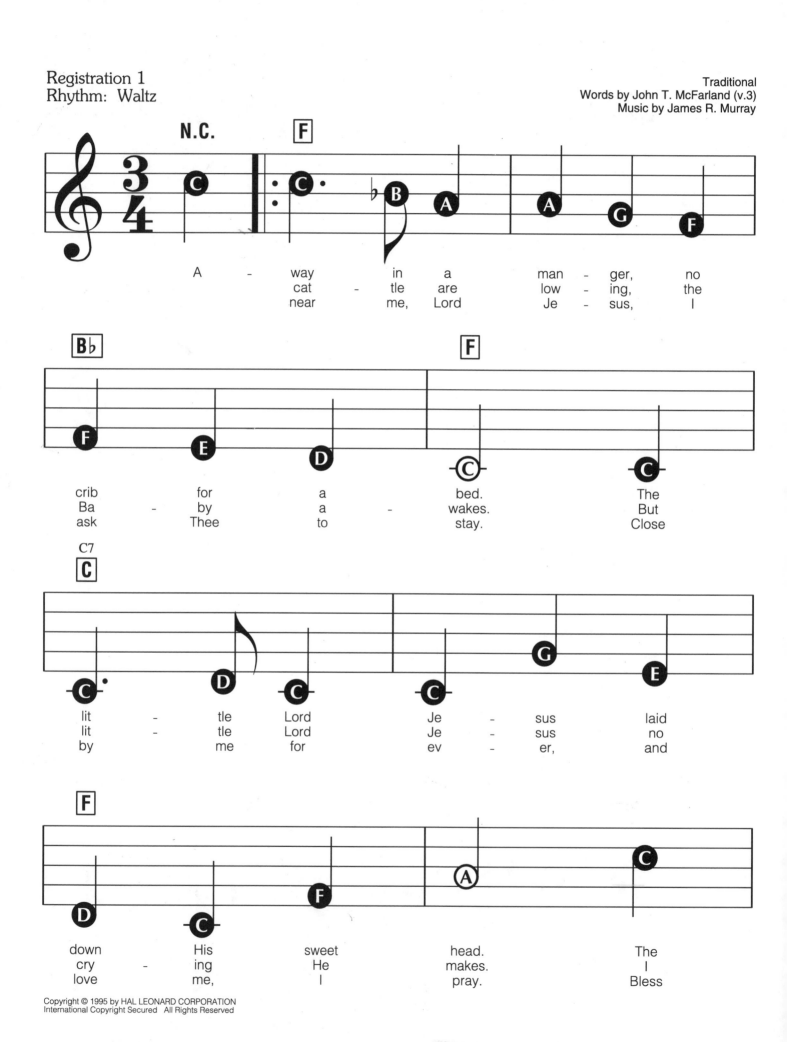

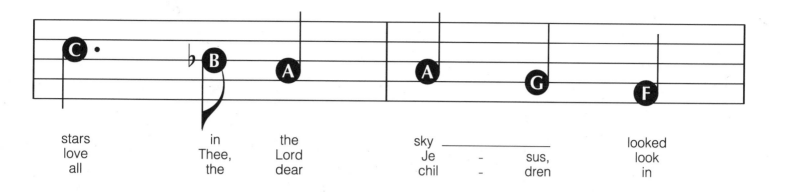

stars   in   the   sky —————— looked
love   Thee,   the Lord   Je - sus,   look
all   the   dear   chil - dren   in

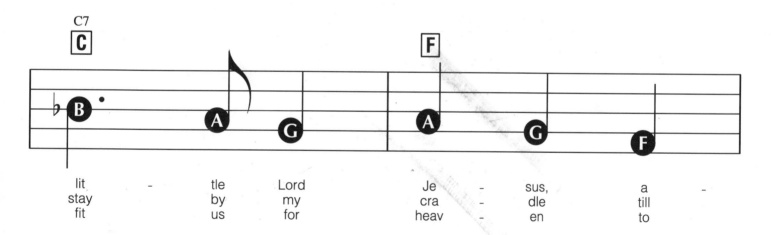

down   where   He   lay.   The
down   from   the   sky.   And
Thy   ten - der   care.   And

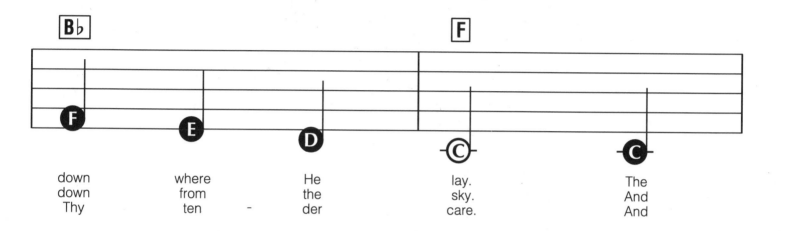

lit - tle   Lord   Je - sus,   a -
stay   by   my   cra - dle   till
fit   us   for   heav - en   to

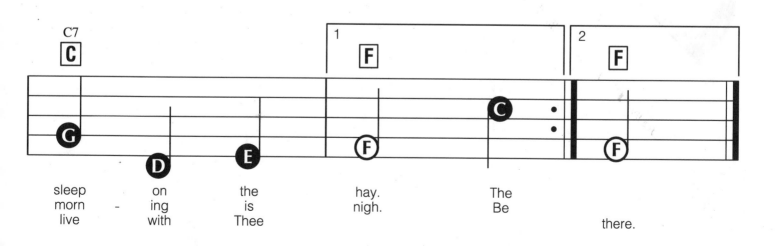

sleep   on   the   hay.   The
morn - ing   is   nigh.   Be
live   with   Thee   there.

Bring a Torch, Jeannette, Isabella

14

Registration 3
Rhythm: None

17th Century French Provençal Carol

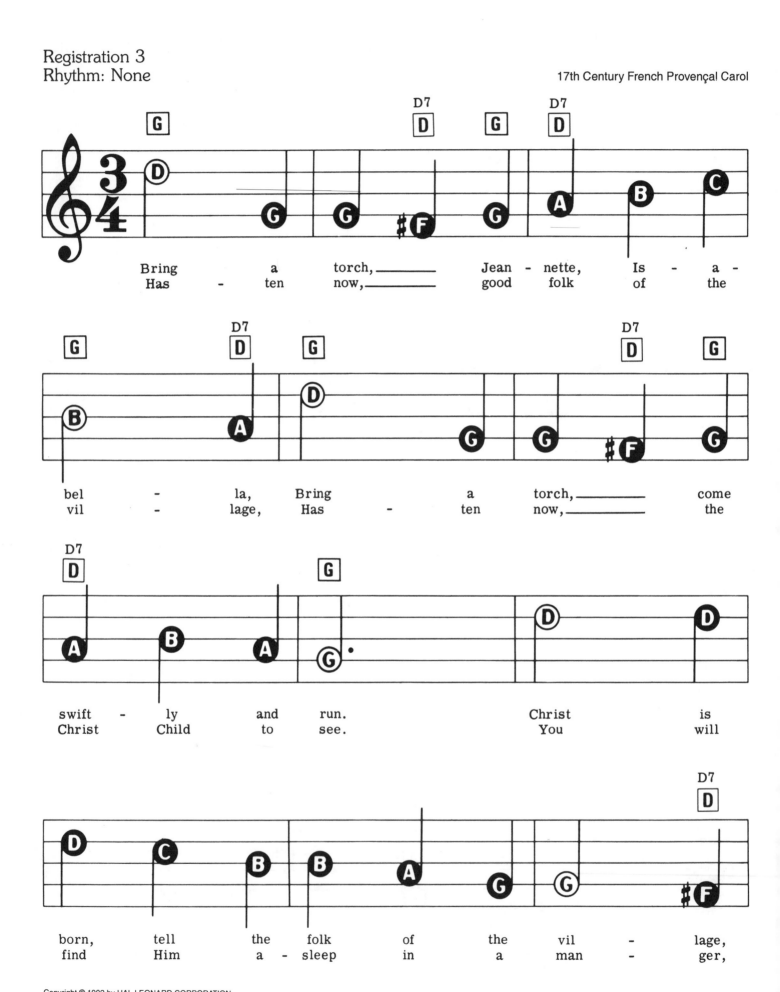

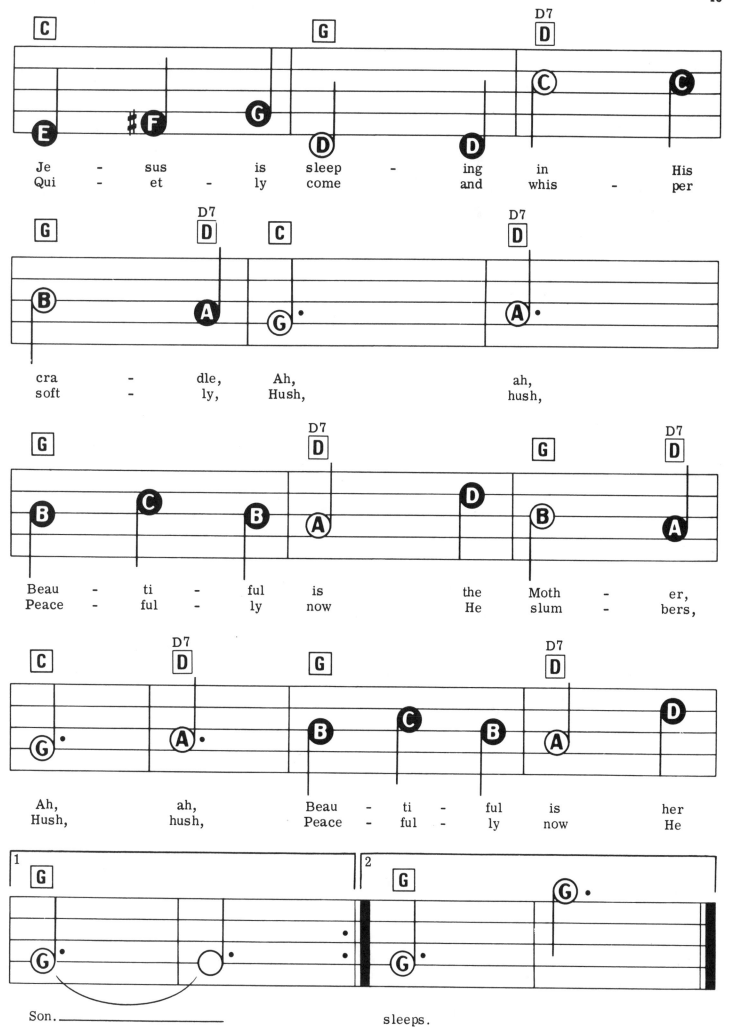

Caroling, Caroling

Registration 5
Rhythm: 6/8 March or Waltz

Words by Wihla Hutson
Music by Alfred Burt

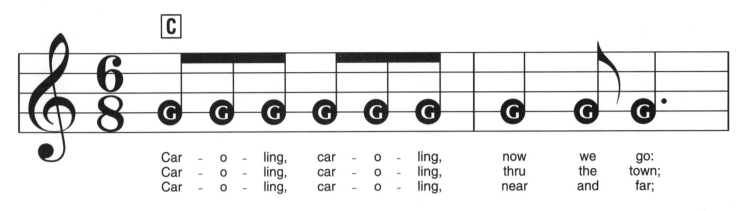

Car - o - ling, car - o - ling, now we go:
Car - o - ling, car - o - ling, thru the town;
Car - o - ling, car - o - ling, near and far;

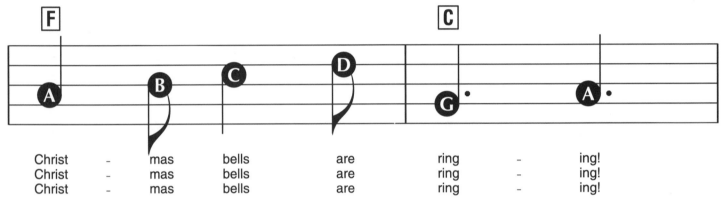

Christ - mas bells are ring - ing!
Christ - mas bells are ring - ing!
Christ - mas bells are ring - ing!

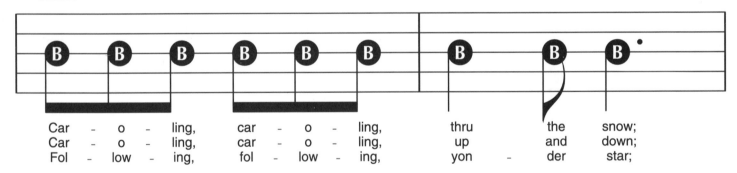

Car - o - ling, car - o - ling, thru the snow;
Car - o - ling, car - o - ling, up and down;
Fol - low - ing, fol - low - ing, yon - der star;

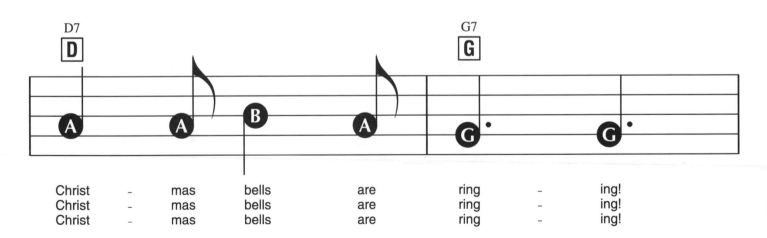

Christ - mas bells are ring - ing!
Christ - mas bells are ring - ing!
Christ - mas bells are ring - ing!

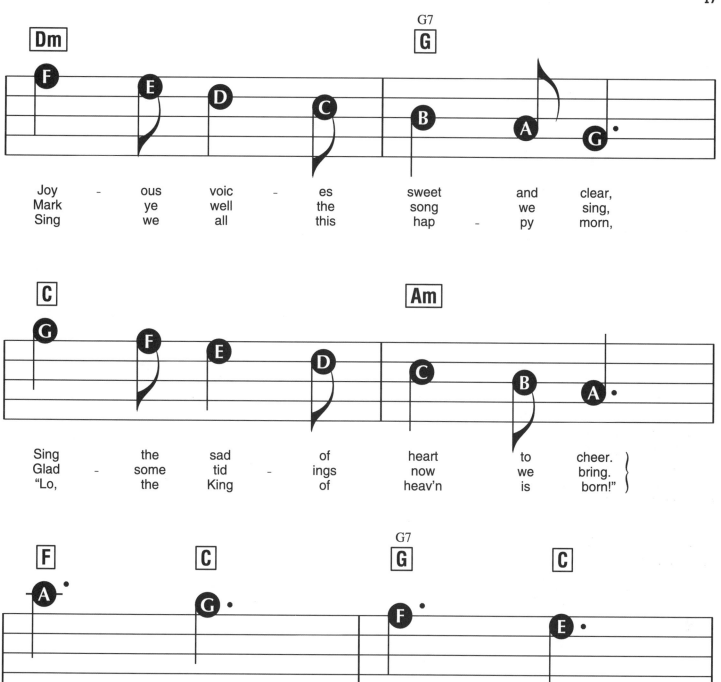

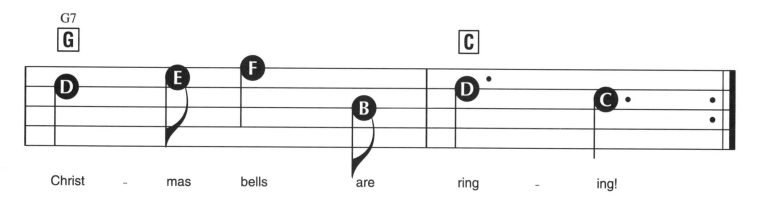

The Chipmunk Song

Registration 3
Rhythm: Waltz

Words and Music by
Ross Bagdasarian

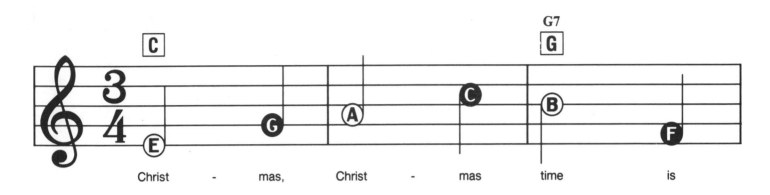

Christ - mas, Christ - mas time is

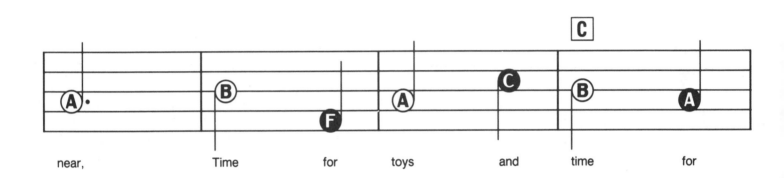

near, Time for toys and time for

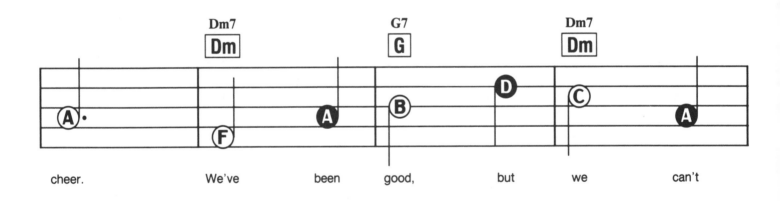

cheer. We've been good, but we can't

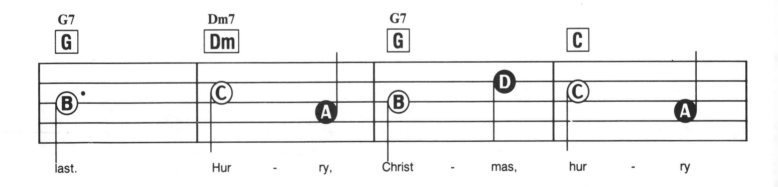

last. Hur - ry, Christ - mas, hur - ry

19

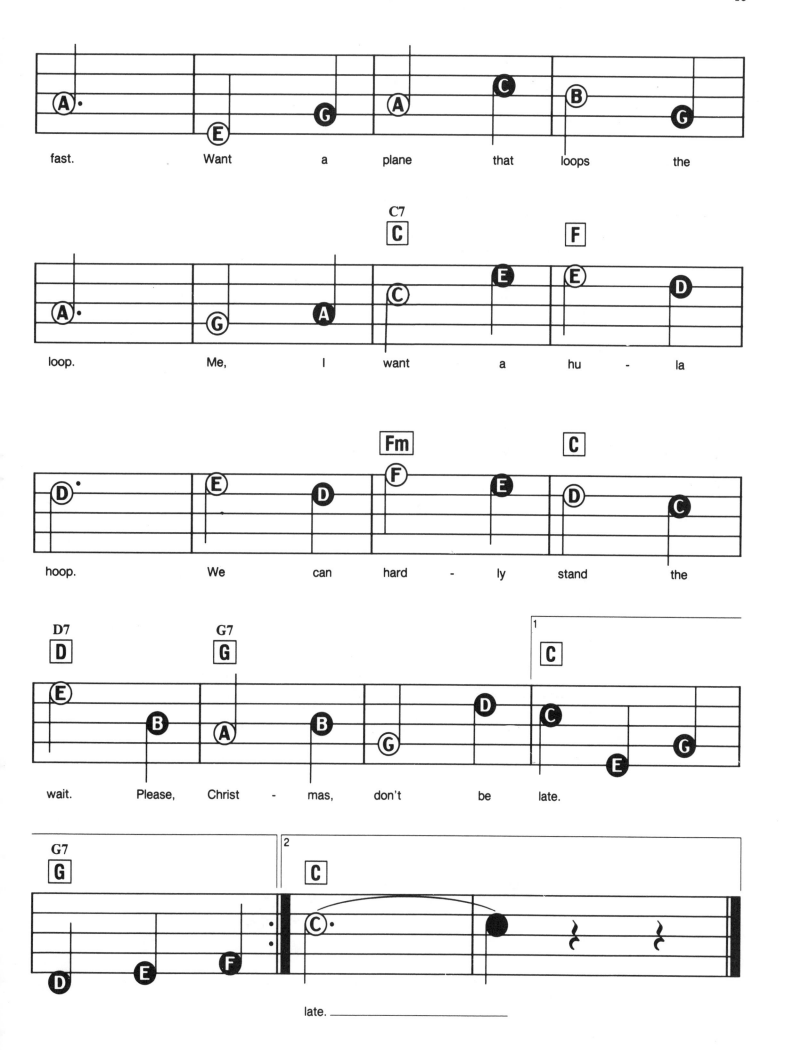

C-H-R-I-S-T-M-A-S

Registration 5
Rhythm: Fox Trot or Ballad

Words by Jenny Lou Carson
Music by Eddy Arnold

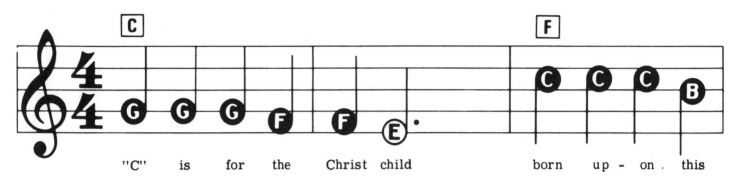

"C" is for the Christ child born up-on this

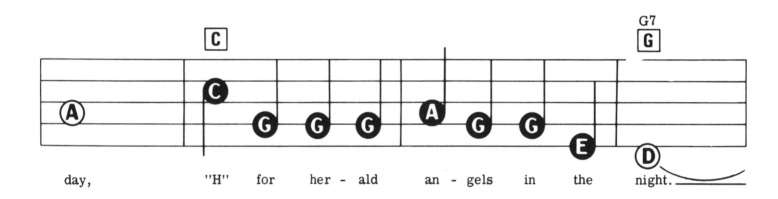

day, "H" for her-ald an-gels in the night.

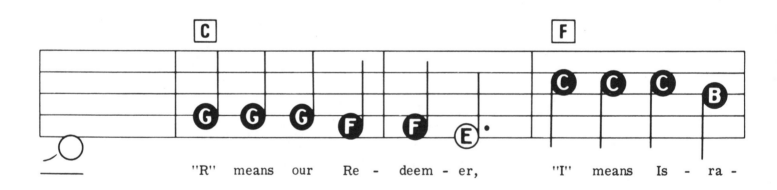

"R" means our Re-deem-er, "I" means Is-ra-

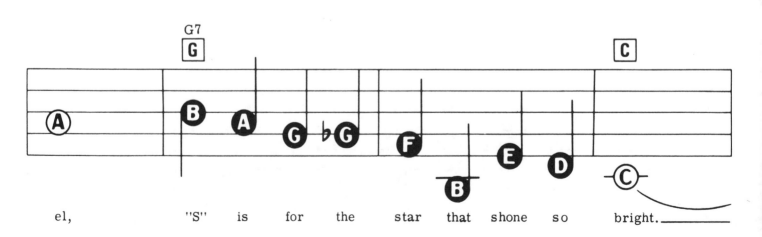

el, "S" is for the star that shone so bright.

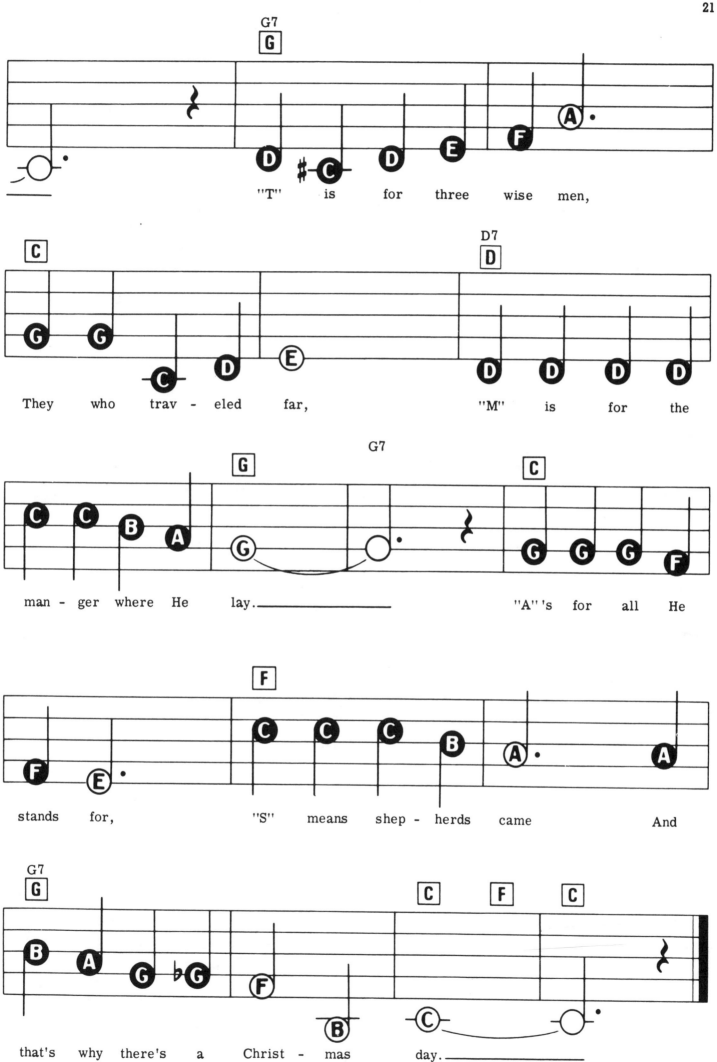

Christmas Time Is Here

Words by Lee Mendelson
Music by Vince Guaraldi

Registration 8
Rhythm: Waltz

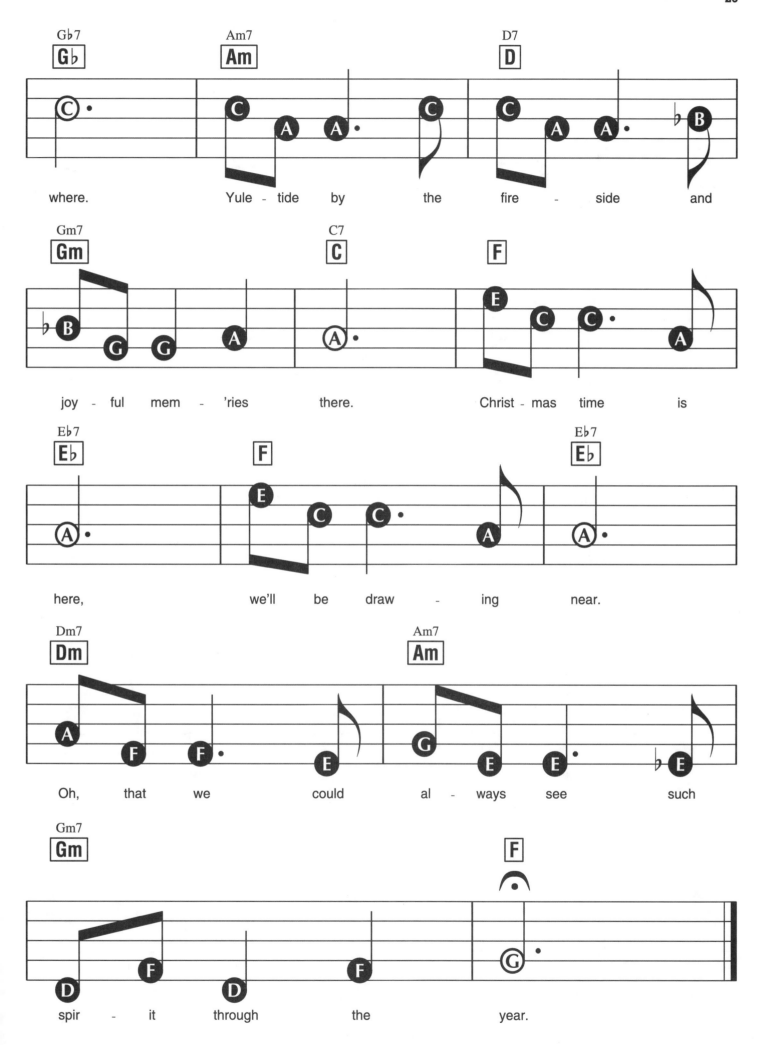

The Christmas Waltz

Words by Sammy Cahn
Music by Jule Styne

Registration 2
Rhythm: Waltz

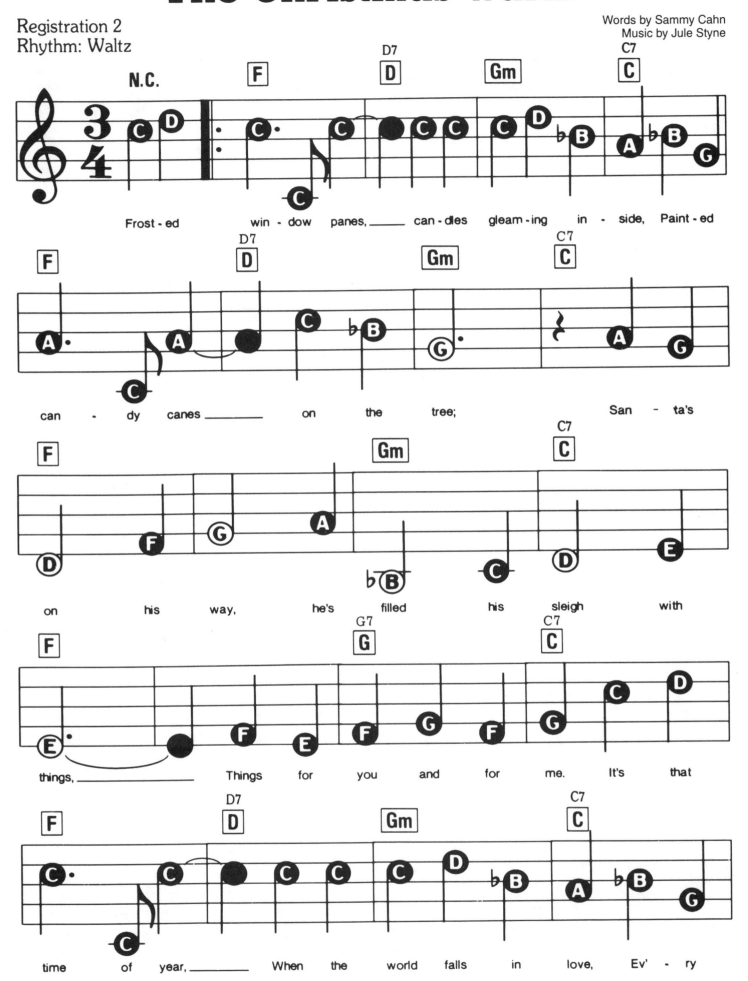

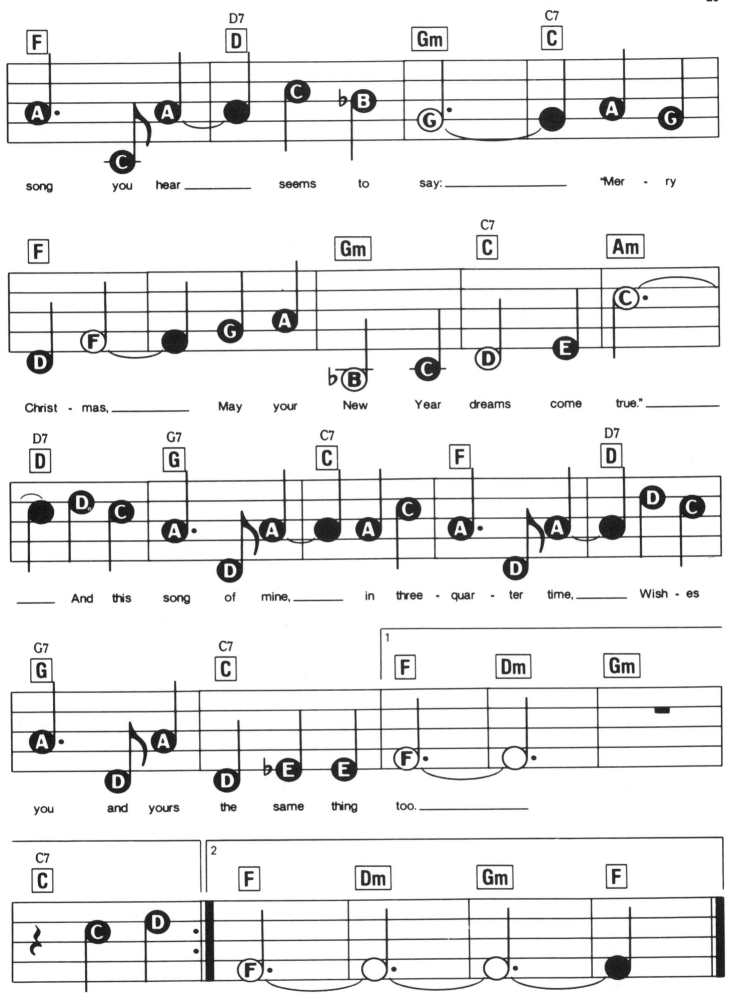

Coventry Carol

Registration 1
Rhythm: None

Words by Robert Croo
Traditional English Melody

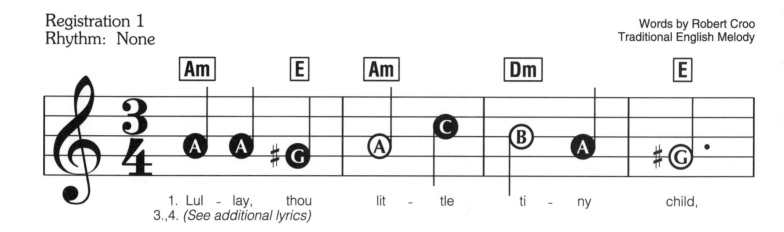

1. Lul - lay, thou lit - tle ti - ny child,
3.,4. *(See additional lyrics)*

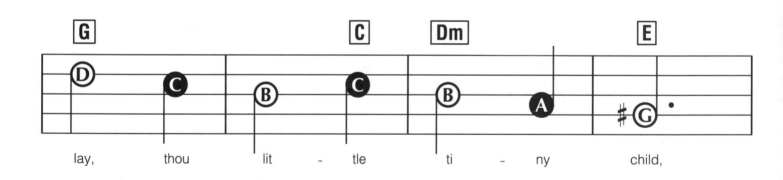

by, by, lul - ly, lul - lay. _____ Lul -

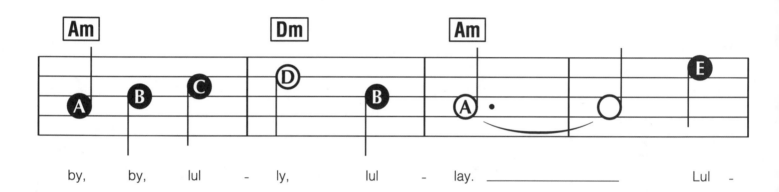

lay, thou lit - tle ti - ny child,

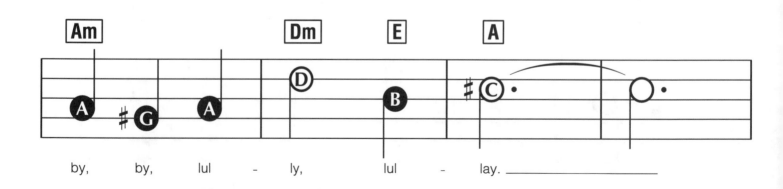

by, by, lul - ly, lul - lay. _____

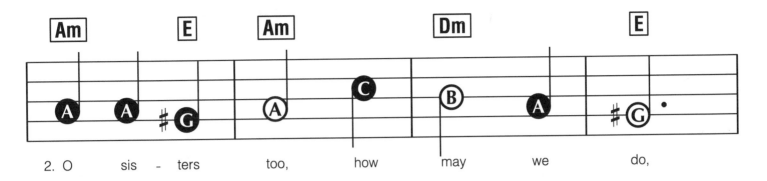

2. O sis - ters too, how may we do,

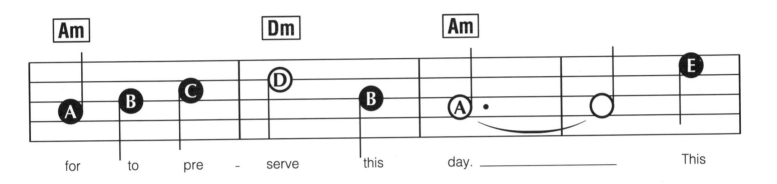

for to pre - serve this day. _____ This

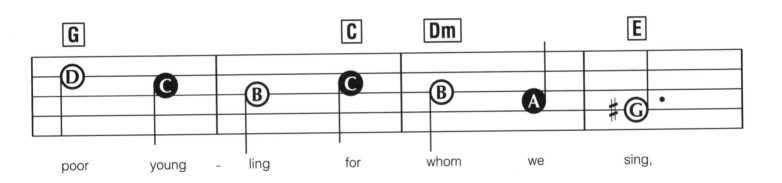

poor young - ling for whom we sing,

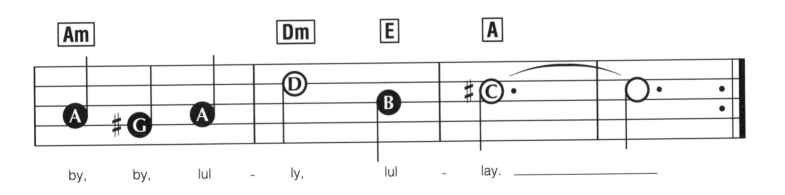

by, by, lul - ly, lul - lay. _____

Additional Lyrics

3. Herod the king, in his raging,
   charged he hath this day.
   His men of might, in his own sight,
   all young children to slay.

4. That woe is me, poor child for thee!
   And ever morn and day.
   For thy parting neither say nor sing,
   by by, lully lullay!

Deck the Hall

Registration 5
Rhythm: Fox Trot

Traditional Welsh Carol

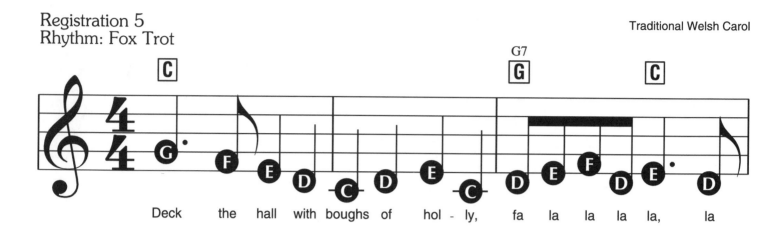

Deck the hall with boughs of hol - ly, fa la la la la, la

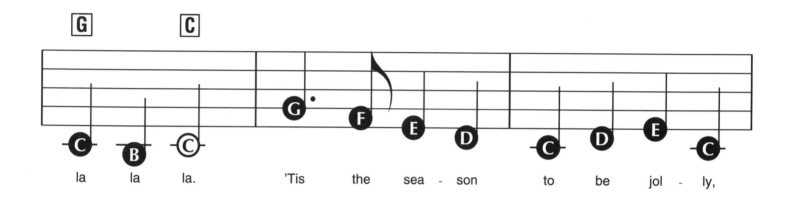

la la la. 'Tis the sea - son to be jol - ly,

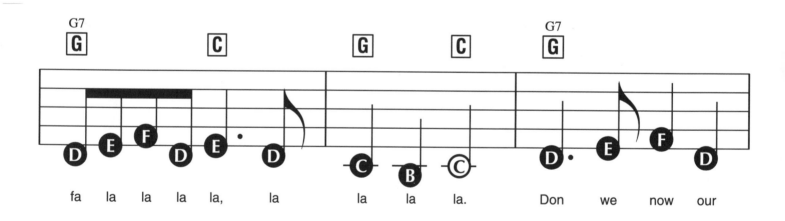

fa la la la la, la la la la. Don we now our

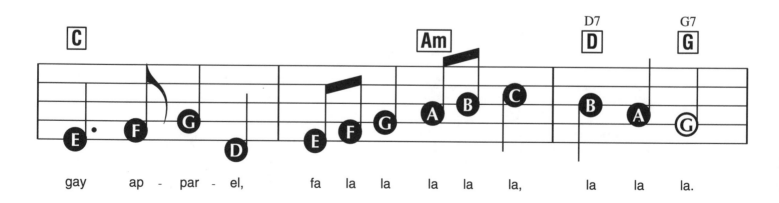

gay ap - par - el, fa la la la la la, la la la la.

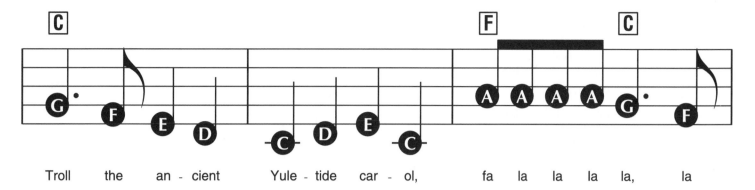

Troll the an - cient Yule - tide car - ol, fa la la la la, la

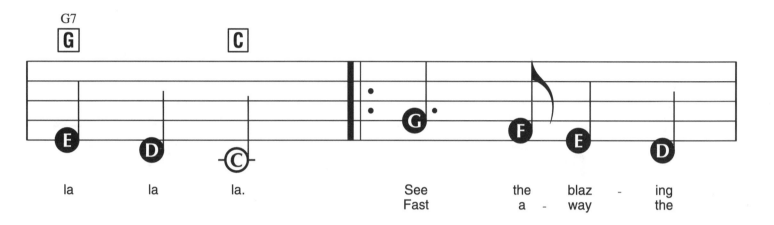

la la la. See the blaz - ing
Fast a - way the

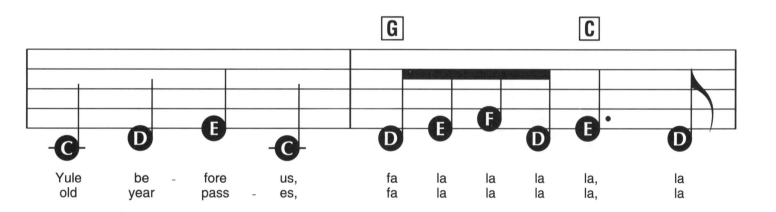

Yule be - fore us, fa la la la la, la
old year pass - es, fa la la la la, la

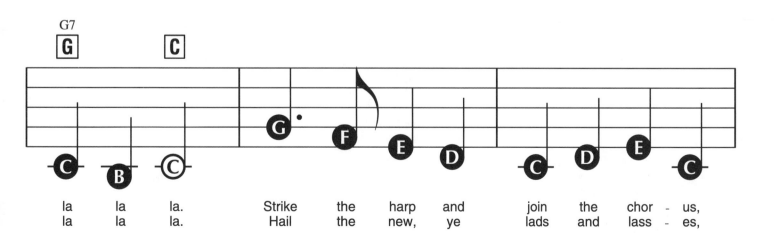

la la la. Strike the harp and join the chor - us,
la la la. Hail the new, ye lads and lass - es,

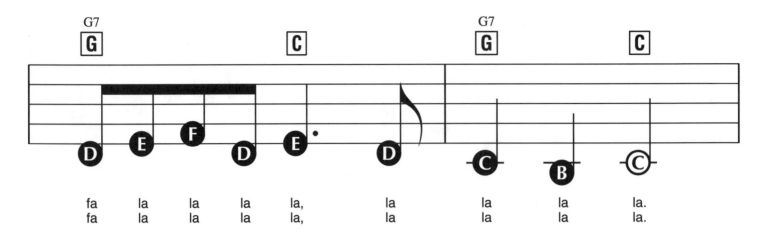

fa la la la la, la la la la.
fa la la la la, la la la la.

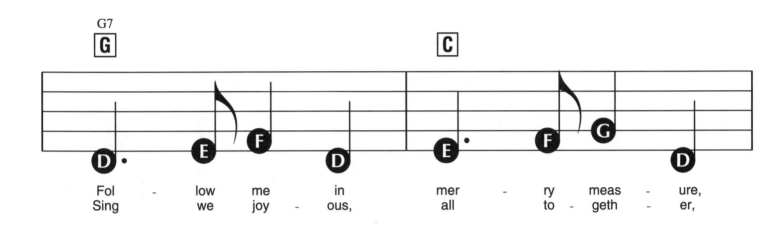

Fol - low me in mer - ry meas - ure,
Sing we joy - ous, all to - geth - er,

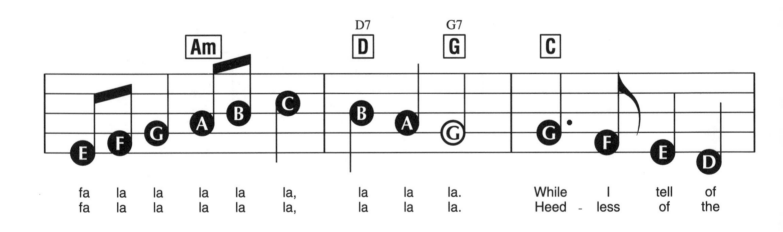

fa la la la la la, la la la. While I tell of
fa la la la la la, la la la. Heed - less of the

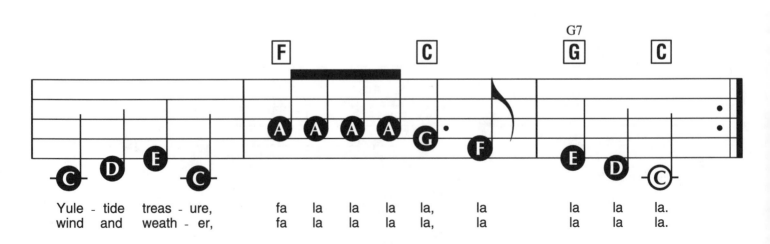

Yule - tide treas - ure, fa la la la la, la la la la.
wind and weath - er, fa la la la la, la la la la.

Do You Hear What I Hear

Registration 4
Rhythm: None

Words and Music by Noel Regney
and Gloria Shayne

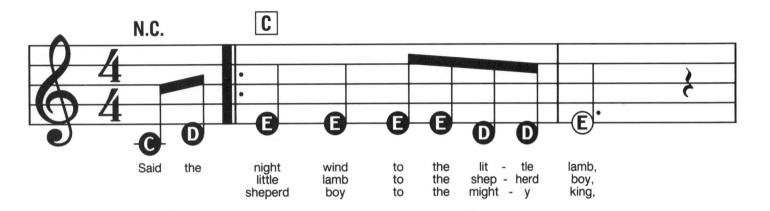

Said the night wind to the lit-tle lamb,
little lamb wind to the shep-herd boy,
sheperd lamb boy to the might-y king,

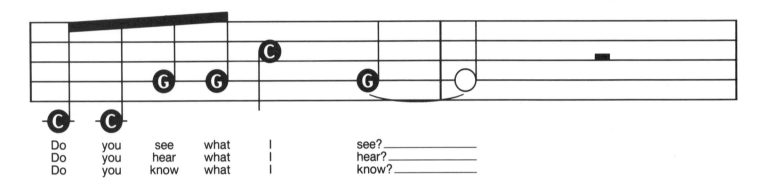

Do you see what I see?
Do you hear what I hear?
Do you know what I know?

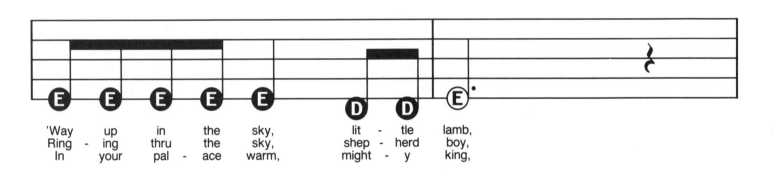

'Way up in the sky, lit-tle lamb,
Ring-ing thru the sky, shep-herd boy,
In your pal-ace warm, might-y king,

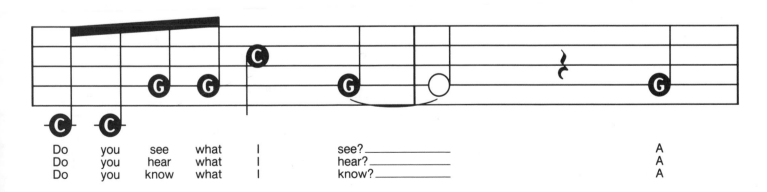

Do you see what I see? A
Do you hear what I hear? A
Do you know what I know? A

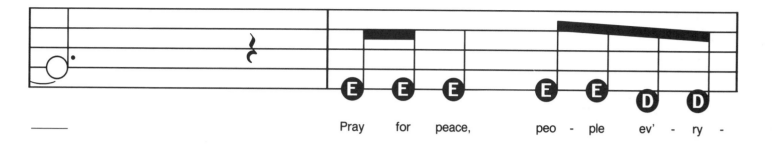

Pray for peace, peo - ple ev' - ry -

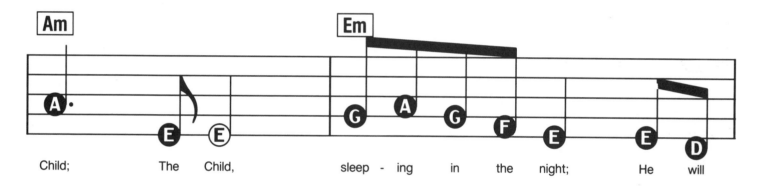

where, Lis - ten to what I say!_____ The

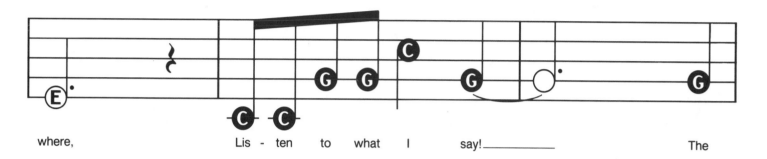

Child; The Child, sleep - ing in the night; He will

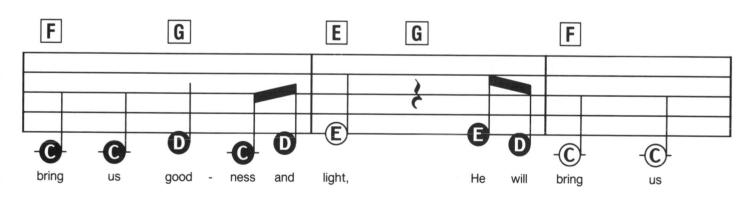

bring us good - ness and light, He will bring us

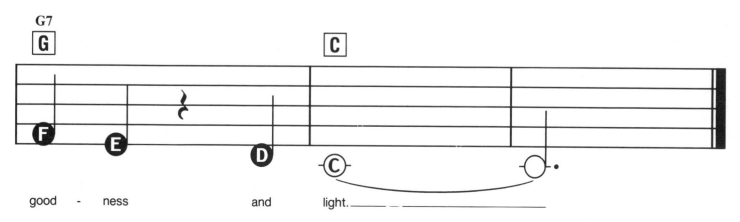

good - ness and light.____ _____

The First Noel

Registration 10
Rhythm: None

17th Century English Carol
Music from *W. Sandys' Christmas Carols*

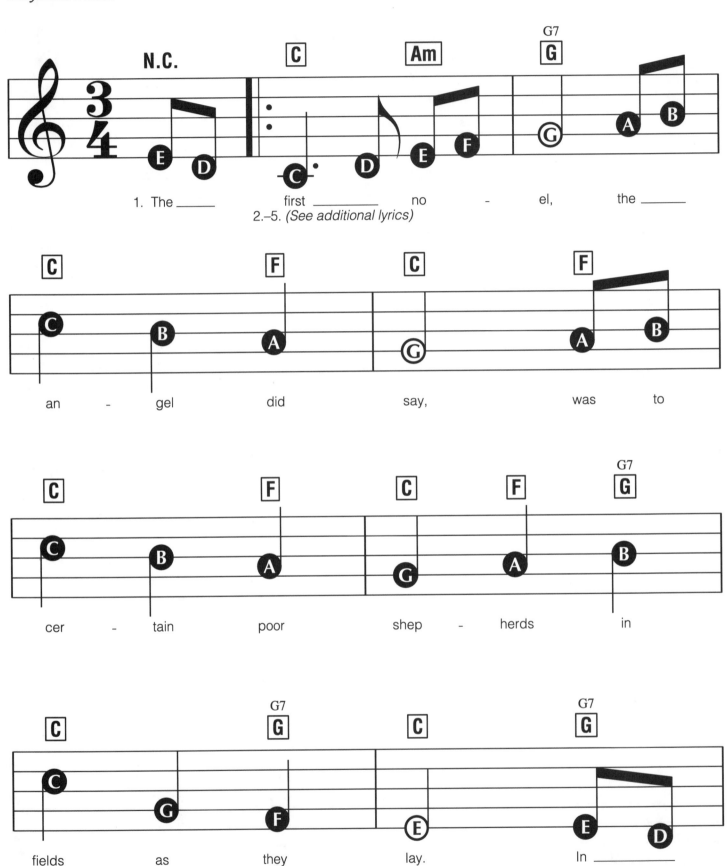

1. The _____ first _____ no - el, the _____
2.–5. *(See additional lyrics)*

an - gel did say, was to

cer - tain poor shep - herds in

fields as they lay. In _____

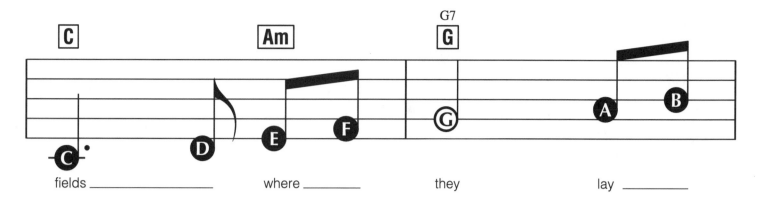

fields _____ where _____ they lay _____

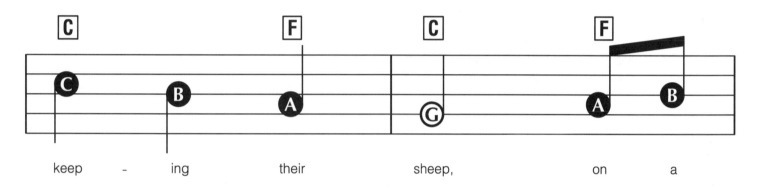

keep - ing their sheep, on a

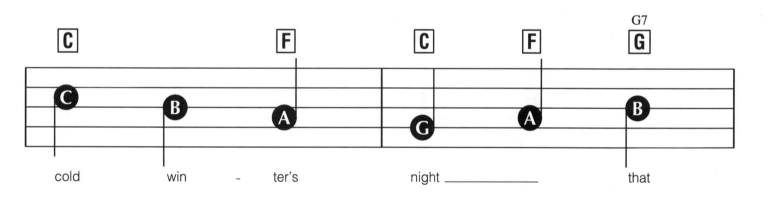

cold win - ter's night _____ that

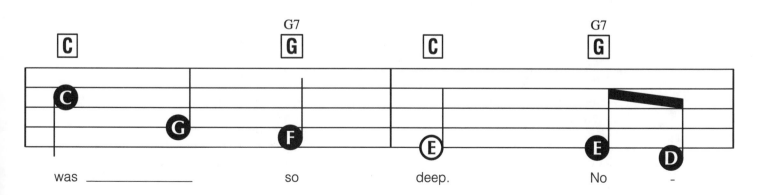

was _____ so deep. No -

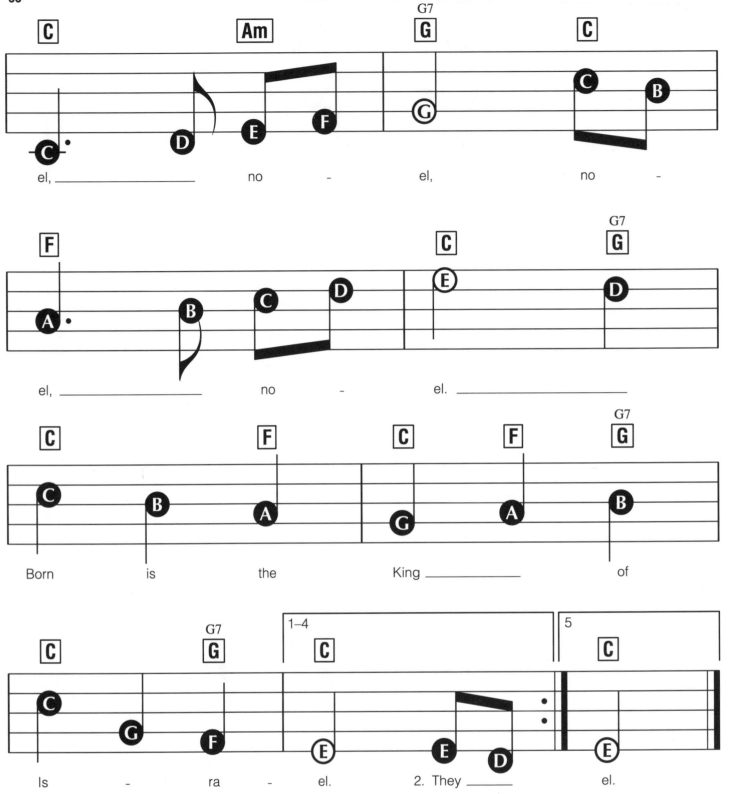

Additional Lyrics

2. They looked up and saw a star,
shining in the east, beyond them far.
And to the earth it gave great light,
and so it continued both day and night.
Noel, noel, noel, noel.
Born is the King of Israel.

3. And by the light of that same star,
three wisemen came from country far.
To seek for a King was their intent,
and to follow the star wherever it went.
Noel, noel, noel, noel.
Born is the King of Israel.

4. This star drew nigh to the northwest,
o'er Bethlehem it took its rest.
And there it did both stop and stay,
right over the place where Jesus lay.
Noel, noel, noel, noel.
Born is the King of Israel.

5. Then entered in those wisemen three,
full reverently upon the knee.
And offered there, in His presence,
their gold, and myrrh, and frankincense.
Noel, noel, noel, noel.
Born is the King of Israel.

Frosty the Snow Man

Registration 2
Rhythm: Fox Trot or Swing

Words and Music by Steve Nelson
and Jack Rollins

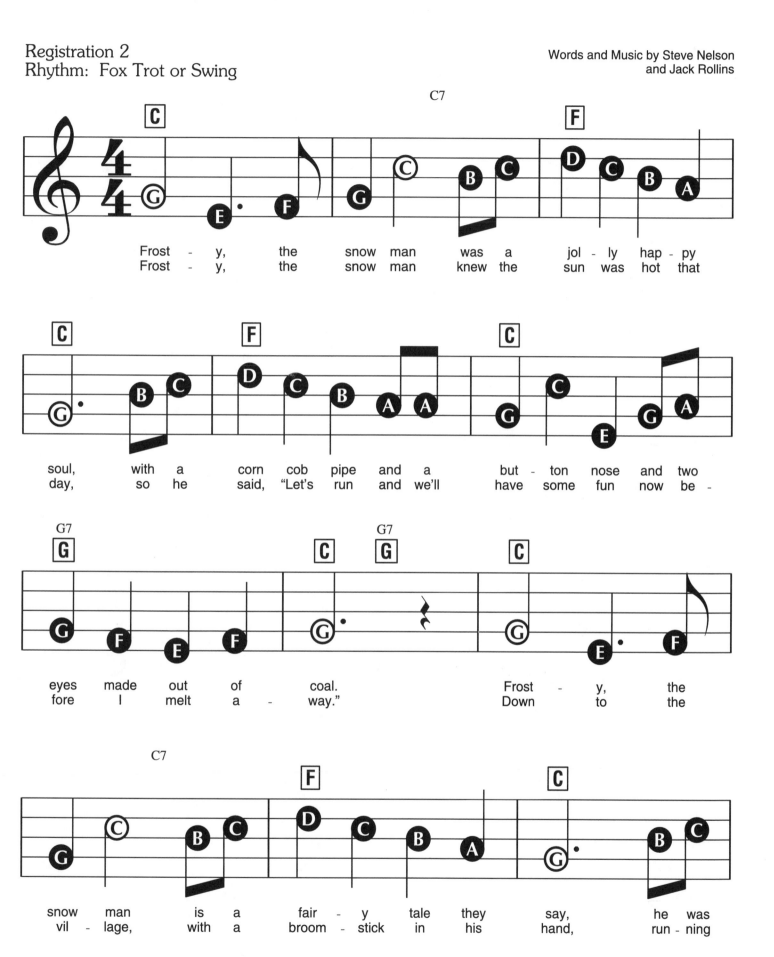

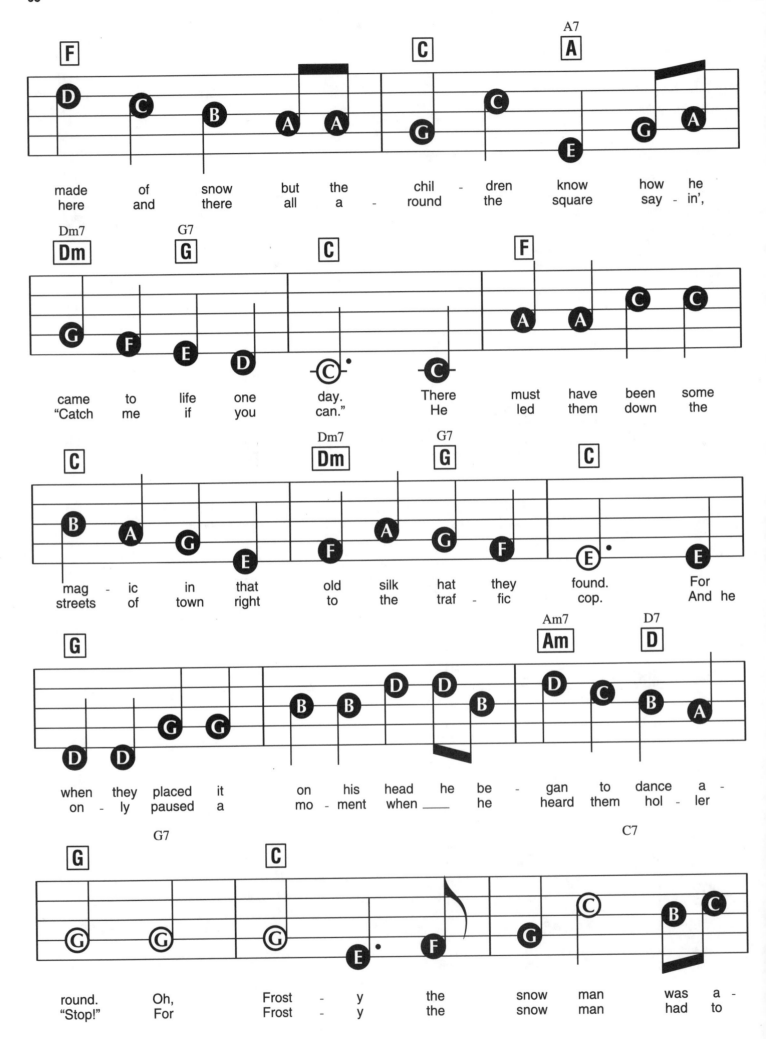

The Friendly Beasts

Registration 2
Rhythm: Waltz

Traditional English Carol

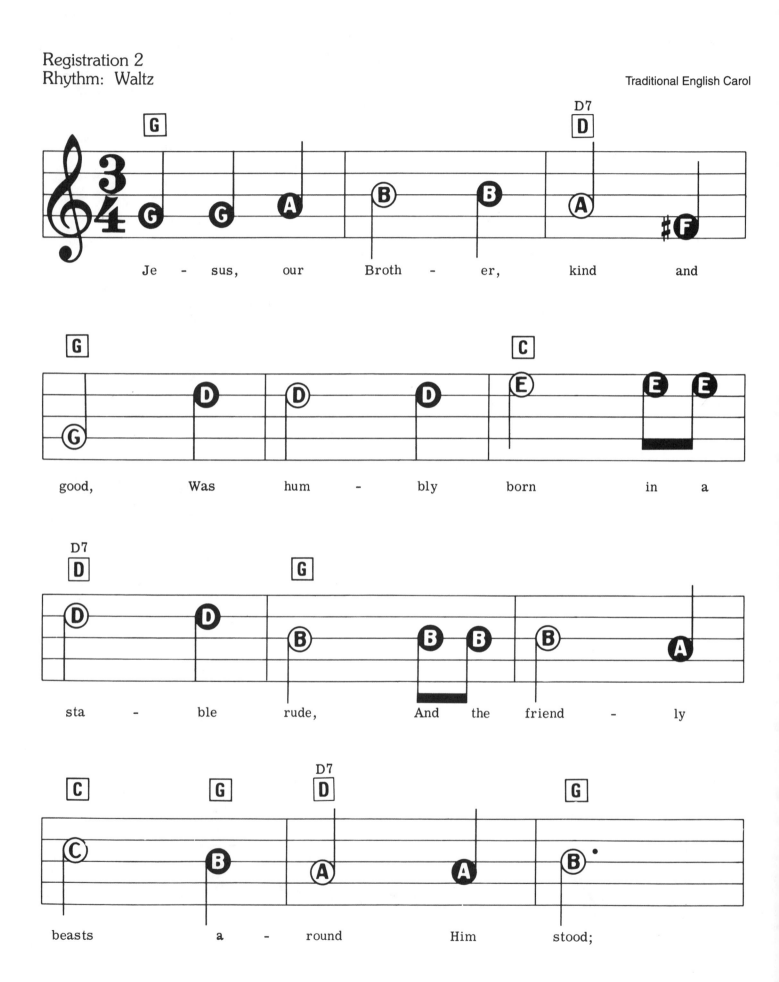

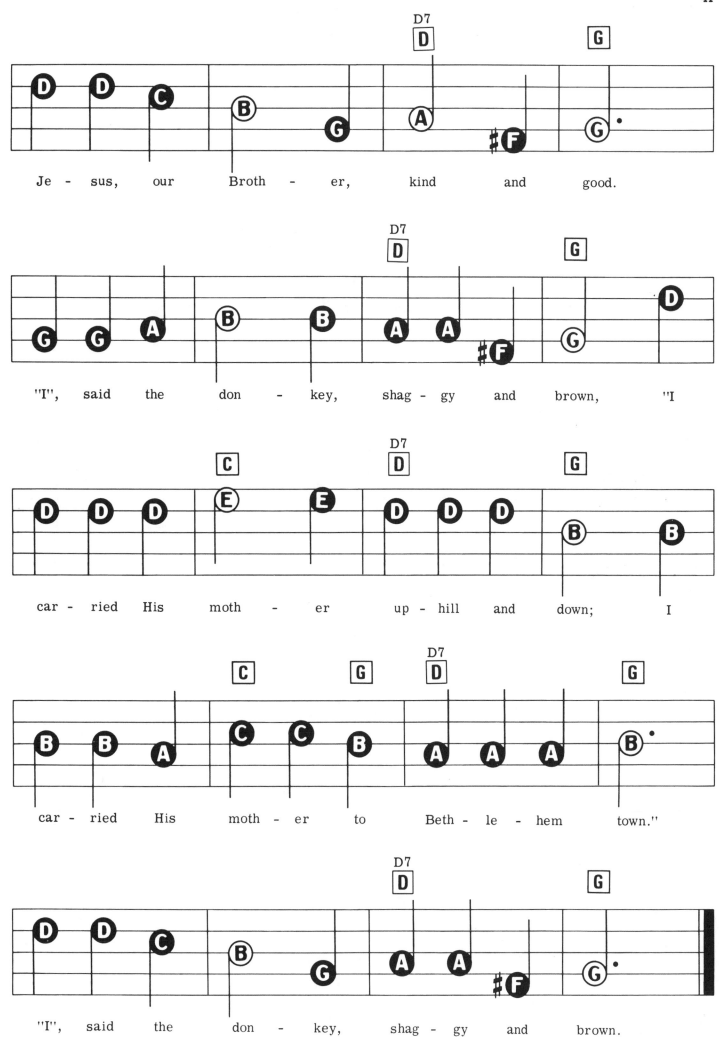

Go, Tell It on the Mountain

Registration 5
Rhythm: Swing

African-American Spiritual
Verses by John W. Work, Jr.

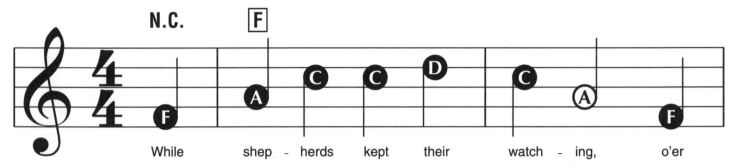

While shep - herds kept their watch - ing, o'er

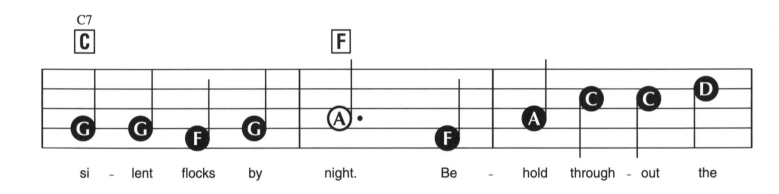

si - lent flocks by night. Be - hold through - out the

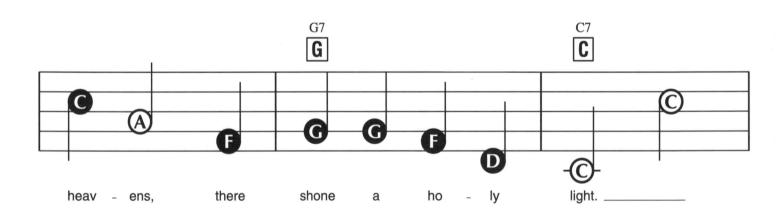

heav - ens, there shone a ho - ly light. _____

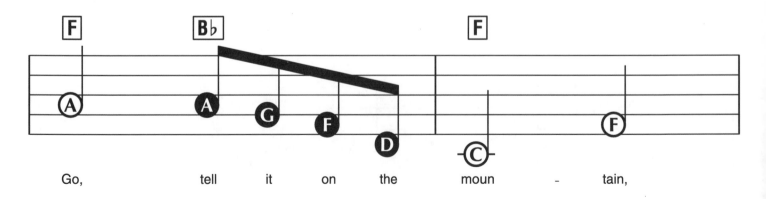

Go, tell it on the moun - tain,

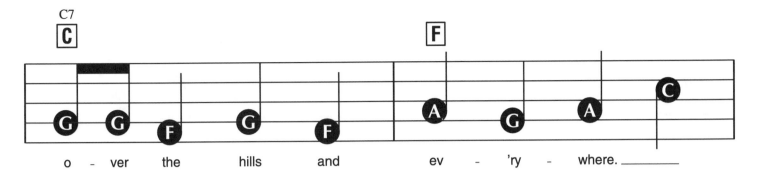

o - ver the hills and ev - 'ry - where. _____

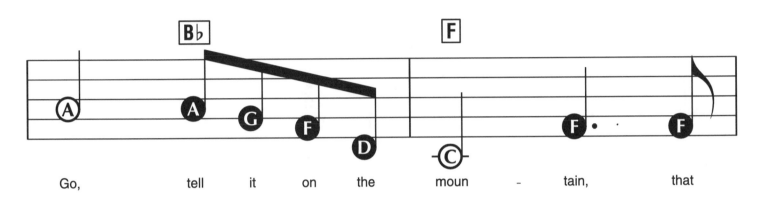

Go, tell it on the moun - tain, that

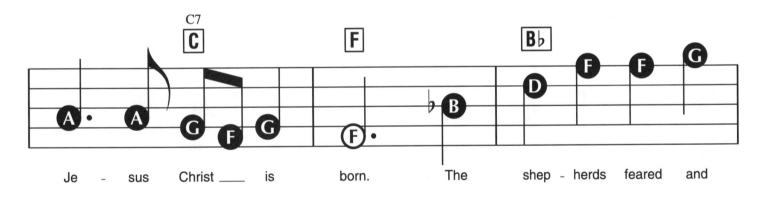

Je - sus Christ ___ is born. The shep - herds feared and

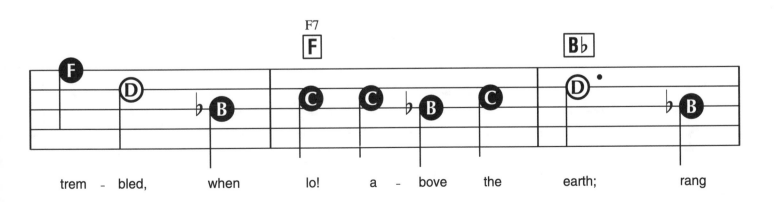

trem - bled, when lo! a - bove the earth; rang

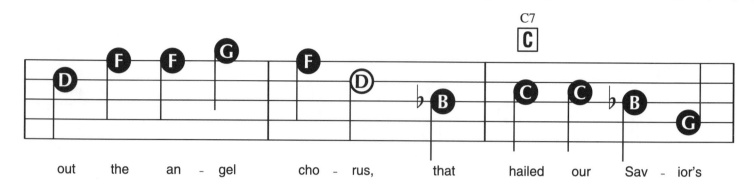

out the an - gel cho - rus, that hailed our Sav - ior's

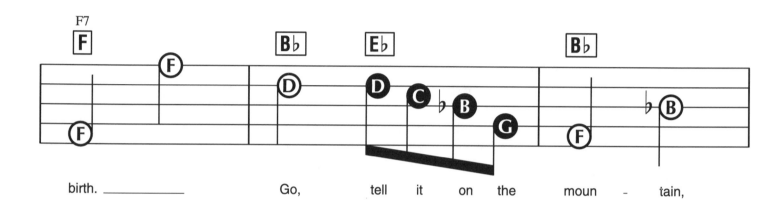

birth. _____ Go, tell it on the moun - tain,

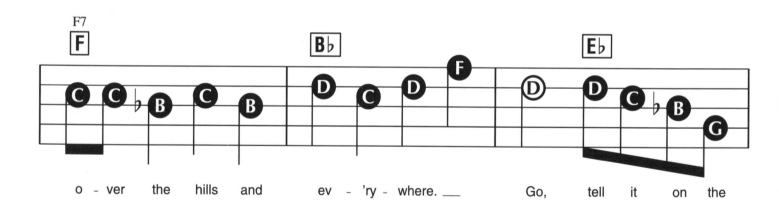

o - ver the hills and ev - 'ry - where. ___ Go, tell it on the

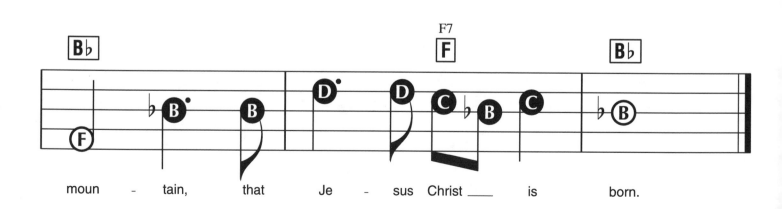

moun - tain, that Je - sus Christ ___ is born.

God Rest Ye Merry, Gentlemen

Registration 6
Rhythm: None

19th Century English Carol

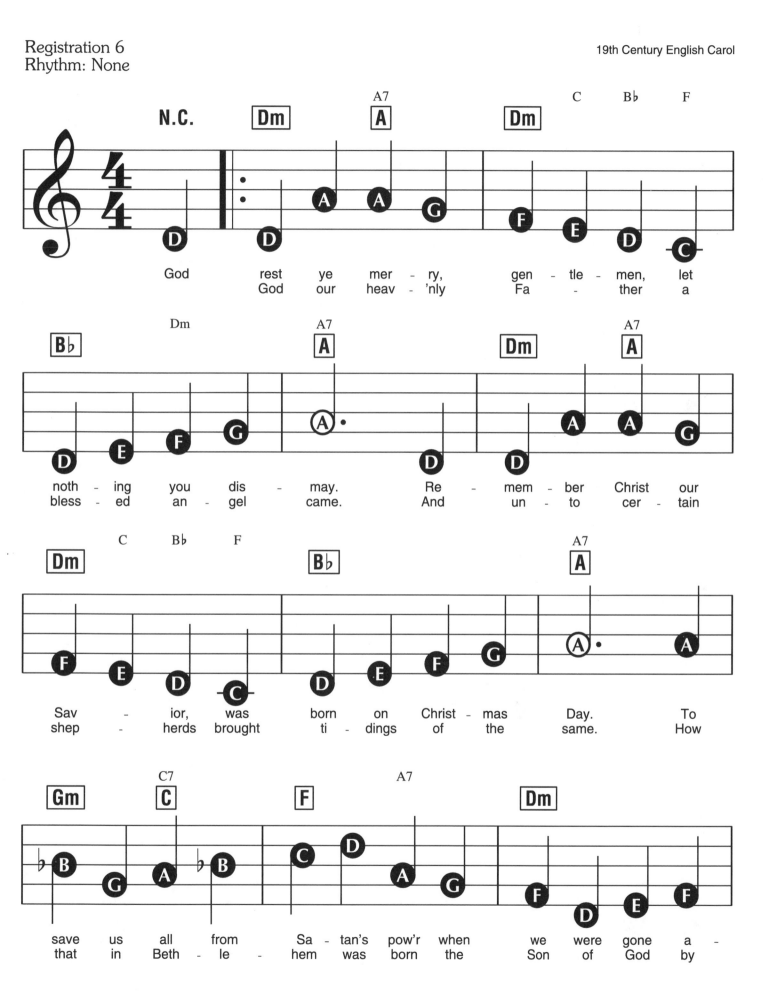

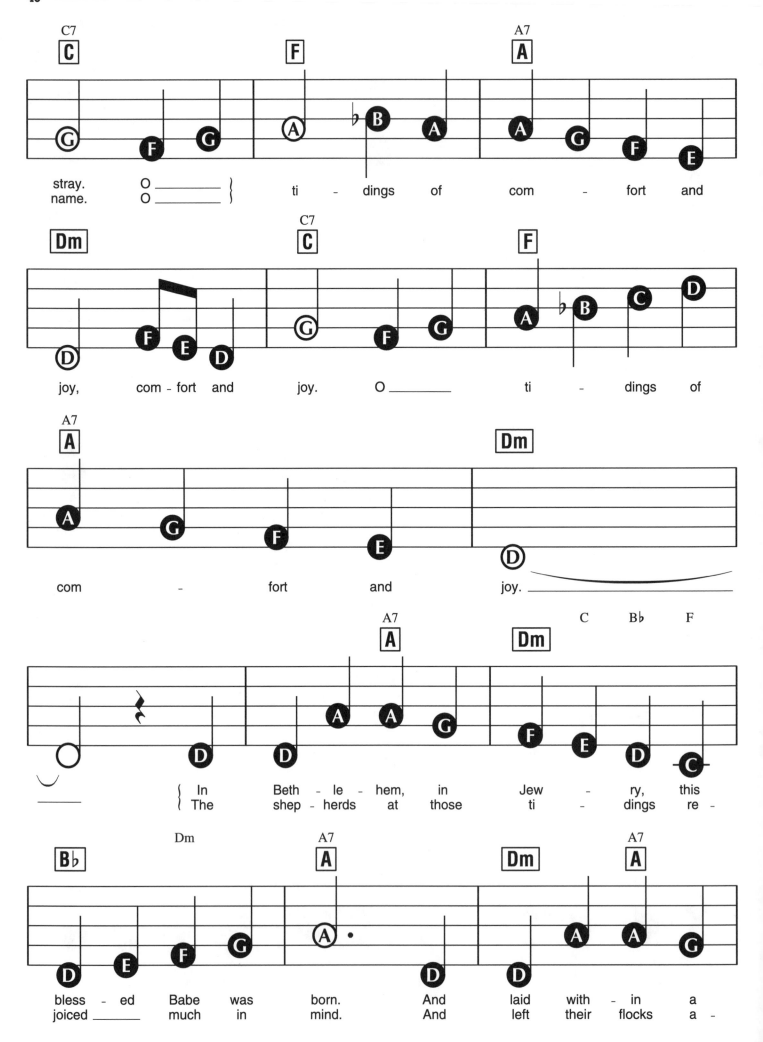

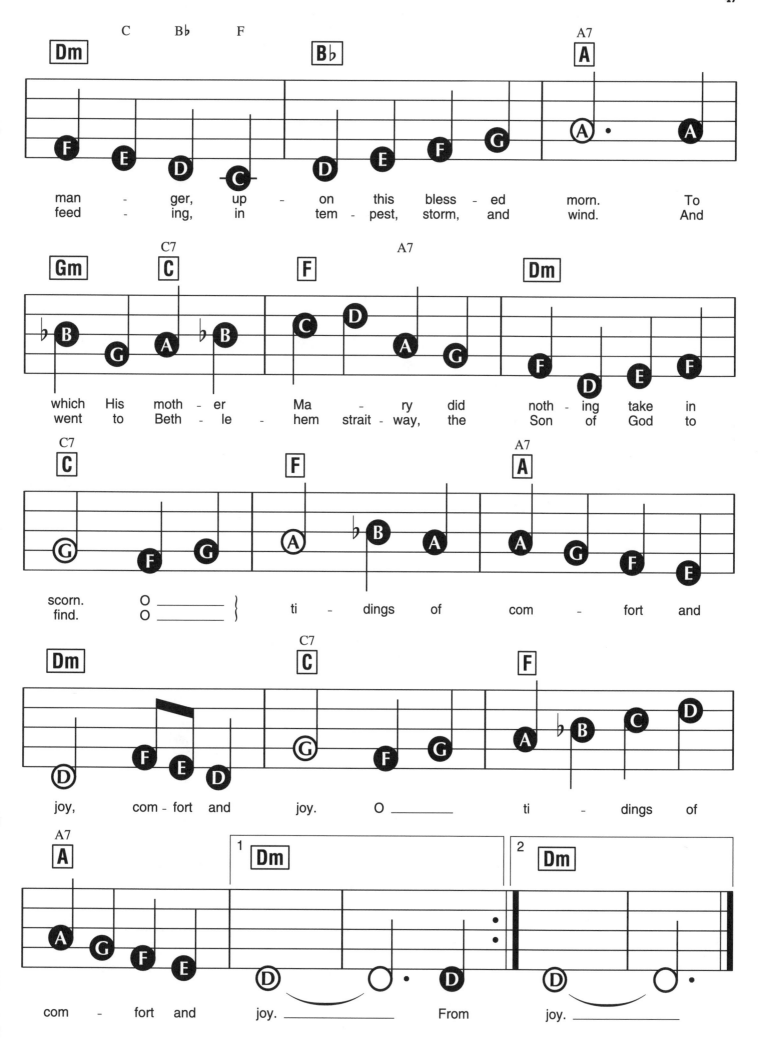

47

Good Christian Men, Rejoice

Registration 6
Rhythm: None

14th Century Latin Text
Translated by John Mason Neale
14th Century German Melody

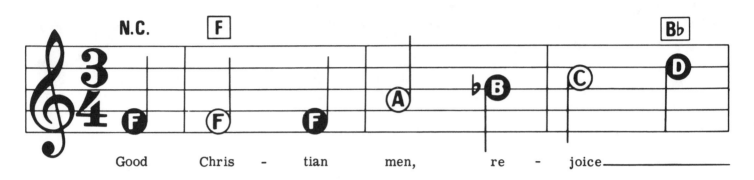

Good Chris - tian men, re - joice____

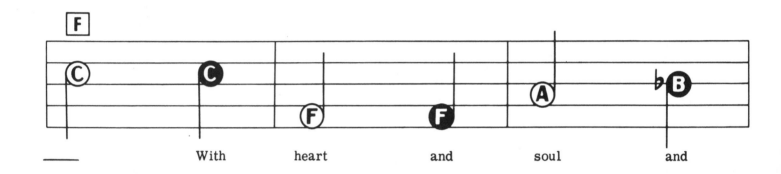

____ With heart and soul and

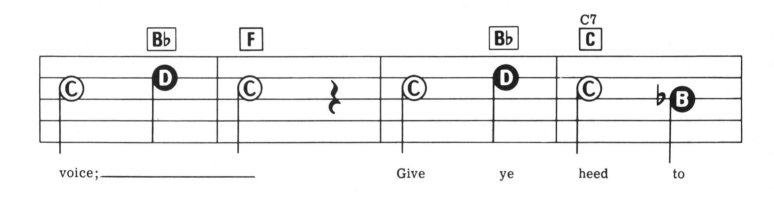

voice;_____ Give ye heed to

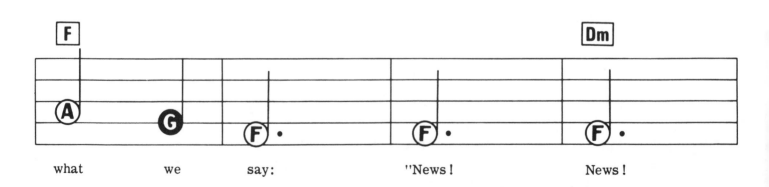

what we say: "News! News!

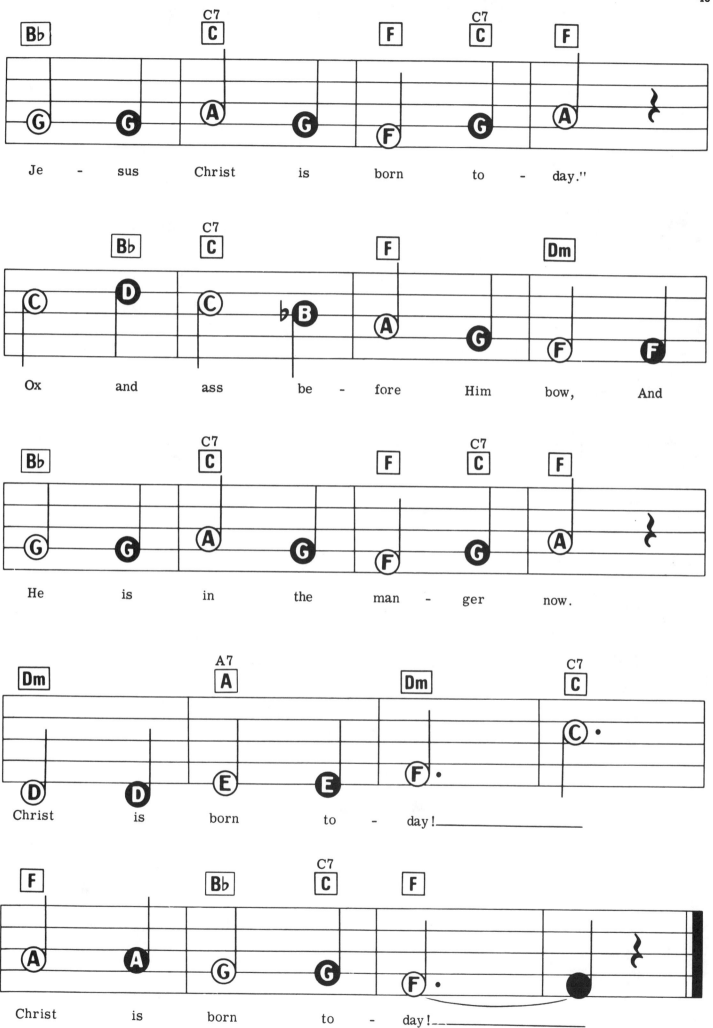

The Greatest Gift of All

Registration 4
Rhythm: Shuffle or Country

Words and Music by
John Jarvis

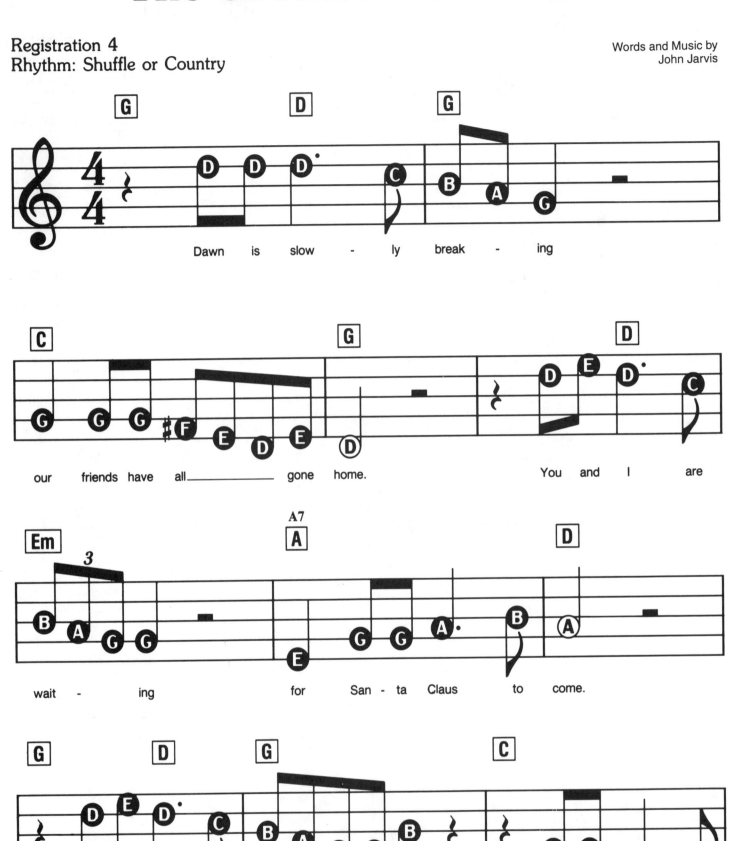

52

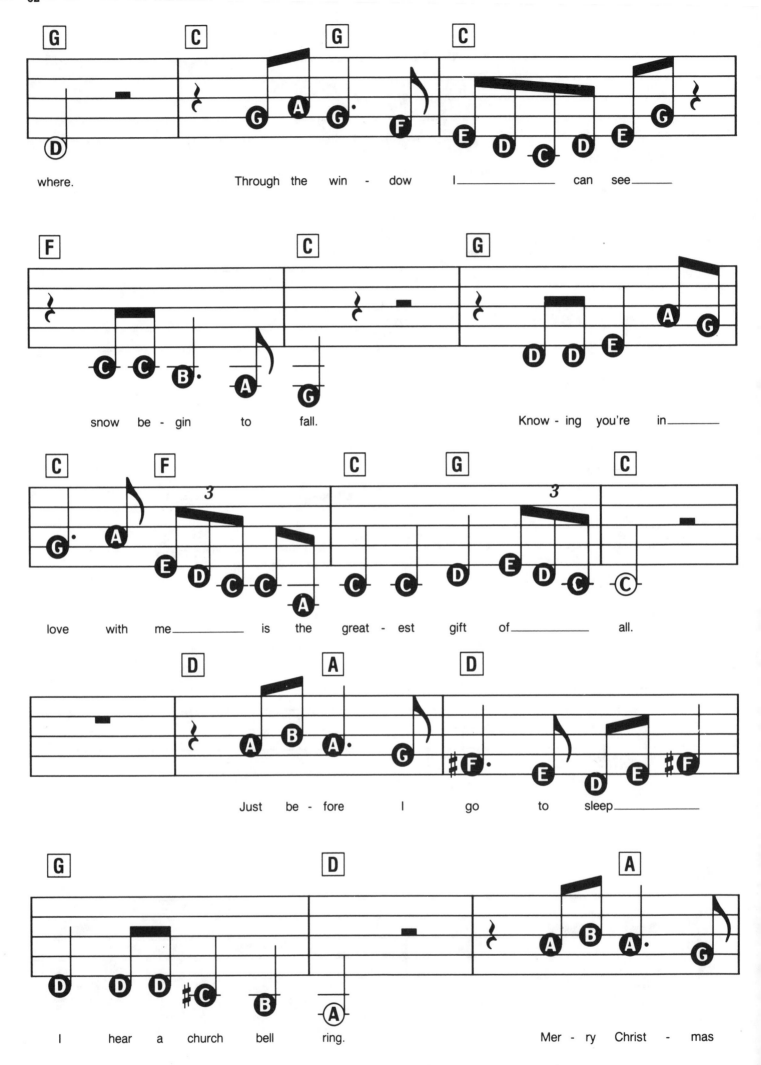

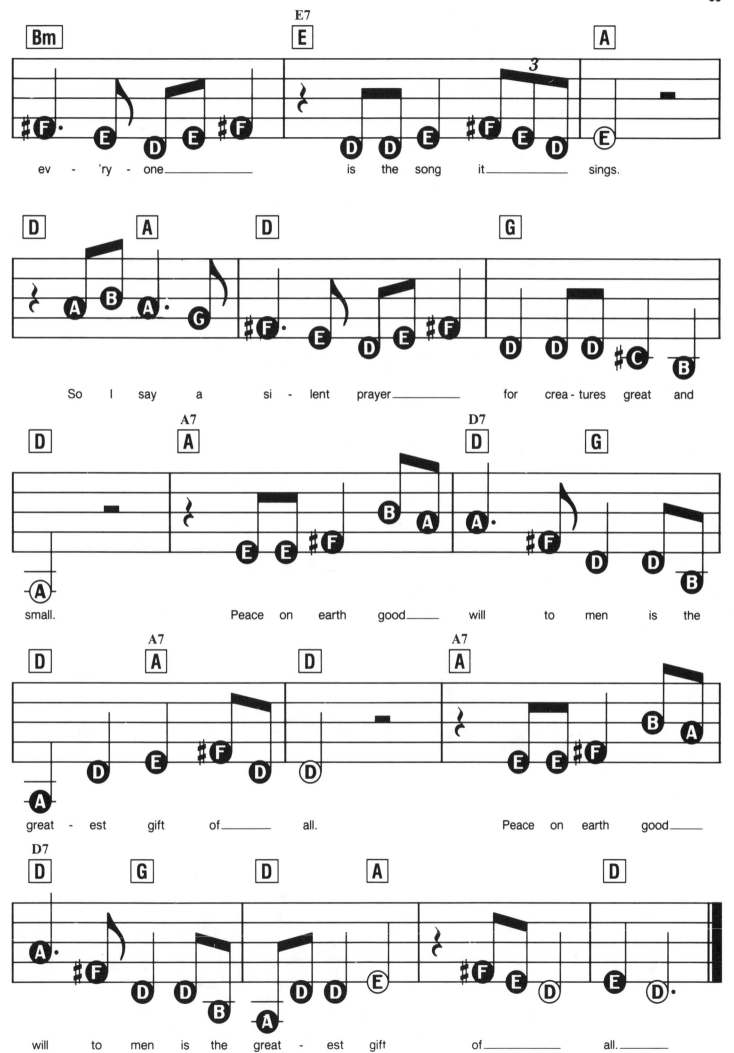

Happy Holiday
from the Motion Picture Irving Berlin's HOLIDAY INN

Registration 4
Rhythm: Fox Trot or Ballad

Words and Music by
Irving Berlin

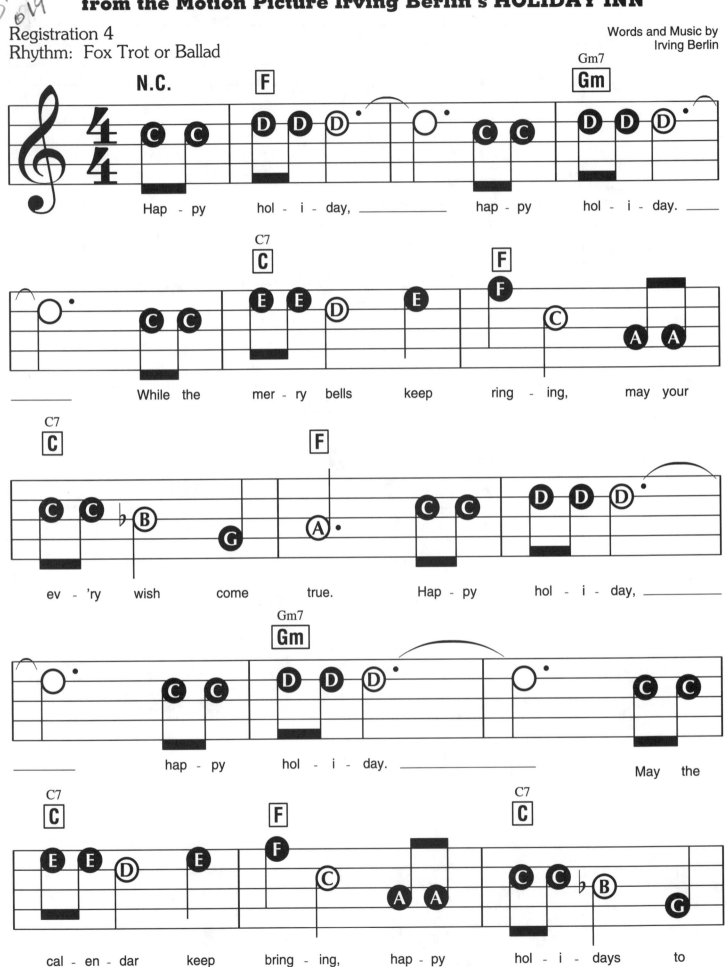

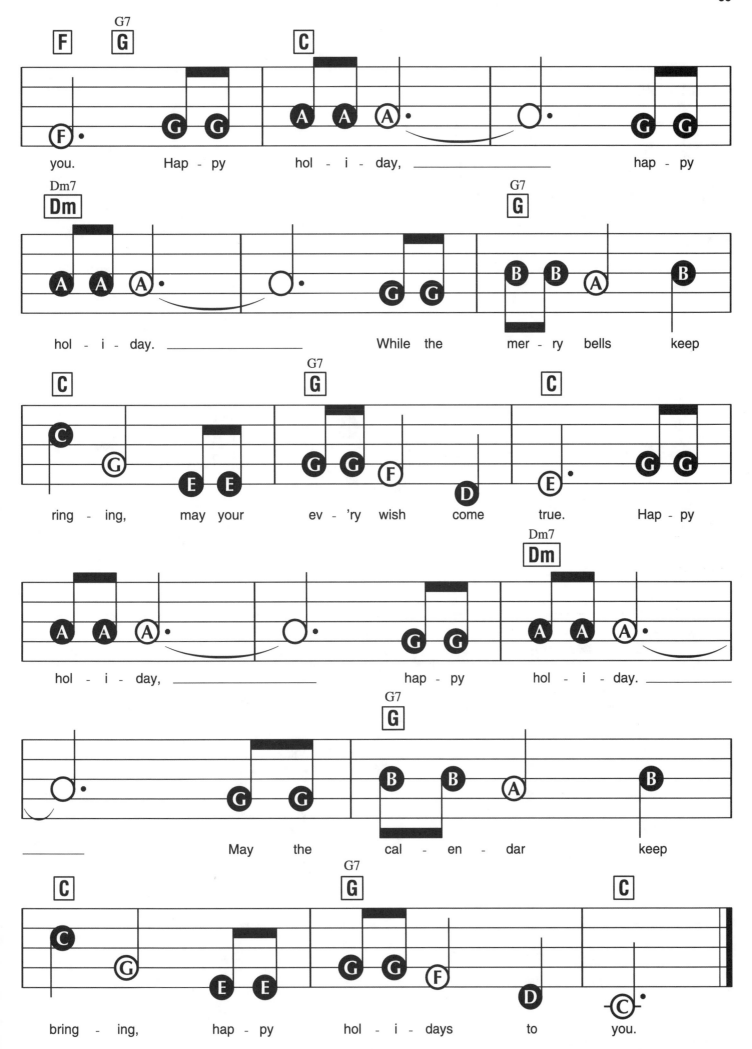

Happy Xmas
(War Is Over)

Registration 1
Rhythm: Slow Rock

Words and Music by John Lennon
and Yoko Ono

So this is X - mas _____ and what have you
X - mas _____ for weak and for
X - mas _____ and what have we

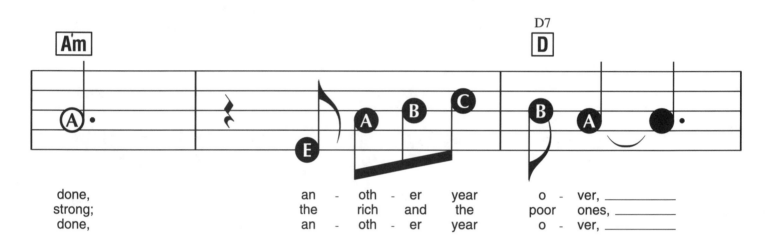

done, an - oth - er year o - ver, _____
strong; the rich and the poor ones, _____
done, an - oth - er year o - ver, _____

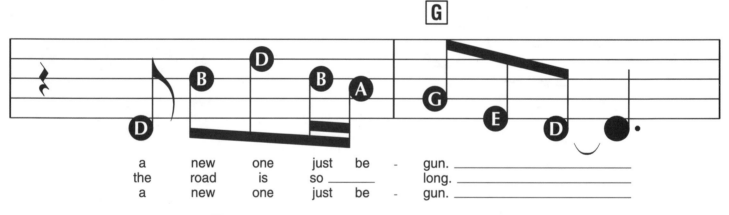

a new one just be - gun. _____
the road is so _____ long. _____
a new one just be - gun. _____

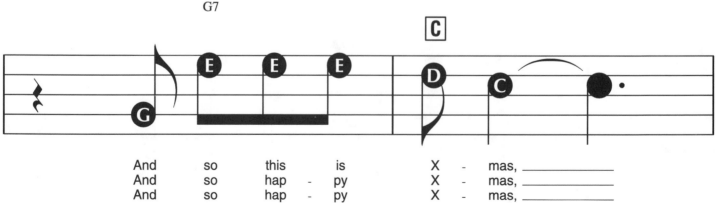

And so this is X - mas, _____
And so hap - py X - mas, _____
And so hap - py X - mas, _____

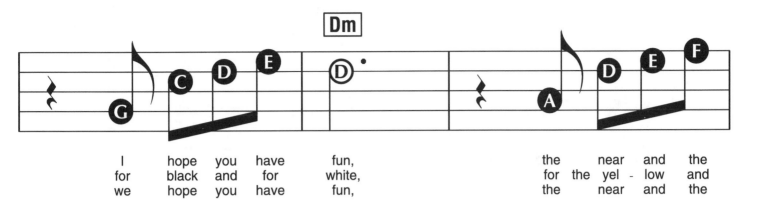

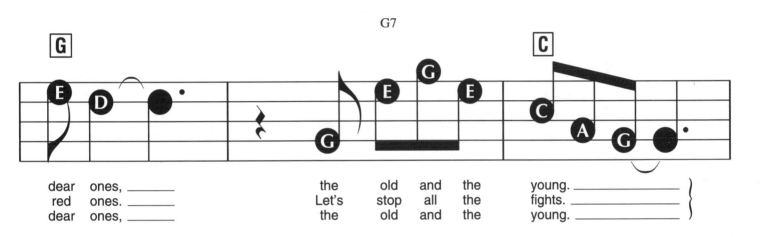

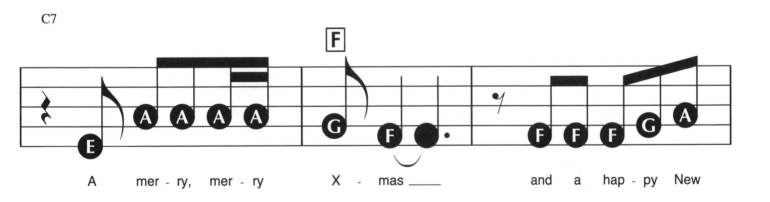

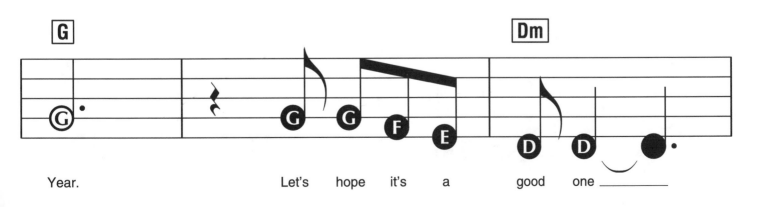

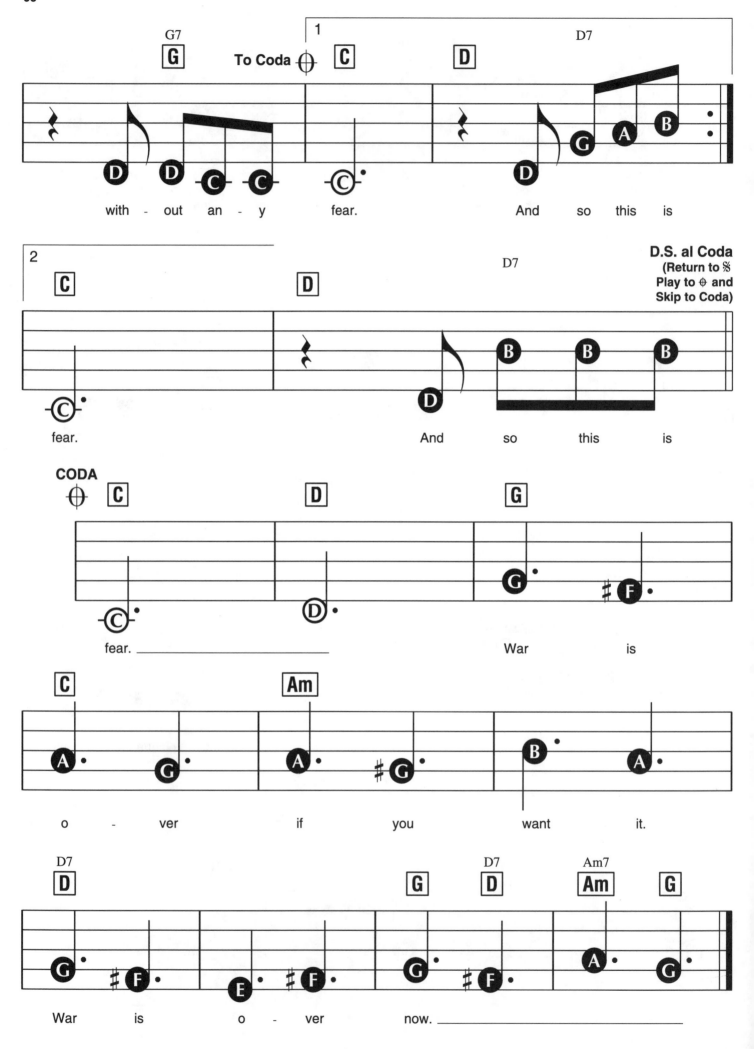

Hark! The Herald Angels Sing

Registration 5
Rhythm: None

Words by Charles Wesley
Altered by George Whitefield
Music by Felix Mendelssohn-Bartholdy
Arranged by William H. Cummings

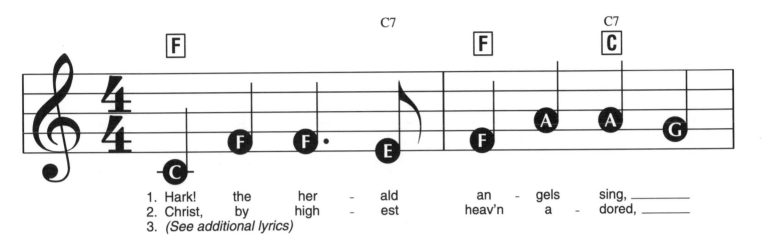

1. Hark! the her - ald an - gels sing, _____
2. Christ, by high - est heav'n a - dored, _____
3. *(See additional lyrics)*

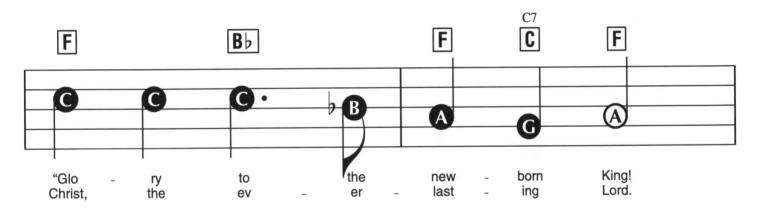

"Glo - ry to the new - born King!
Christ, the ev - er - last - ing Lord.

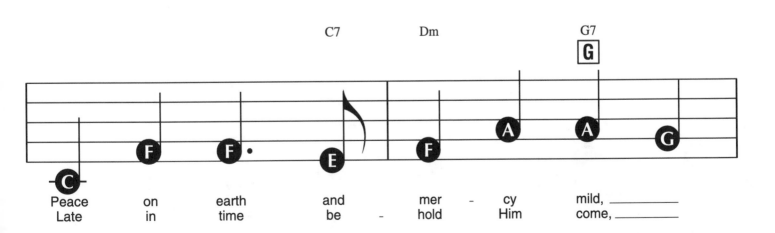

Peace on earth and mer - cy mild, _____
Late in time be - hold Him come, _____

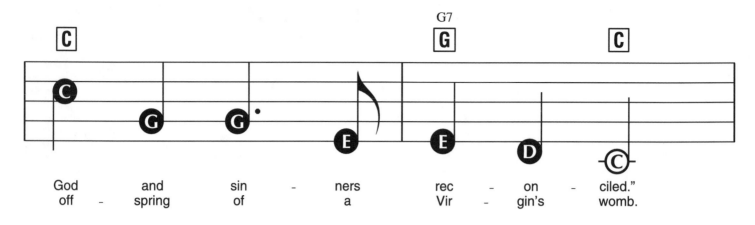

God — and sin — ners rec — on — ciled."
off — spring of a Vir — gin's womb.

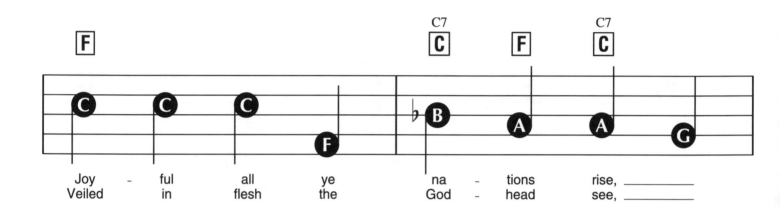

Joy — ful all ye na — tions rise, _____
Veiled in flesh the God — head see, _____

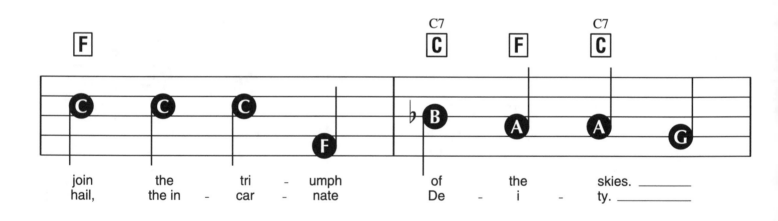

join the tri — umph of the skies. _____
hail, the in — car — nate De — i — ty. _____

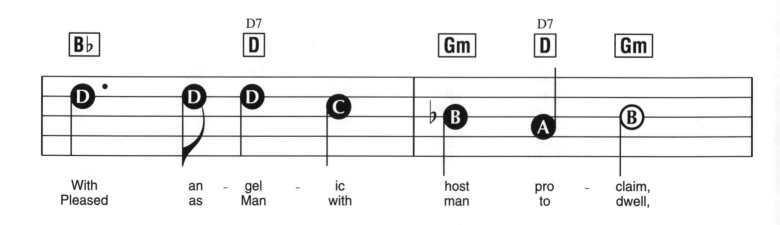

With an — gel — ic host pro — claim,
Pleased as Man with man to dwell,

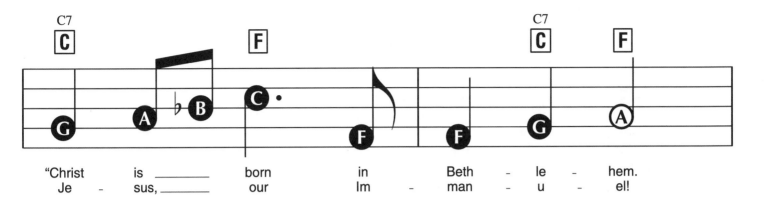

"Christ is _____ born in Beth - le - hem.
Je - sus, _____ our Im - man - u - el!

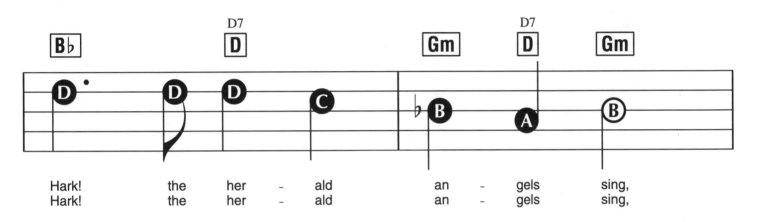

Hark! the her - ald an - gels sing,
Hark! the her - ald an - gels sing,

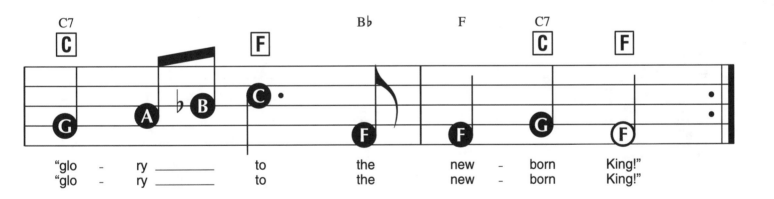

"glo - ry _____ to the new - born King!"
"glo - ry _____ to the new - born King!"

Additional Lyrics

3. Hail, the heaven-born Prince of Peace!
   Hail, the Sun of Righteousness!
   Light and life to all He brings,
   Risen with healing in His wings.
   Mild He lays His glory by,
   Born that man no more may die.
   Born to raise the sons of earth,
   Born to give them second birth.

   Hark! the herald angels sing,
   "Glory to the newborn King!"

Here We Come A-Wassailing

Registration 3
Rhythm: None

Traditional

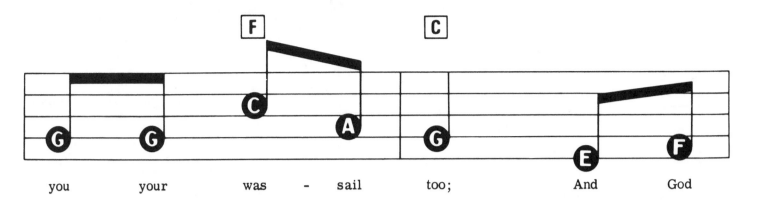

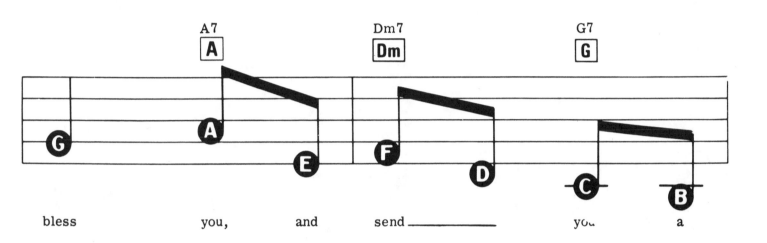

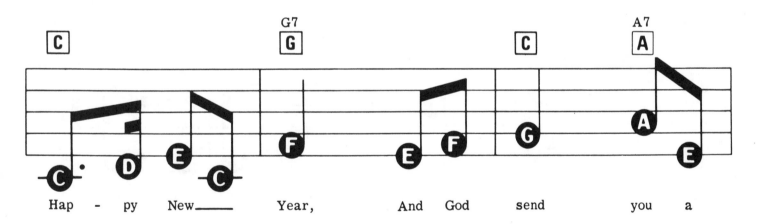

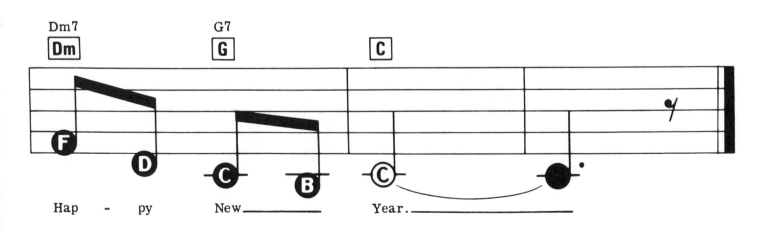

The Holly and the Ivy

Registration 1
Rhythm: None

18th Century English Carol

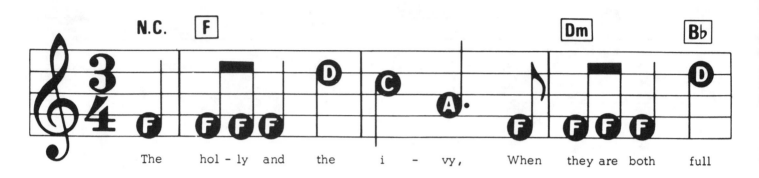

The hol - ly and the i - vy, When they are both full

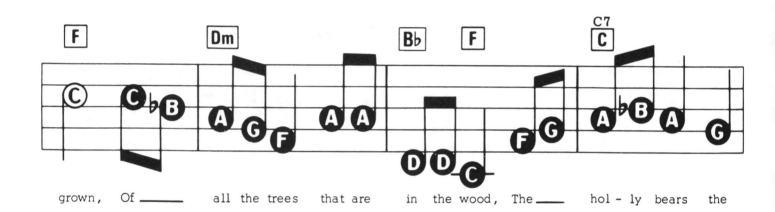

grown, Of ____ all the trees that are in the wood, The ____ hol - ly bears the

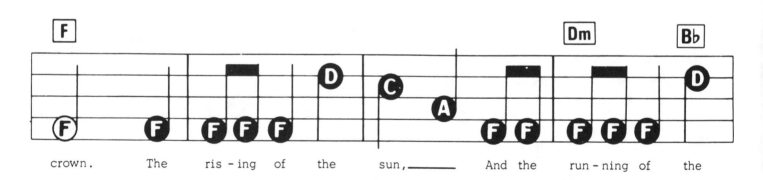

crown. The ris - ing of the sun, ____ And the run - ning of the

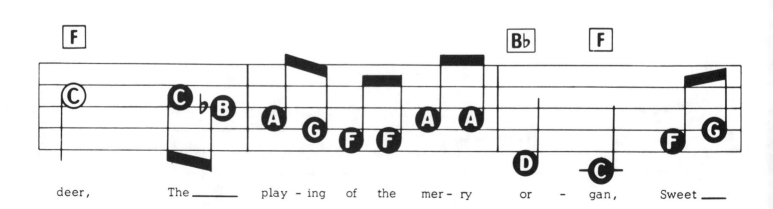

deer, The ____ play - ing of the mer - ry or - gan, Sweet ____

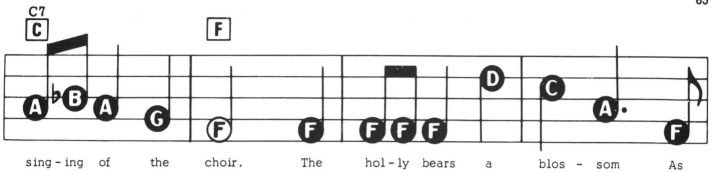

sing - ing of the choir. The hol - ly bears a blos - som As

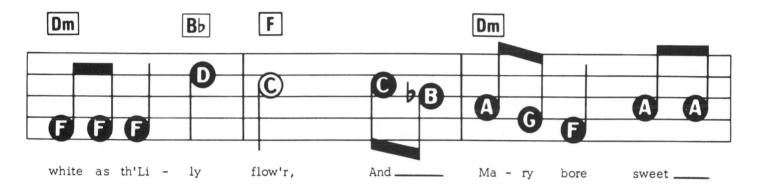

white as th'Li - ly flow'r, And Ma - ry bore sweet

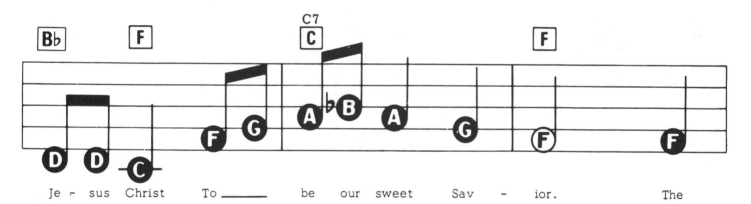

Je - sus Christ To be our sweet Sav - ior. The

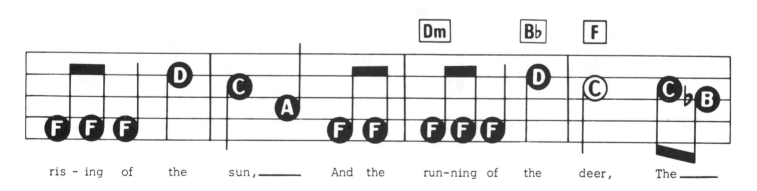

ris - ing of the sun, And the run - ning of the deer, The

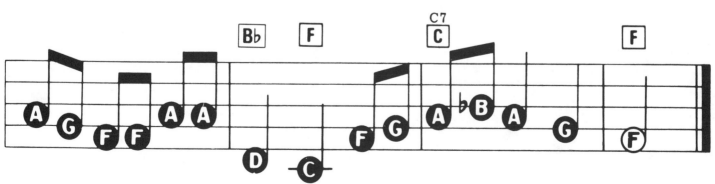

play - ing of the mer - ry or - gan, Sweet sing - ing of the choir.

A Holly Jolly Christmas

Registration 9
Rhythm: Fox Trot or Swing

Music and Lyrics by
Johnny Marks

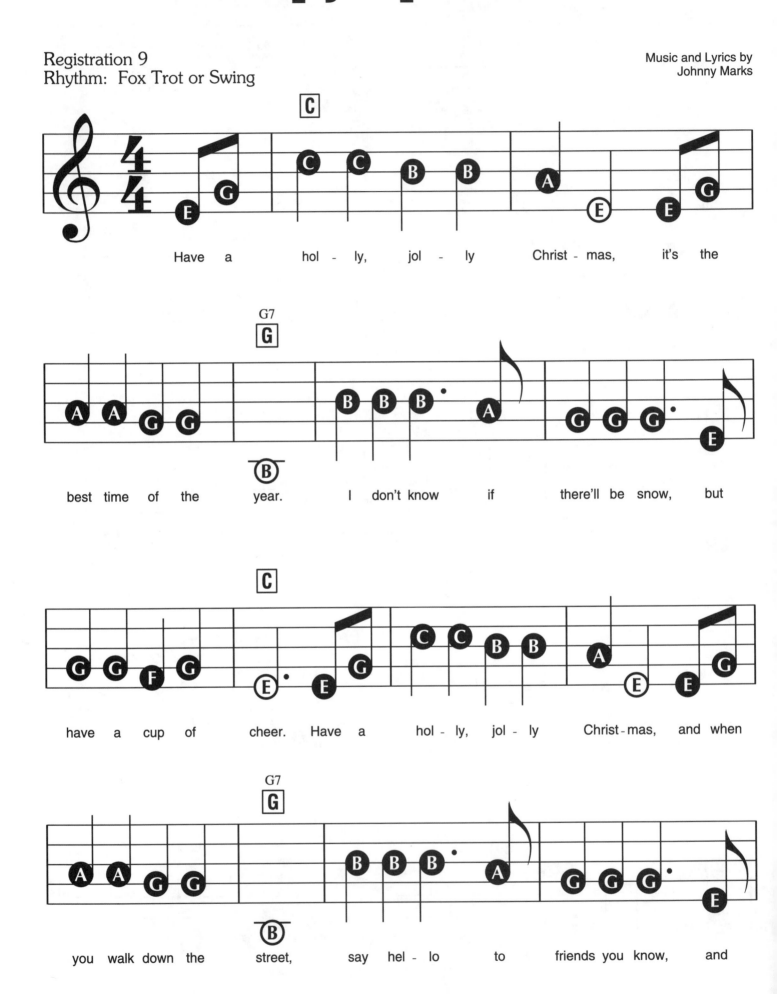

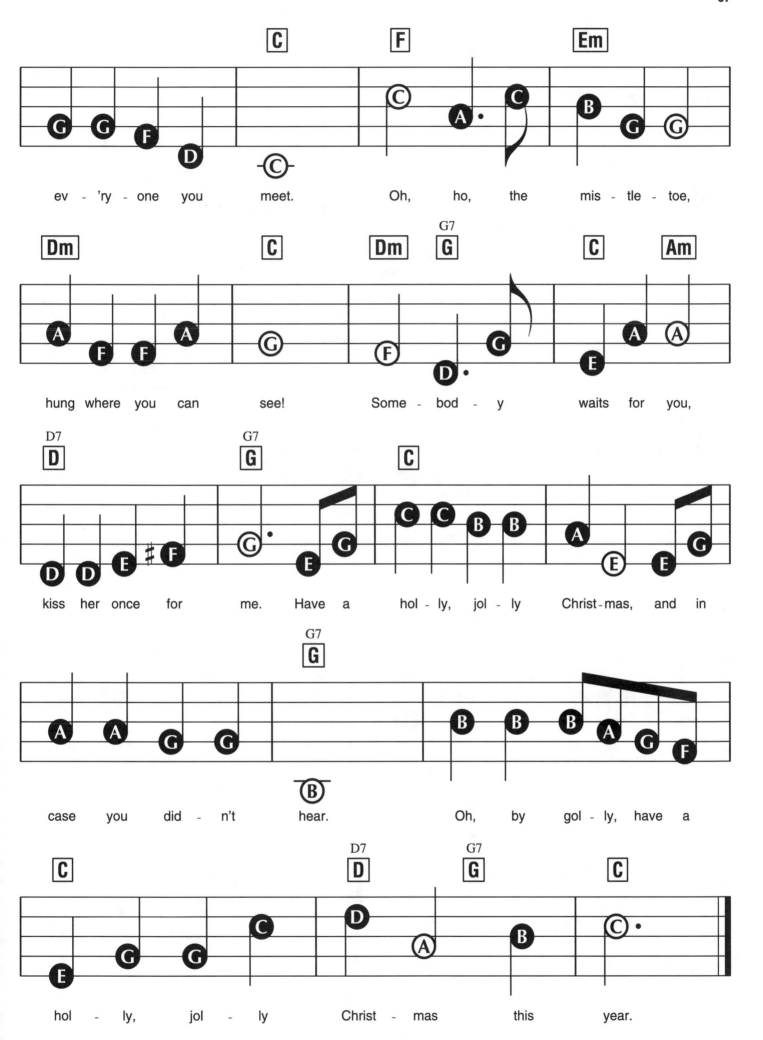

(There's No Place Like)
Home for the Holidays

Registration 5
Rhythm: Fox Trot or Swing

Words by Al Stillman
Music by Robert Allen

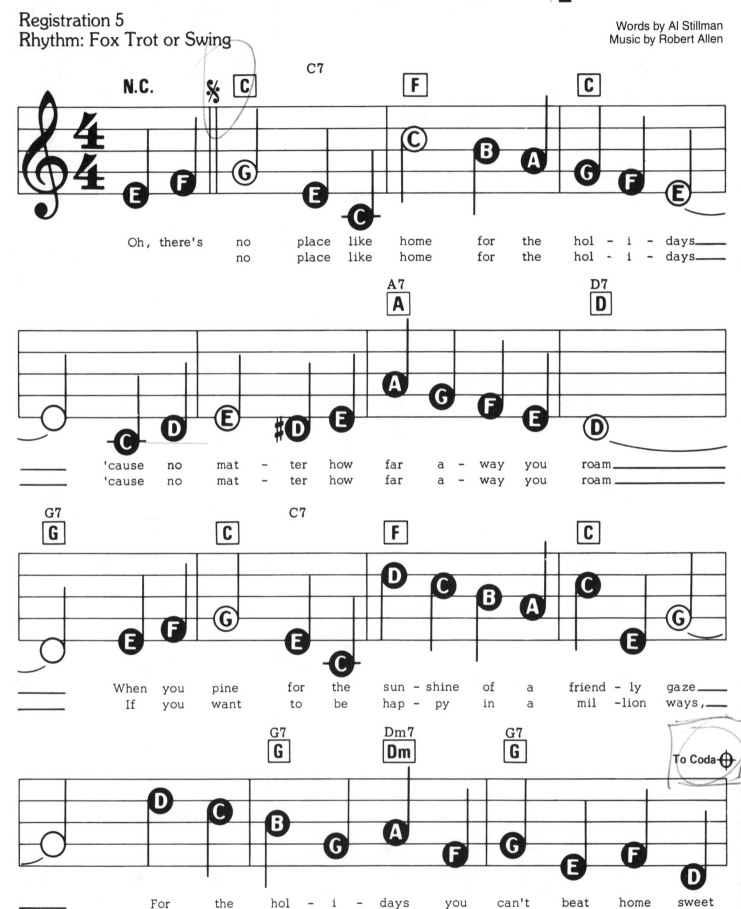

Oh, there's no place like home for the hol - i - days___
no place like home for the hol - i - days___

___ 'cause no mat - ter how far a - way you roam___
___ 'cause no mat - ter how far a - way you roam

___ When you pine for the sun - shine of a friend - ly gaze___
___ If you want to be hap - py in a mil - lion ways,___

To Coda

___ For the hol - i - days you can't beat home sweet
___ For the hol - i - days you can't beat home, sweet

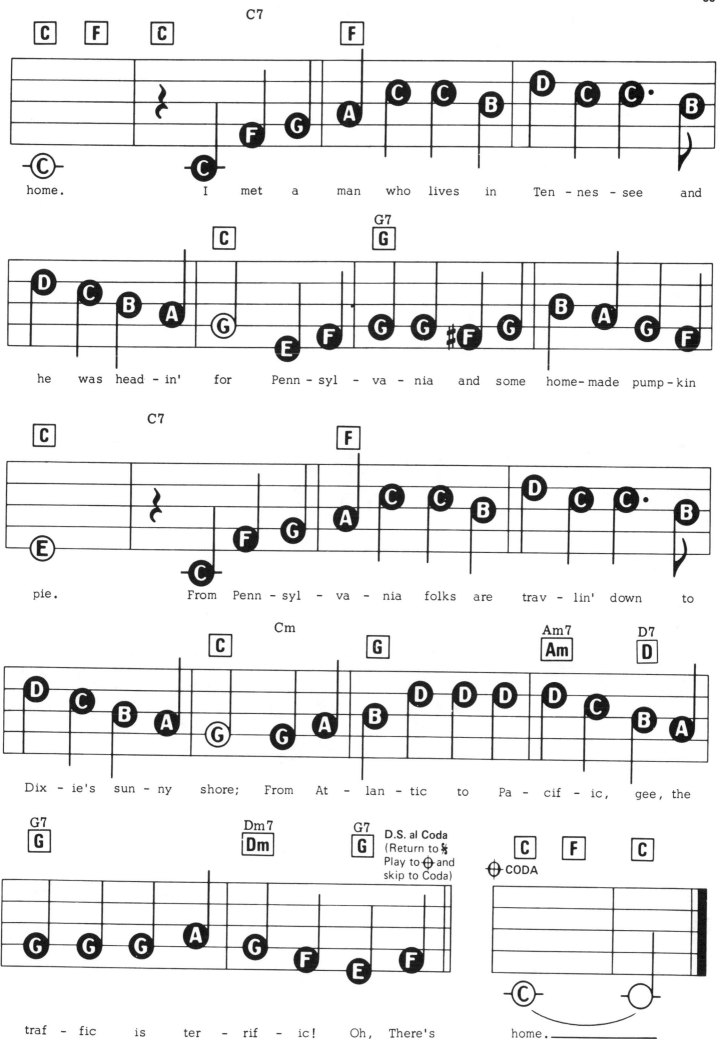

Voice
D96

I Heard the Bells on Christmas Day

Registration 7
Rhythm: Ballad or Fox Trot

Words by Henry Wadsworth Longfellow
Music by John Baptiste Calkin

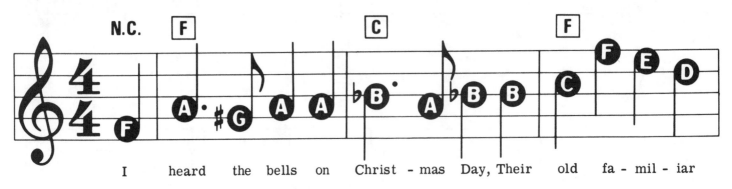

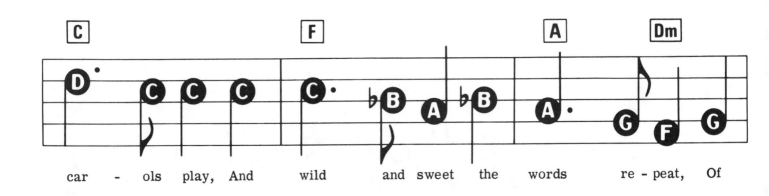

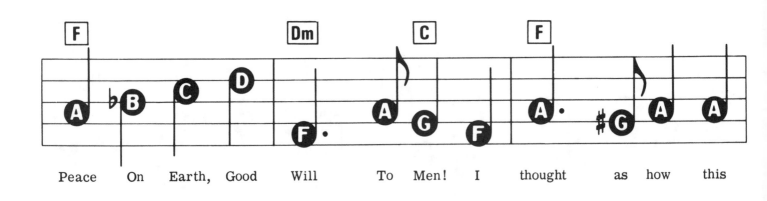

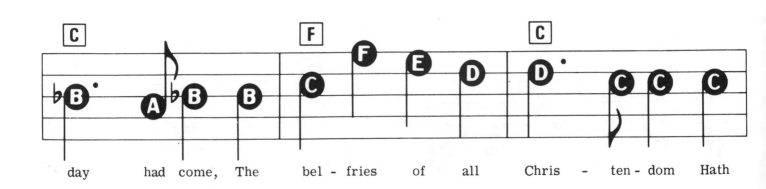

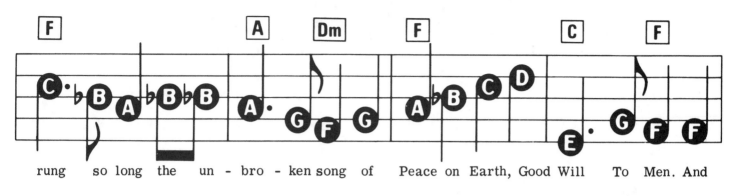

rung   so long   the   un - bro - ken song of   Peace on Earth, Good Will   To   Men. And

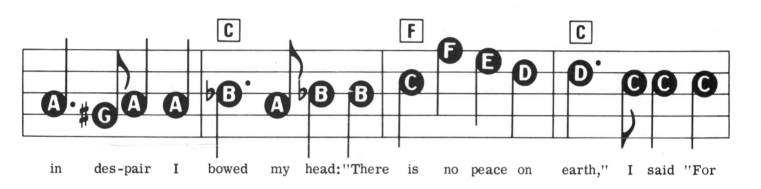

in   des-pair   I   bowed   my   head:"There   is   no   peace on   earth,"   I   said "For

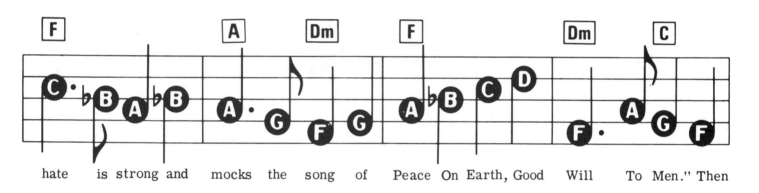

hate   is strong and   mocks   the   song   of   Peace On Earth, Good   Will   To Men." Then

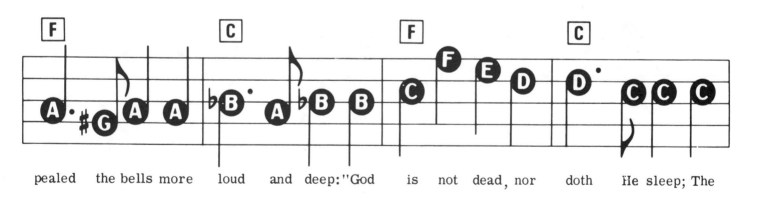

pealed   the bells more   loud   and   deep:"God   is   not dead, nor   doth   He sleep; The

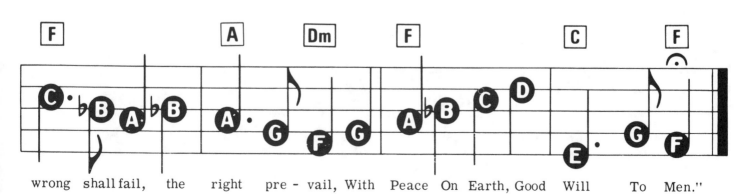

wrong shall fail,   the   right   pre - vail,   With   Peace On Earth, Good   Will   To   Men."

I Heard the Bells on Christmas Day

Registration 9
Rhythm: Fox Trot

Words by Henry Wadsworth Longfellow
Adapted by Johnny Marks
Music by Johnny Marks

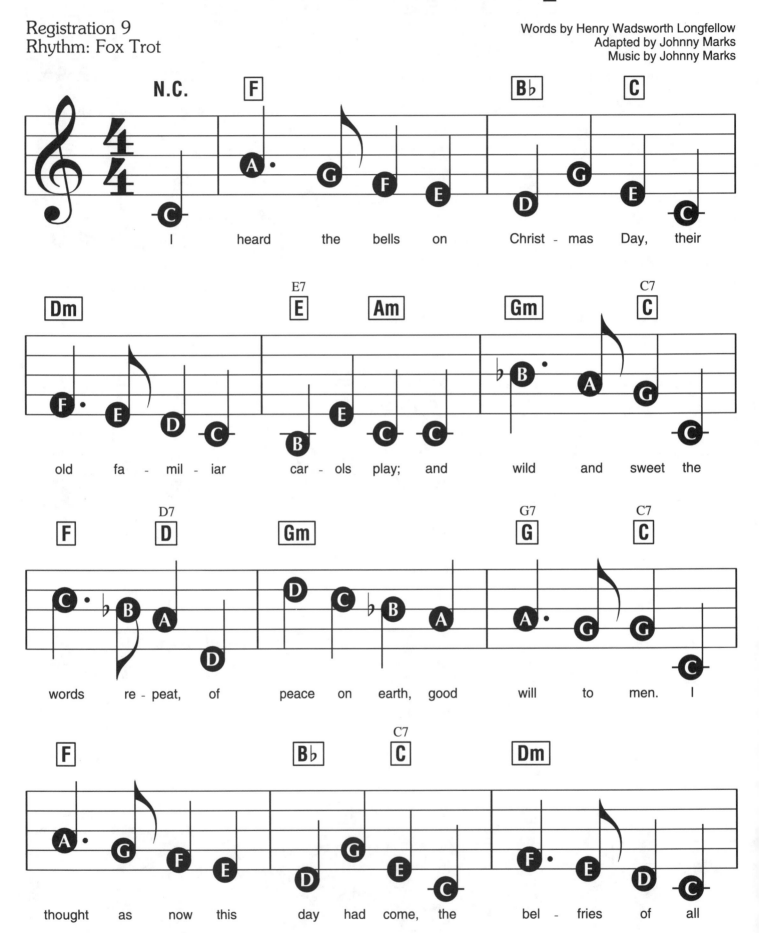

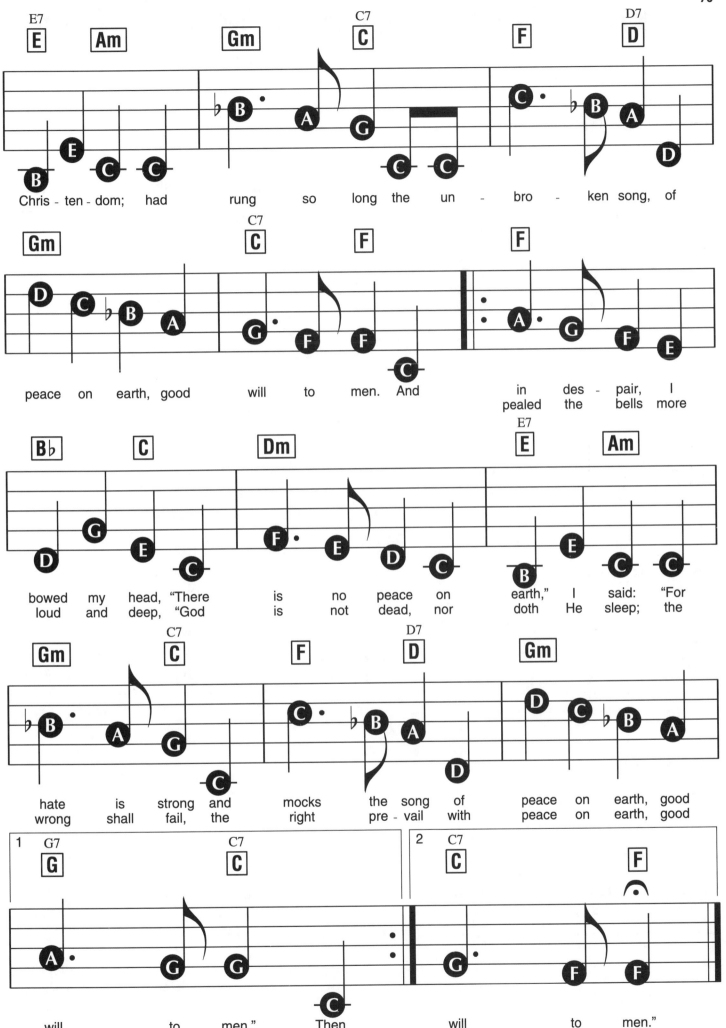

I Saw Mommy Kissing Santa Claus

Registration 5
Rhythm: Fox Trot or Swing

Words and Music by
Tommie Connor

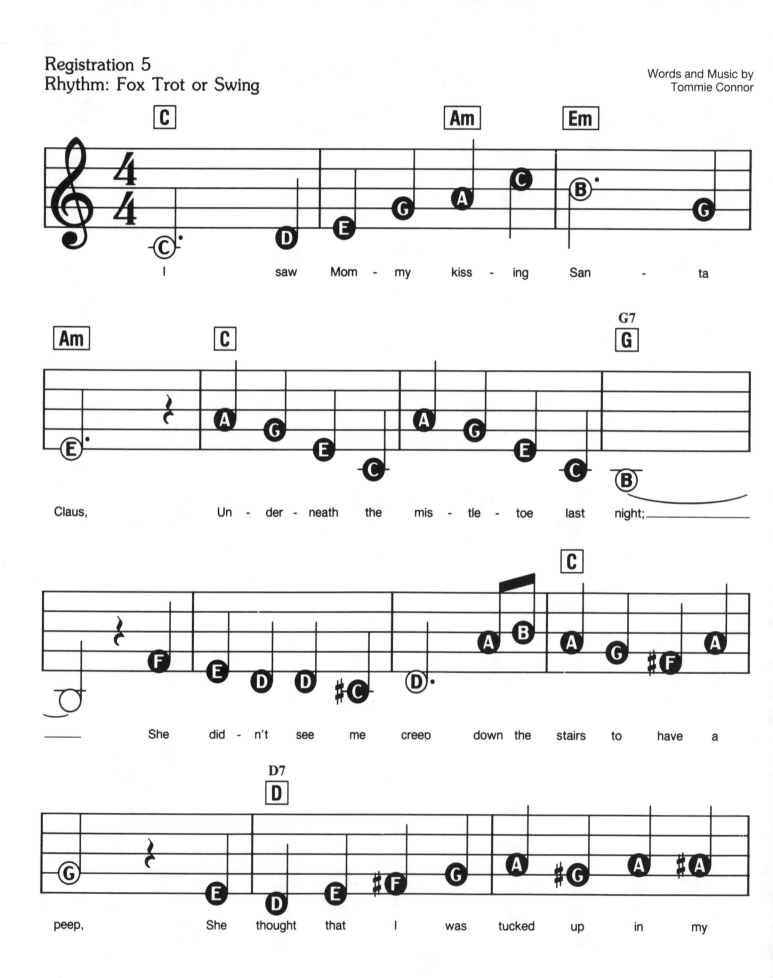

I Saw Three Ships

Registration 2
Rhythm: 6/8 March or Waltz

Traditional English Carol

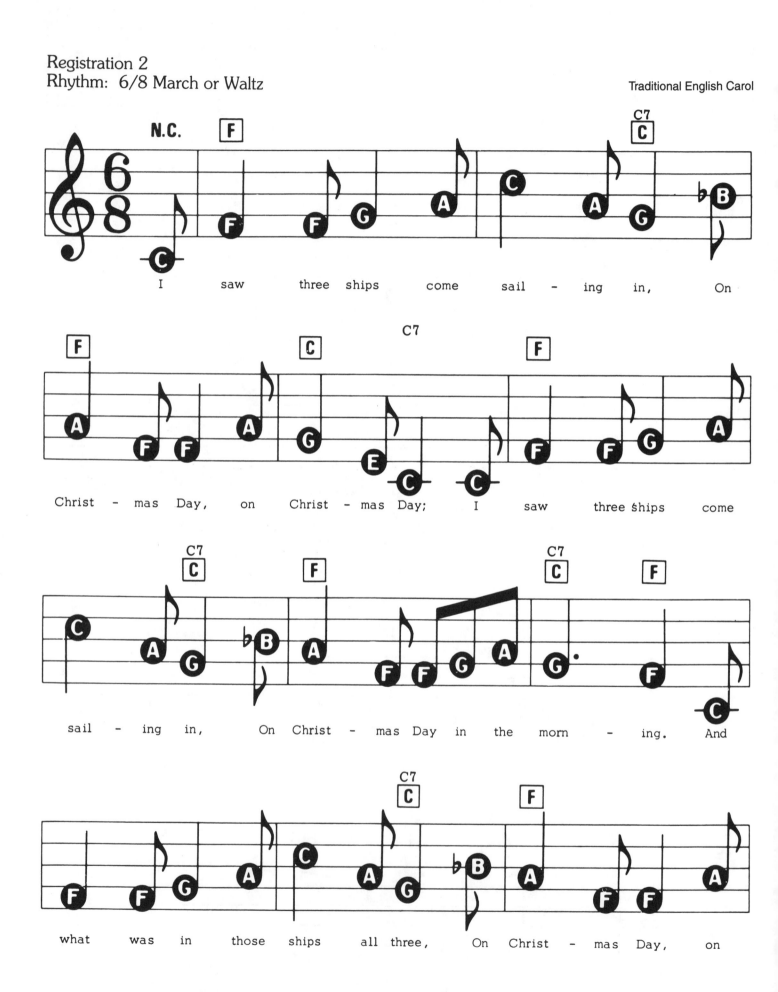

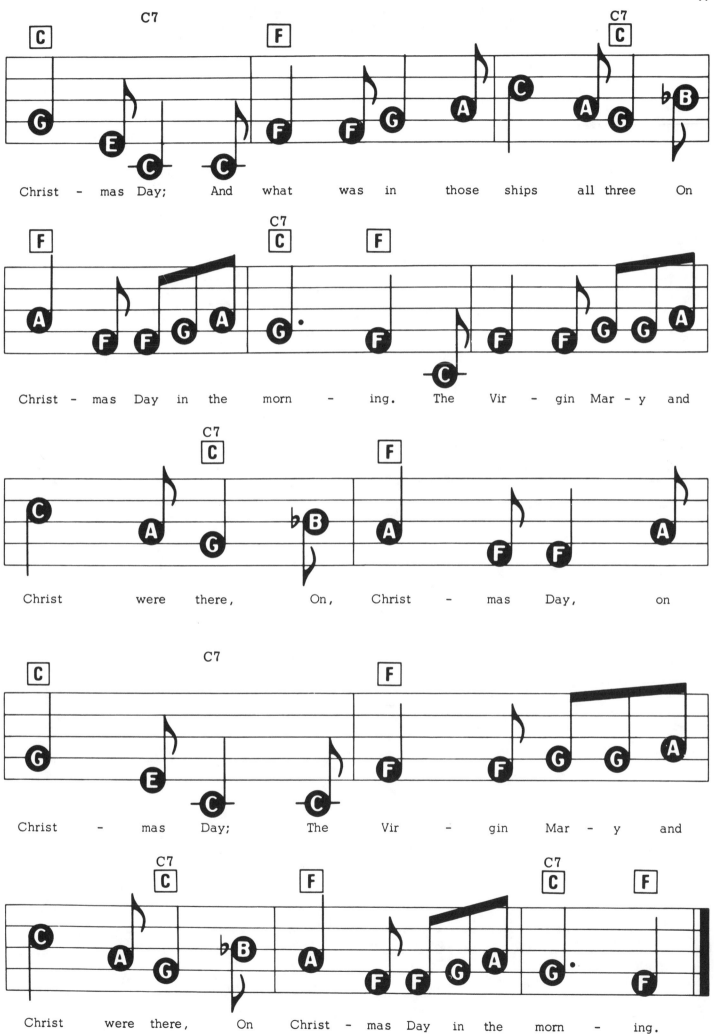

I'll Be Home for Christmas

Registration 1
Rhythm: Fox Trot

Words and Music by Kim Gannon
and Walter Kent

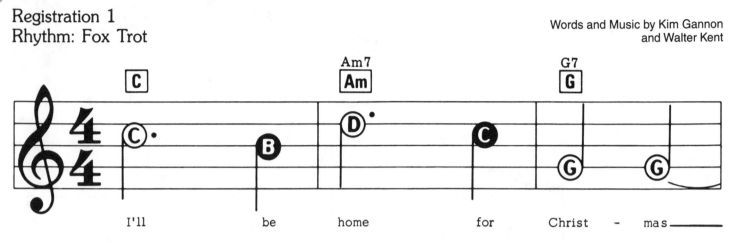

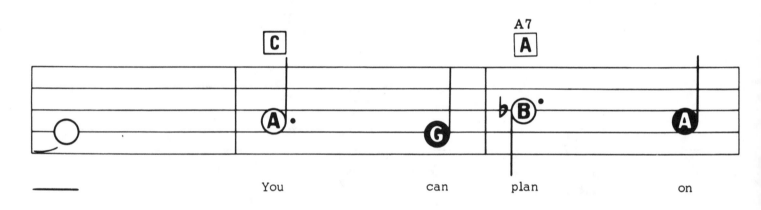

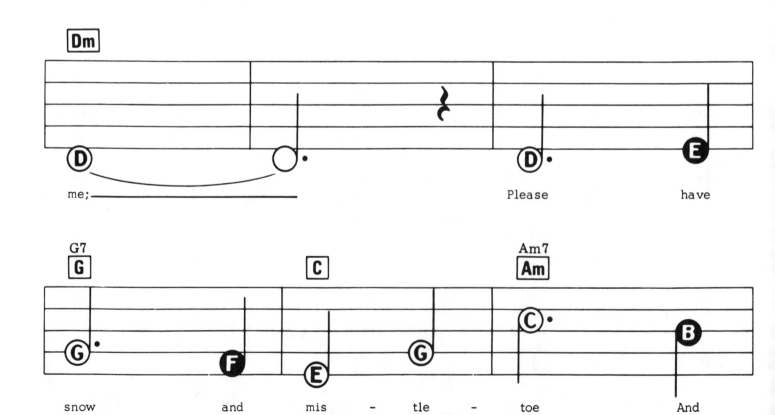

79

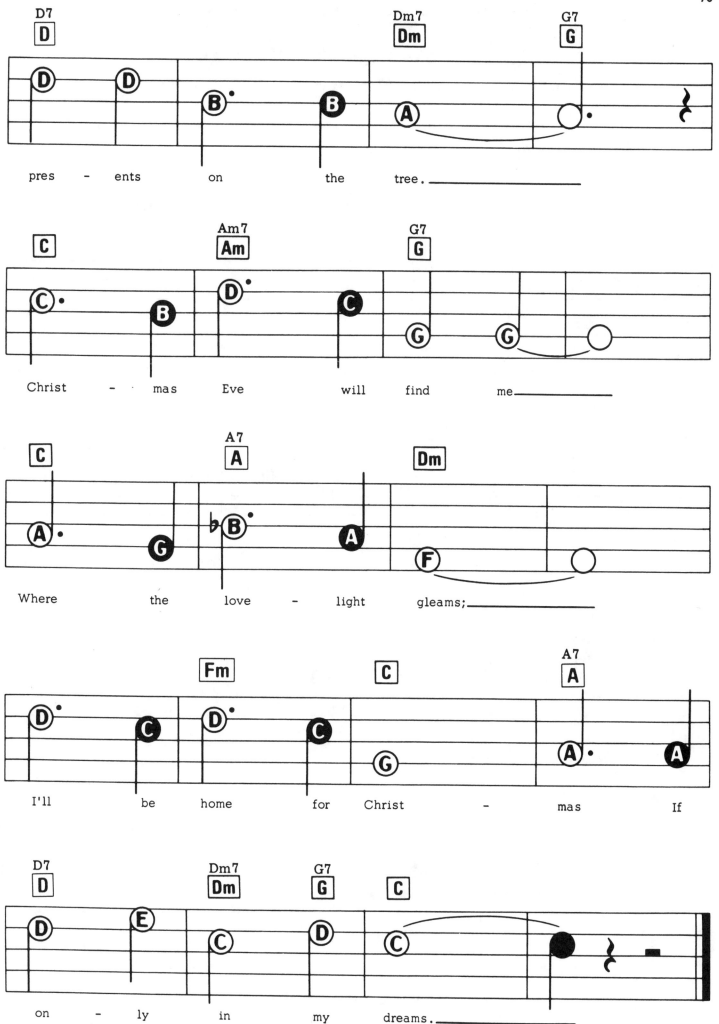

I've Got My Love to Keep Me Warm

from the 20th Century Fox Motion Picture ON THE AVENUE

Registration 4
Rhythm: Fox Trot or Swing

Words and Music by
Irving Berlin

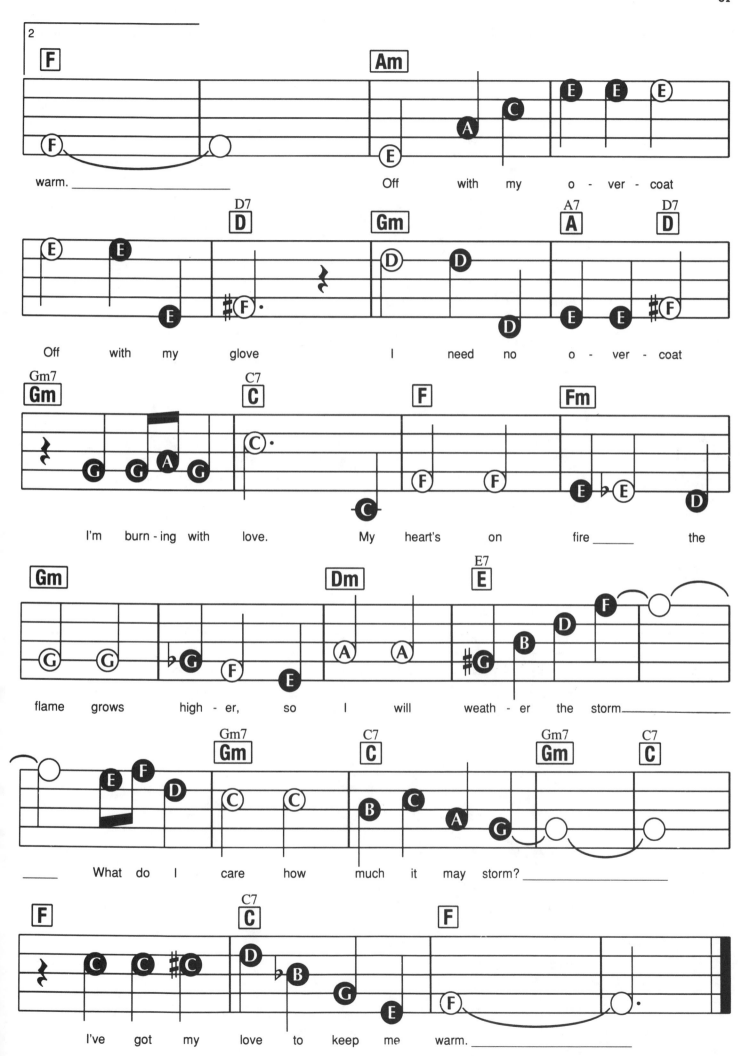

It Came Upon the Midnight Clear

Registration 1
Rhythm: None

Words by Edmund Hamilton Sears
Music by Richard Storrs Willis

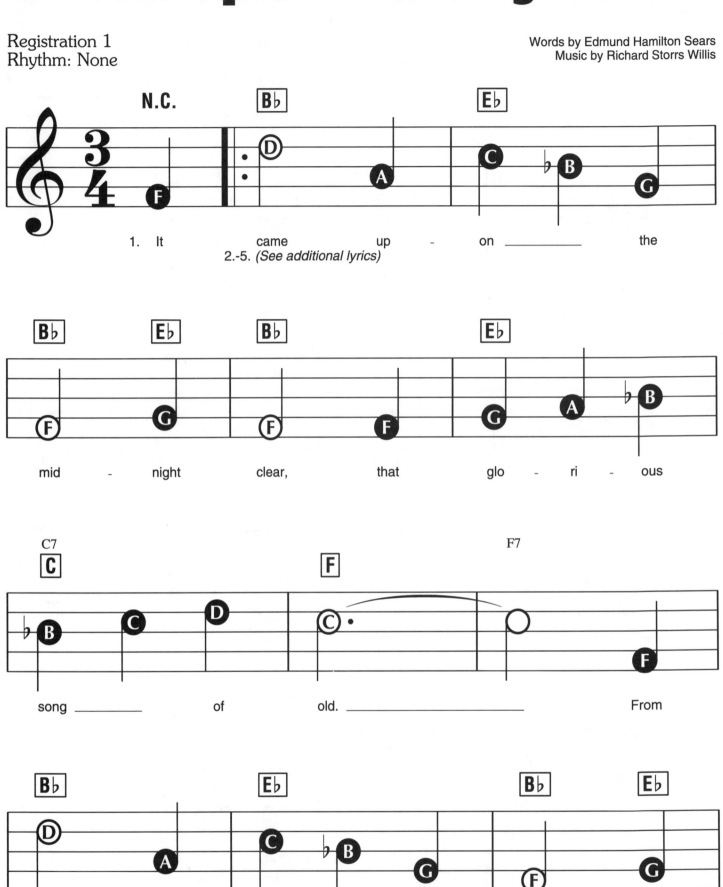

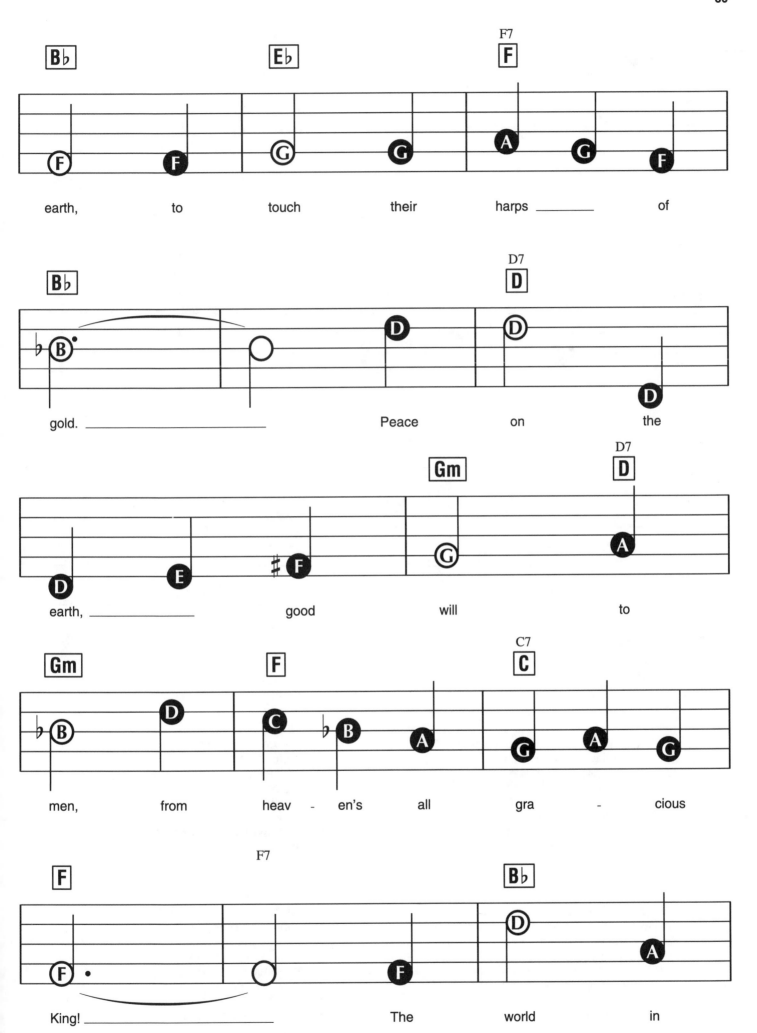

earth,   to   touch   their   harps _____ of

gold. _____   Peace   on   the

earth, _____   good   will   to

men,   from   heav - en's   all   gra - cious

King! _____   The   world   in

83

84

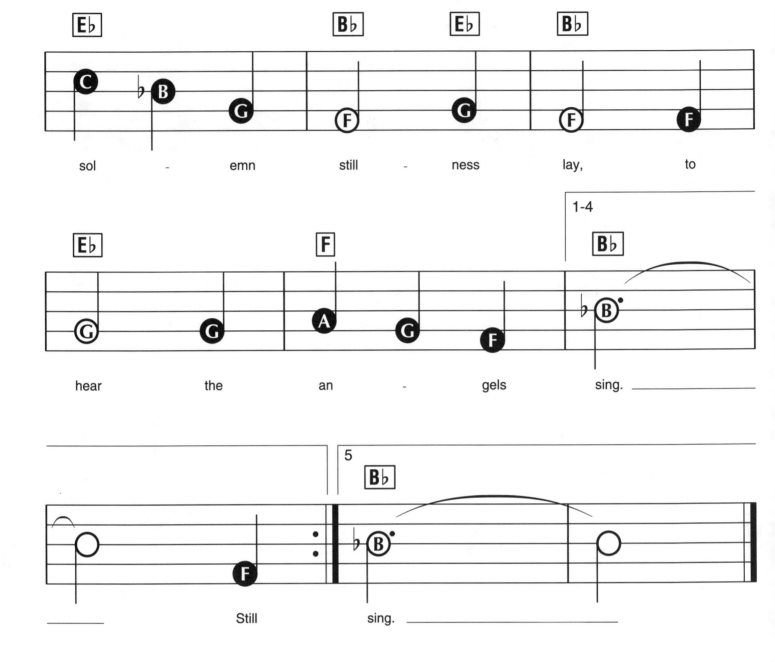

Additional Lyrics

2. Still through the cloven skies they come,
   with peaceful wings unfurled.
   And still their heavenly music floats,
   o'er all the weary world.
   Above its sad and lowly plains,
   they bend on hovering wing,
   And ever o'er its Babel sounds,
   the blessed angels sing.

3. Yet with the woes of sin and strife,
   the world hath suffered long.
   Beneath the angel-strain have rolled,
   two thousand years of wrong.
   And man, at war with man, hears not,
   the love song which they bring.
   O hush the noise, ye men of strife,
   and hear the angels sing.

4. And ye, beneath life's crushing load,
   whose forms are bending low.
   Who toil along the climbing way,
   with painful steps and slow.
   Look now! for glad and golden hours,
   come swiftly on the wing.
   O rest beside the weary road,
   and hear the angels sing.

5. For lo! the days are hastening on,
   by prophet-bards foretold.
   When, with the ever-circling years,
   shall come the Age of Gold,
   When peace shall over all the earth,
   its heavenly splendors fling.
   And all the world give back the song,
   which now the angels sing.

Jesus Born on This Day

Registration 2
Rhythm: 8 Beat or Rock

Words and Music by Mariah Carey
and Walter Afanasieff

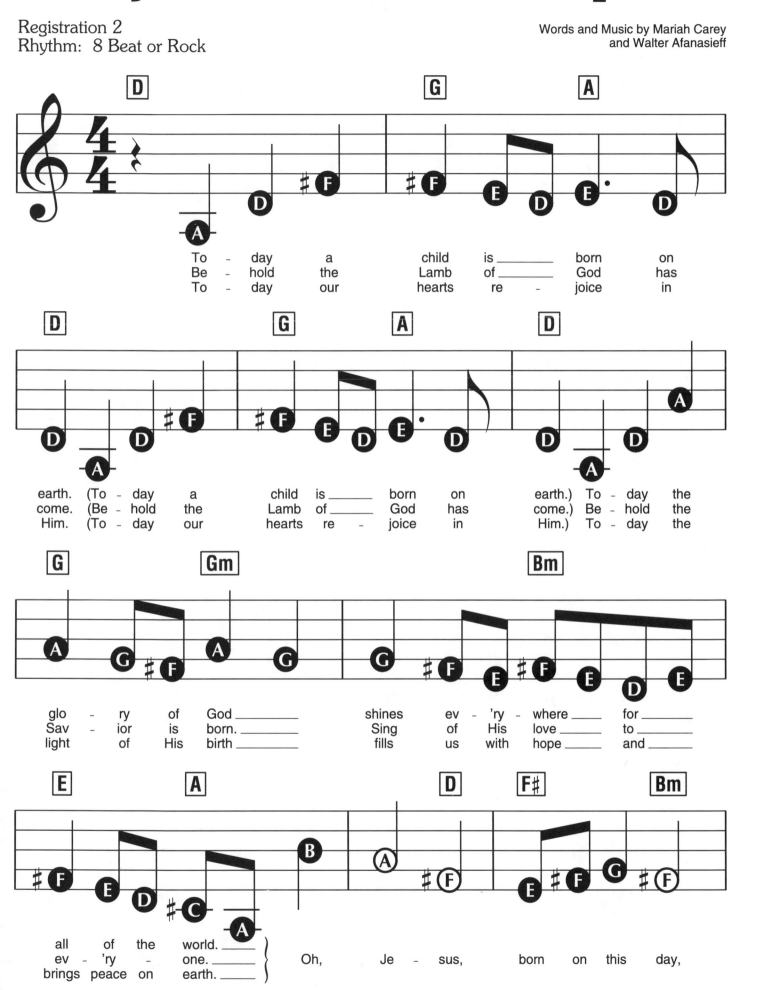

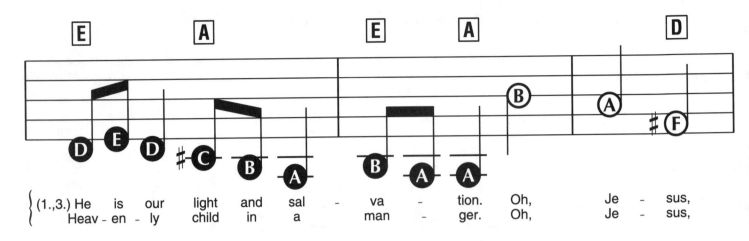

(1.,3.) He is our light and sal - va - tion. Oh, Je - sus,
Heav - en - ly child in a man - ger. Oh, Je - sus,

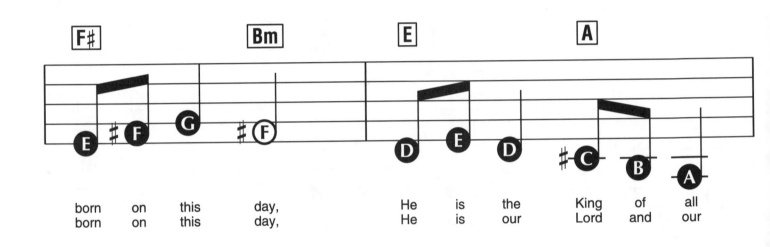

born on this day, He is the King of all
born on this day, He is our Lord and our

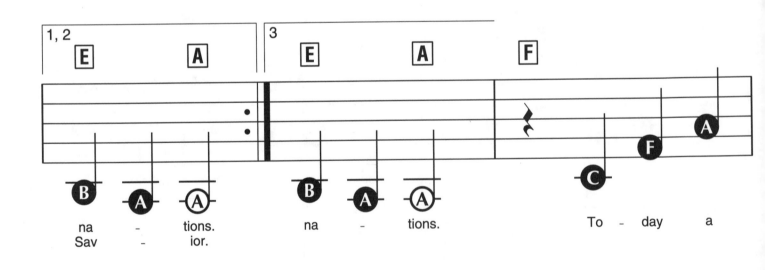

1, 2	3

na - tions. na - tions. To - day a
Sav - ior.

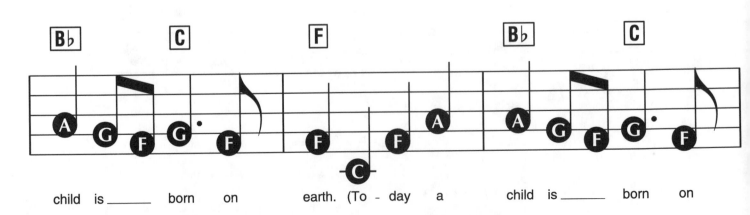

child is _____ born on earth. (To - day a child is _____ born on

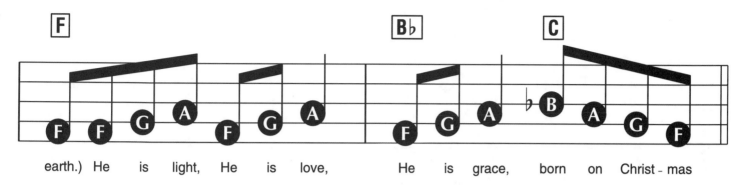

earth.) He is light, He is love, He is grace, born on Christ - mas

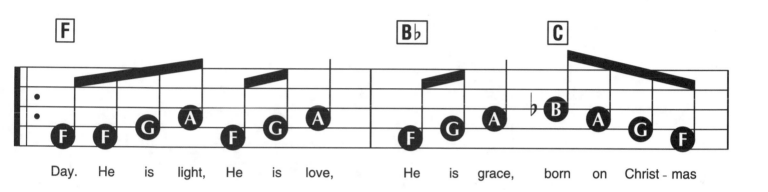

Day. He is light, He is love, He is grace, born on Christ - mas

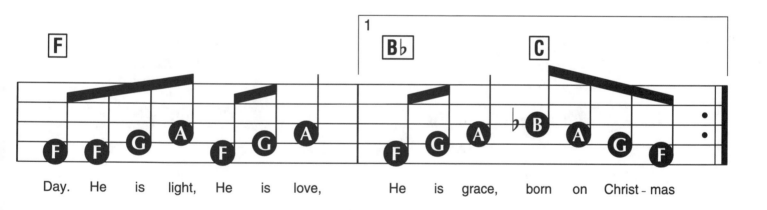

Day. He is light, He is love, He is grace, born on Christ - mas

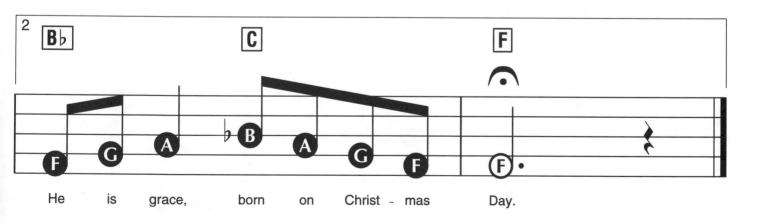

He is grace, born on Christ - mas Day.

Jingle-Bell Rock

Registration 5
Rhythm: Rock or Fox Trot

Words and Music by Joe Beal
and Jim Boothe

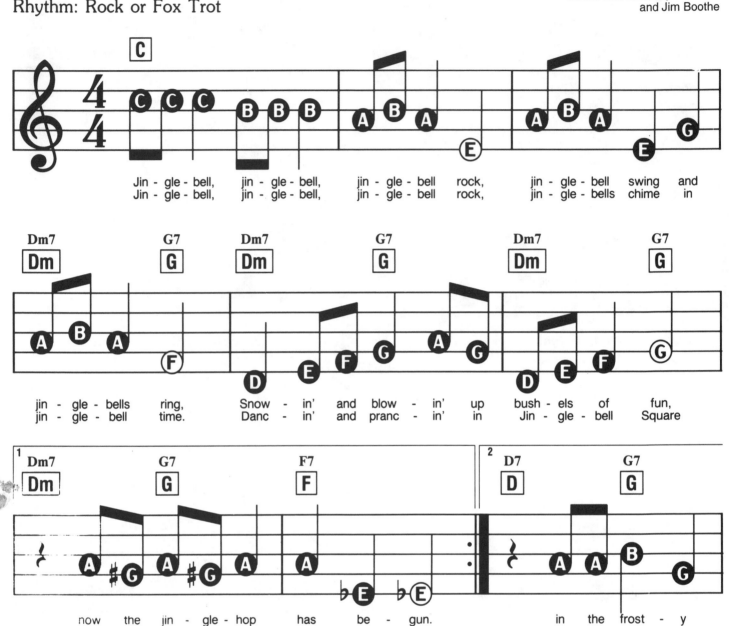

Jin - gle - bell, jin - gle - bell, jin - gle - bell rock, jin - gle - bell swing and
Jin - gle - bell, jin - gle - bell, jin - gle - bell rock, jin - gle - bells chime in

jin - gle - bells ring, Snow - in' and blow - in' up bush - els of fun,
jin - gle - bell time. Danc - in' and pranc - in' in Jin - gle - bell, Square

now the jin - gle - hop has be - gun. in the frost - y

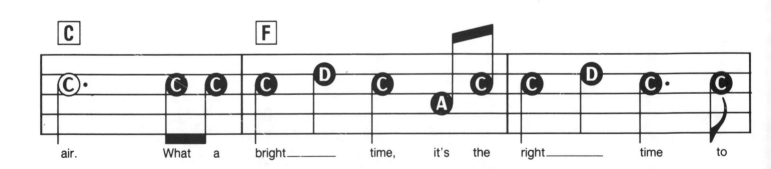

air. What a bright_____ time, it's the right_____ time to

Jingle Bells

Registration 5
Rhythm: Fox Trot or Swing

Words and Music by
J. Pierpont

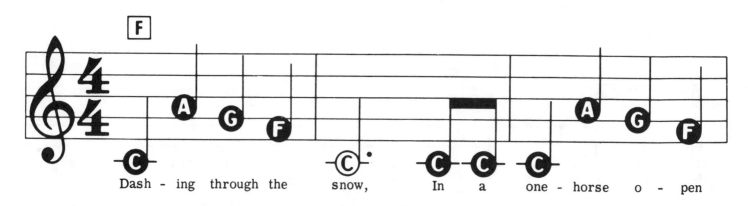

Dash - ing through the snow, In a one - horse o - pen

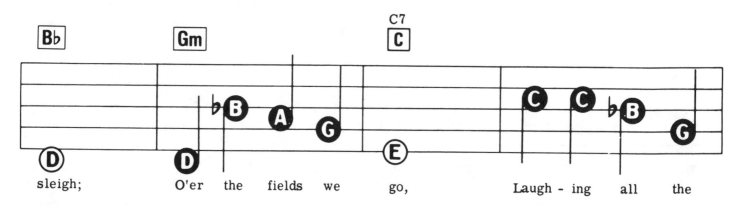

sleigh; O'er the fields we go, Laugh - ing all the

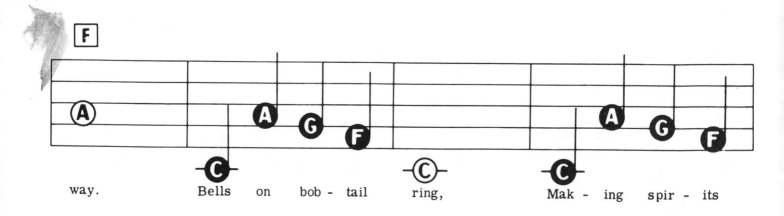

way. Bells on bob - tail ring, Mak - ing spir - its

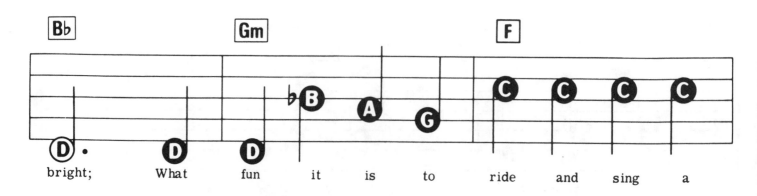

bright; What fun it is to ride and sing a

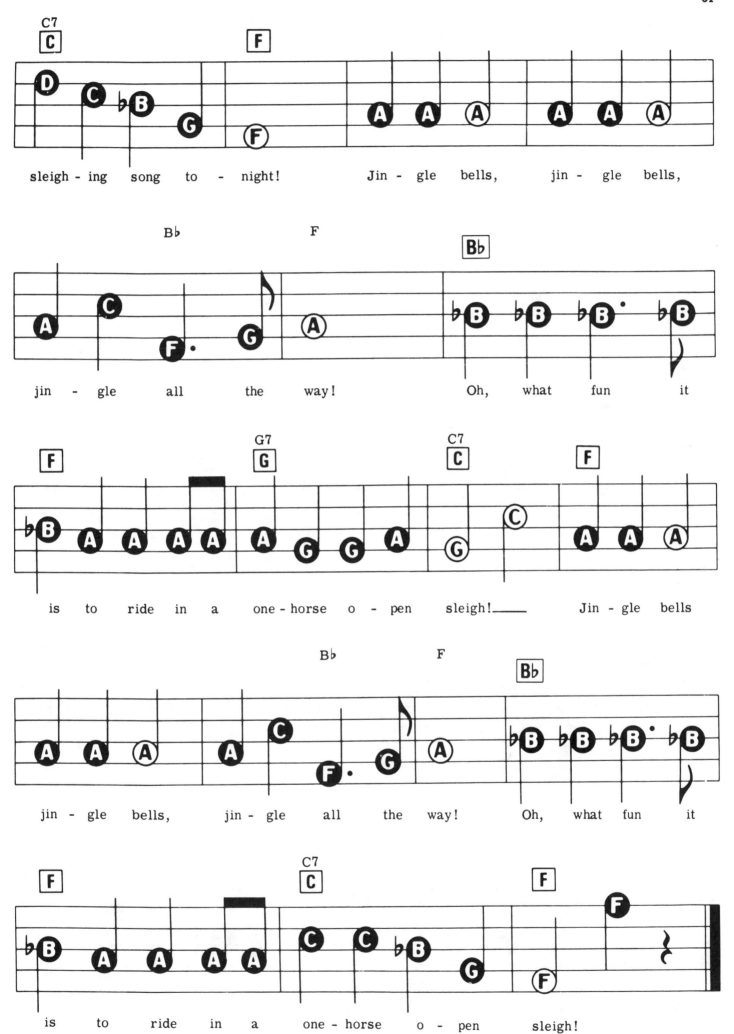

Jingle, Jingle, Jingle

Registration 9
Rhythm: Swing

Music and Lyrics by
Johnny Marks

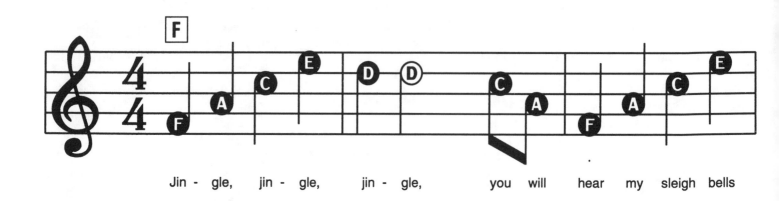

Jin - gle, jin - gle, jin - gle, you will hear my sleigh bells

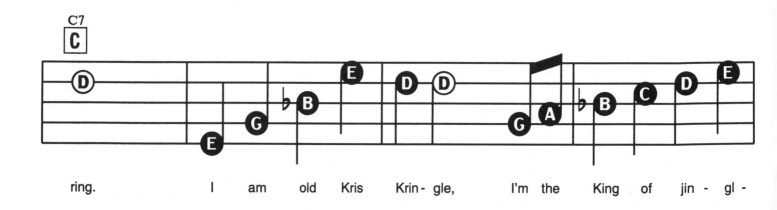

ring. I am old Kris Krin - gle, I'm the King of jin - gl-

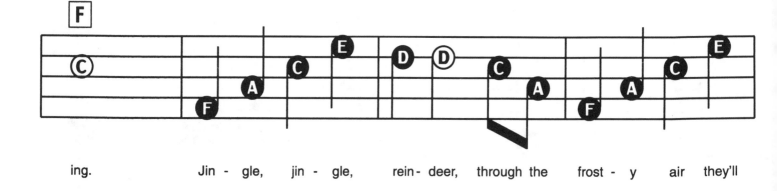

ing. Jin - gle, jin - gle, rein - deer, through the frost - y air they'll

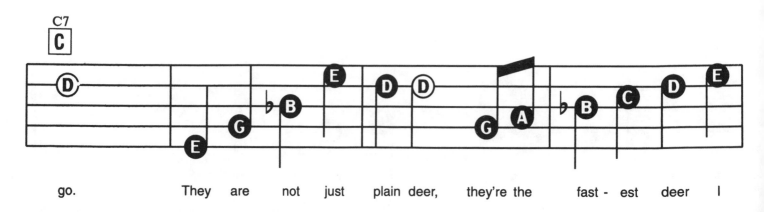

go. They are not just plain deer, they're the fast - est deer I

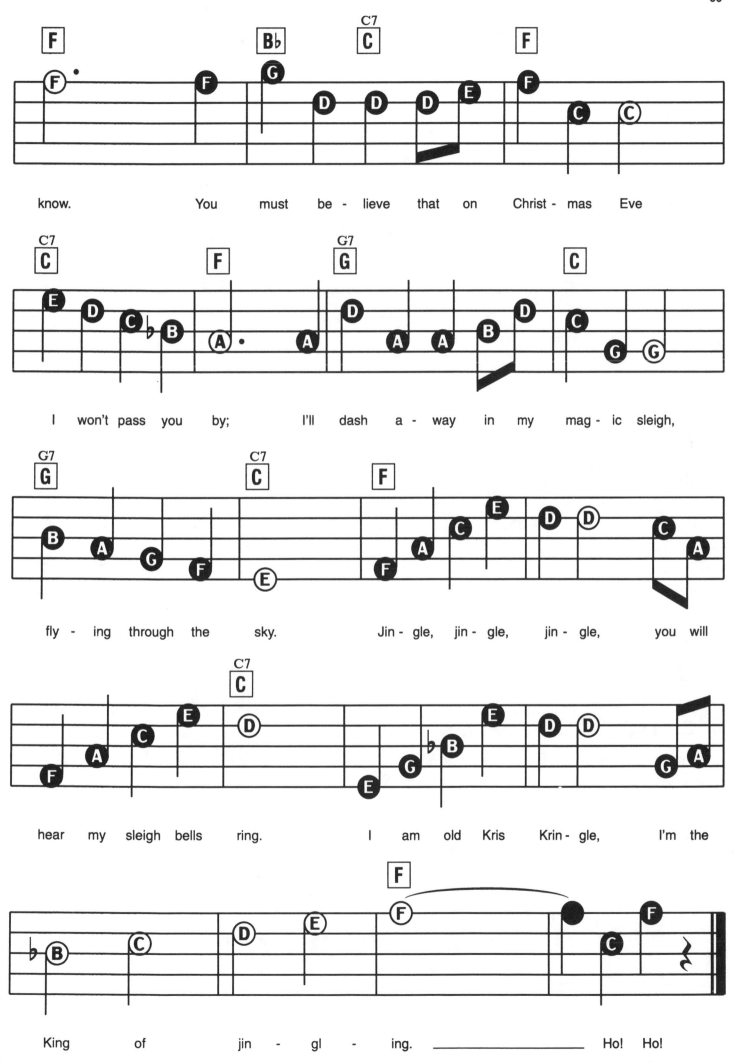

know.   You   must   be - lieve   that   on   Christ - mas   Eve

I   won't   pass   you   by;   I'll   dash   a - way   in   my   mag - ic   sleigh,

fly - ing   through   the   sky.   Jin - gle,   jin - gle,   jin - gle,   you   will

hear   my   sleigh   bells   ring.   I   am   old   Kris   Krin - gle,   I'm   the

King   of   jin - gl - ing. _____   Ho!   Ho!

Jolly Old St. Nicholas

Registration 2
Rhythm: Fox Trot or Swing

Traditional 19th Century American Carol

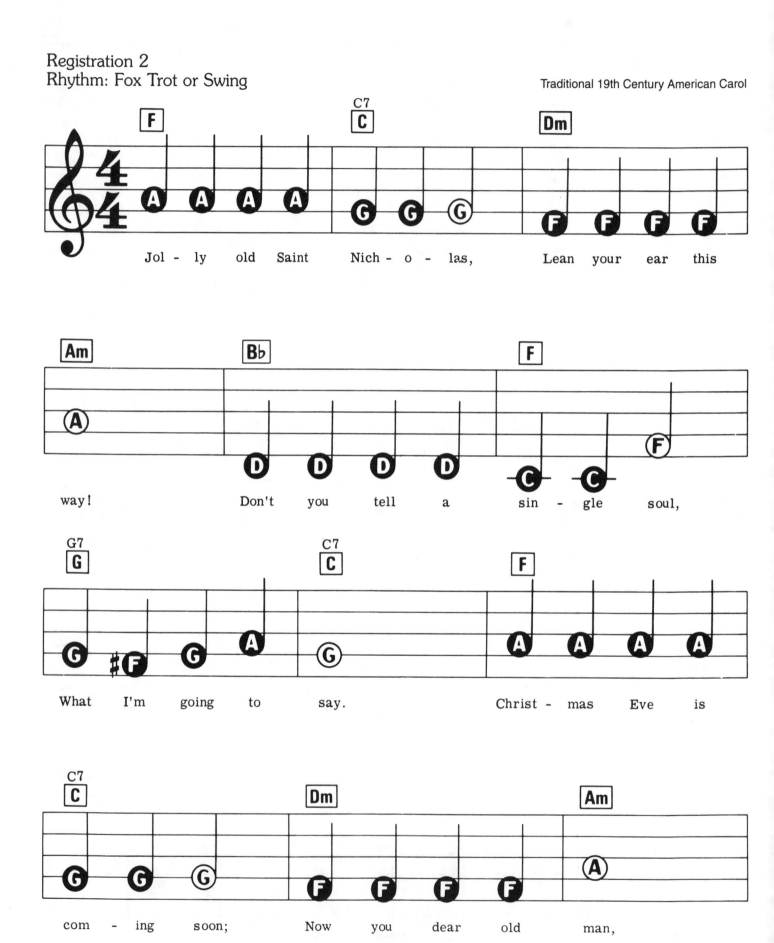

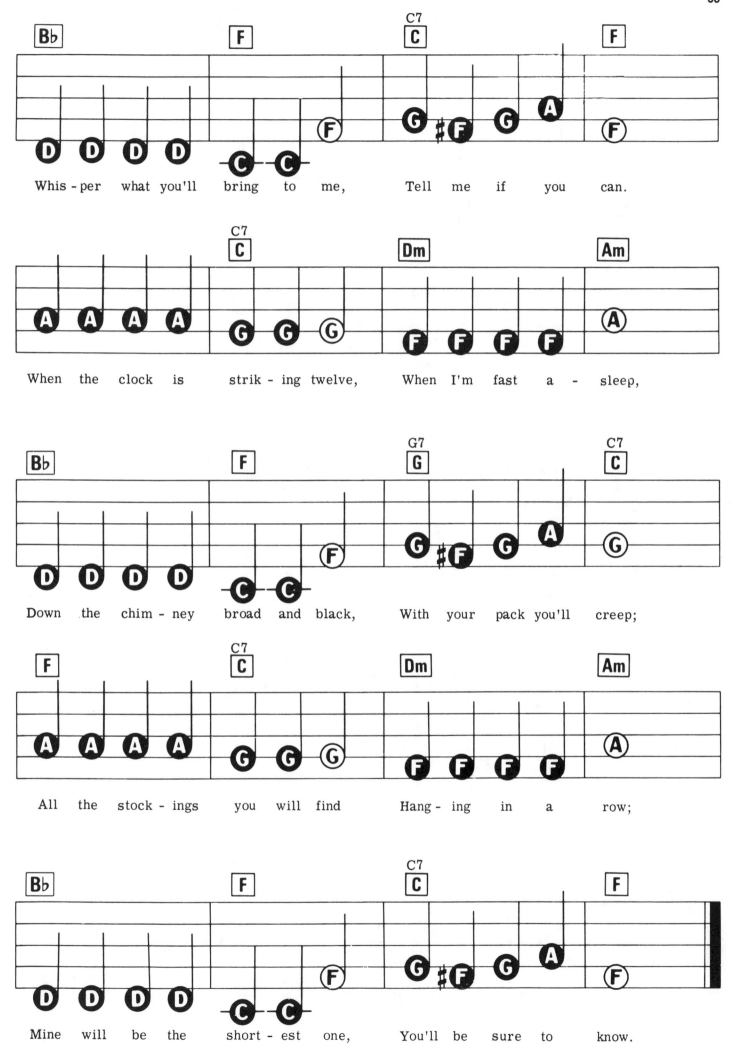

Joy to the World

Registration 2
Rhythm: None

Words by Isaac Watts
Music by George Frideric Handel
Arranged by Lowell Mason

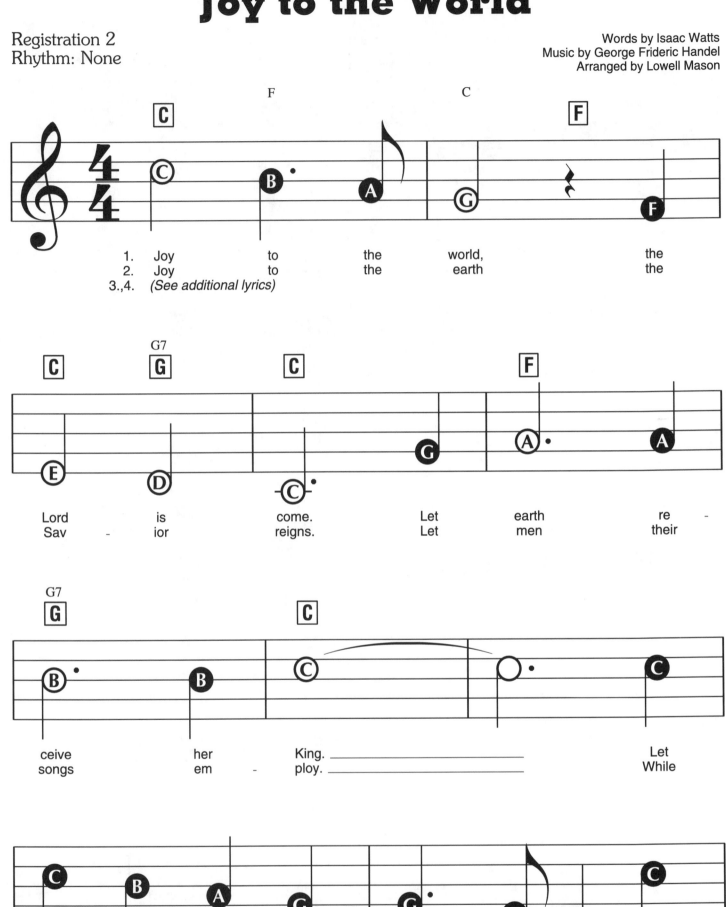

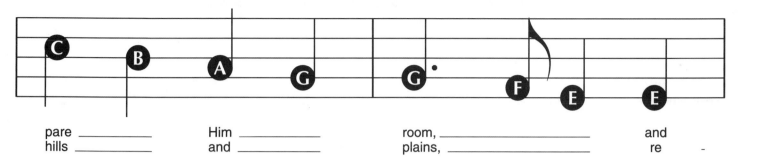

pare _____ Him _____ room, _____ and
hills _____ and _____ plains, _____ re -

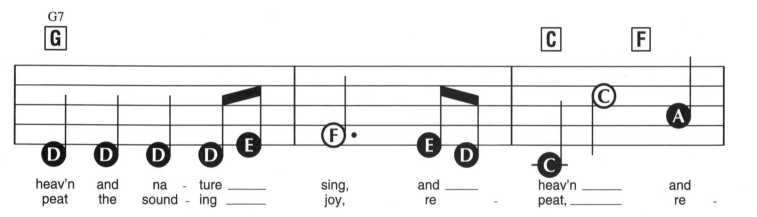

heav'n and na - ture _____ sing, and _____
peat and the sound - ing _____ joy, re -

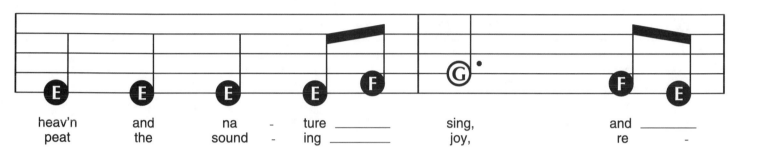

G7

| G | | | | | C | F |

heav'n and na - ture _____ sing, and _____ heav'n _____ and
peat the sound - ing _____ joy, re - peat, _____ re -

| C | | F | | C | G | C |
| | | | | | G7 | |

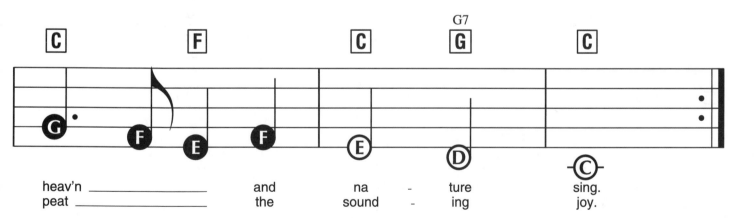

heav'n _____ and na - ture sing.
peat _____ the sound - ing joy.

Additional Lyrics

3. No more let sins and sorrows grow,
   nor thorns infest the ground.
   He comes to make His blessings flow,
   far as the curse is found,
   far as the curse is found,
   far as, far as the curse is found.

4. He rules the world with truth and grace,
   and makes the nations prove;
   the glories of His righteousness,
   and wonders of His love,
   and wonders of His love,
   and wonders, wonders of His love.

The Last Month of the Year
(What Month Was Jesus Born In?)

Registration 10
Rhythm: Pops or Country

Words and Music by Vera Hall
Adapted and Arranged by Ruby Pickens Tartt and Alan Lomax

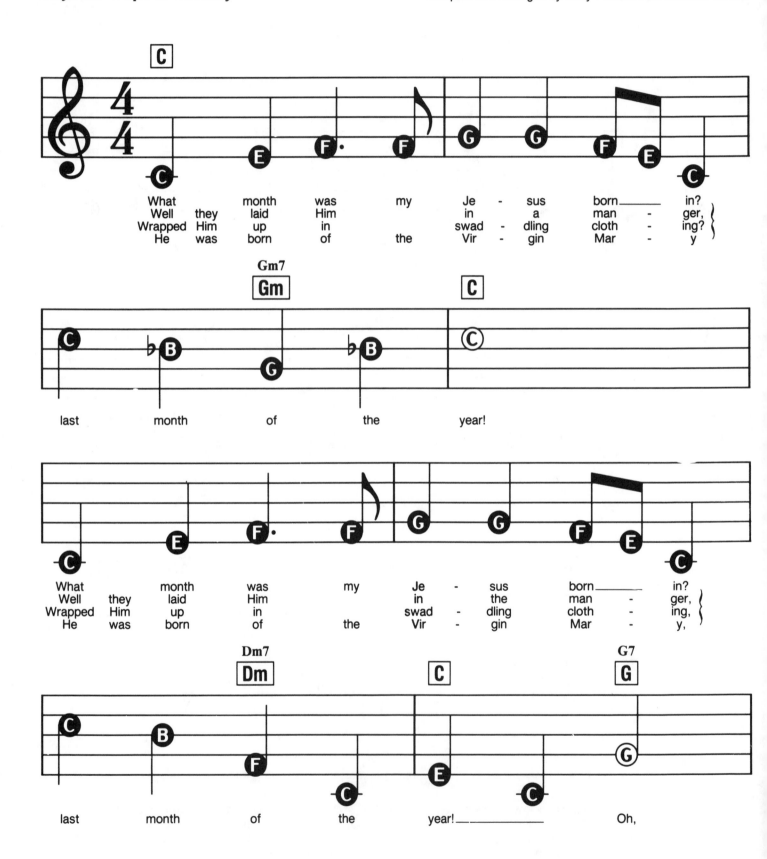

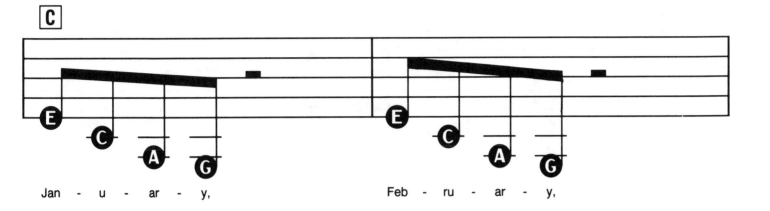

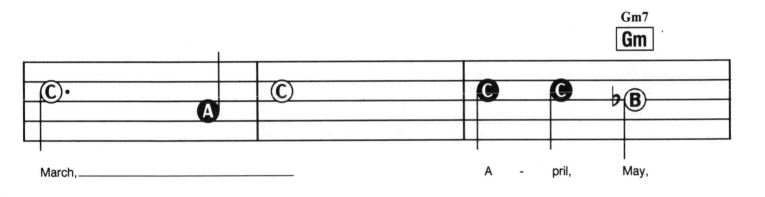

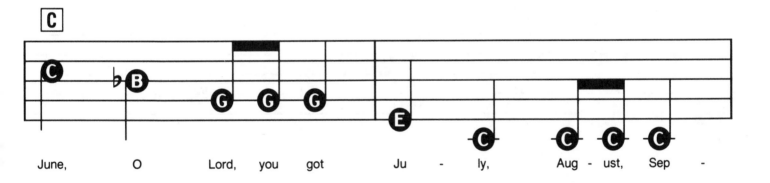

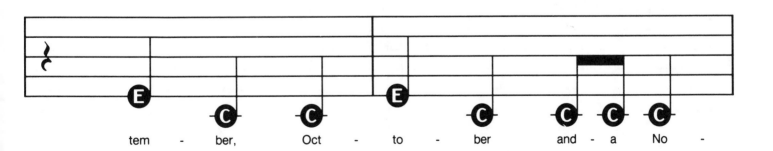

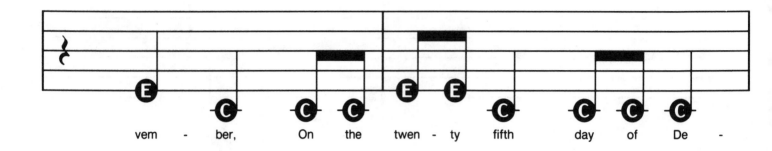

vem - ber, On the twen - ty fifth day of De -

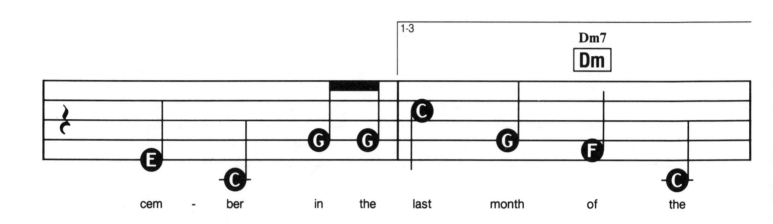

cem - ber in the last month of the

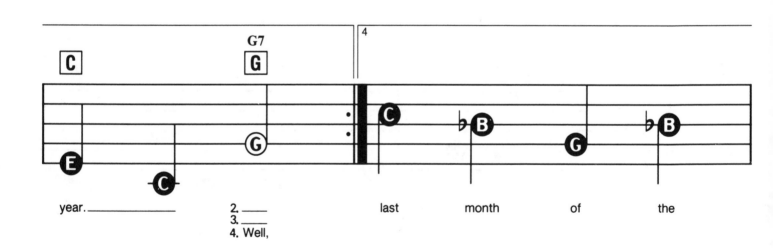

year._____ 2.___ 3.___ 4. Well, last month of the

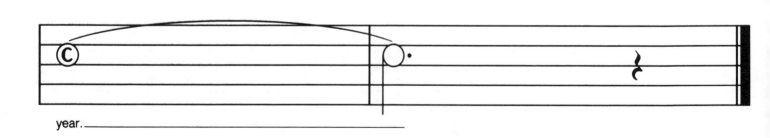

year._____

Merry Christmas, Darling

Registration 9
Rhythm: 4/4 Ballad

Words and Music by Richard Carpenter
and Frank Pooler

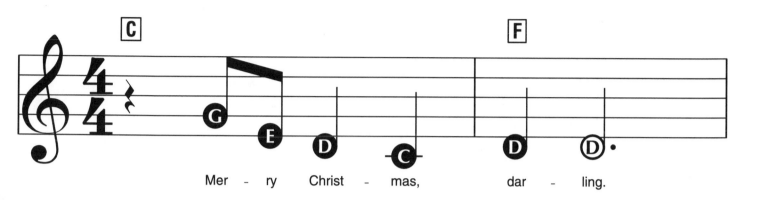

Mer - ry Christ - mas, dar - ling.

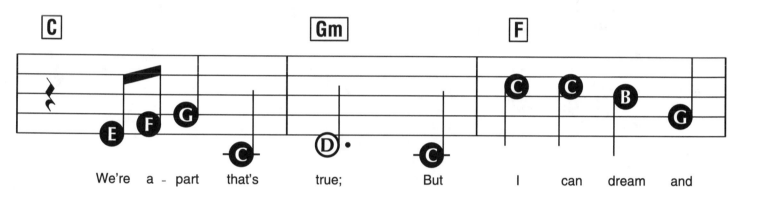

We're a - part that's true; But I can dream and

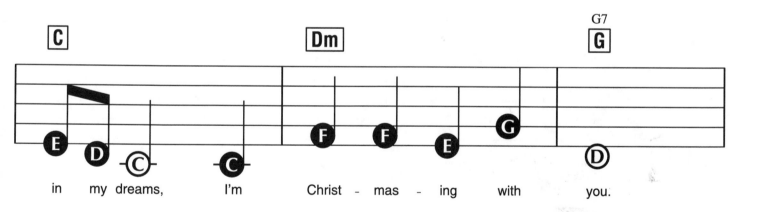

in my dreams, I'm Christ - mas - ing with you.

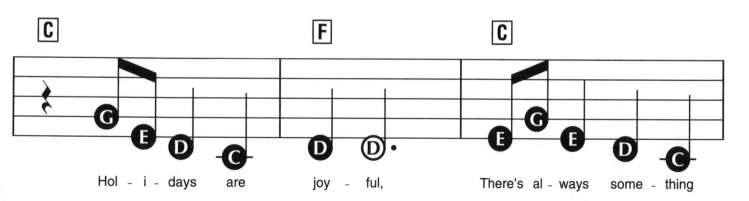

Hol - i - days are joy - ful, There's al - ways some - thing

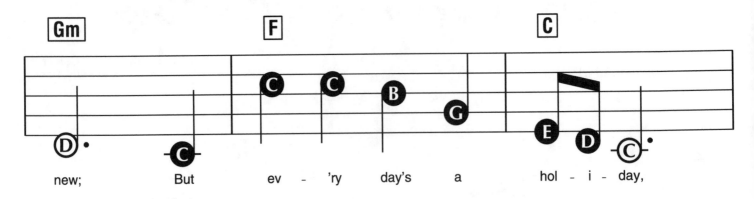

new;   But   ev - 'ry   day's   a   hol - i - day,

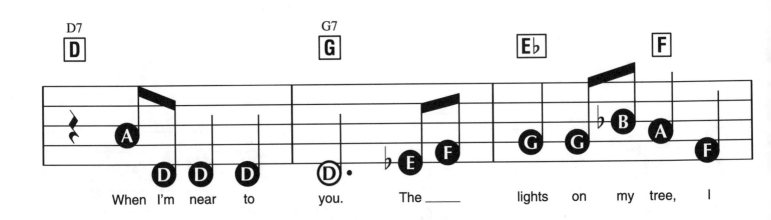

When I'm near   to   you.   The _____   lights on my tree, I

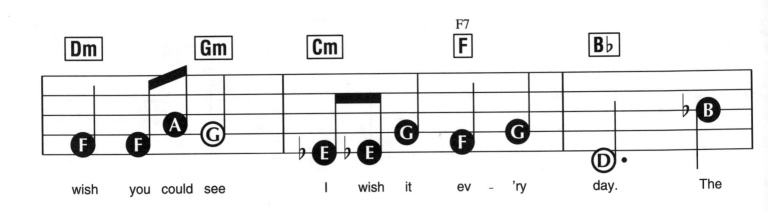

wish you could see   I wish it ev - 'ry   day.   The

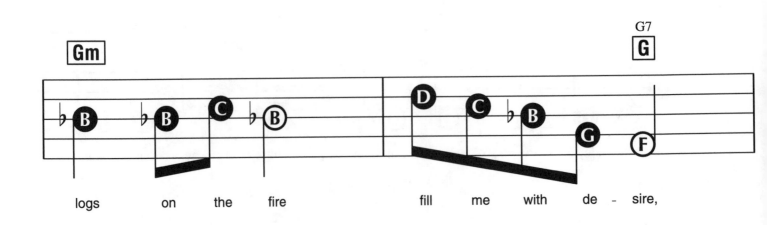

logs   on   the   fire   fill   me with de - sire,

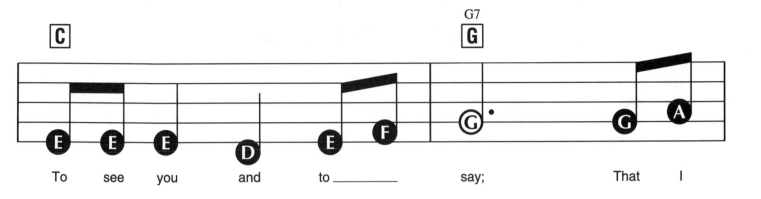

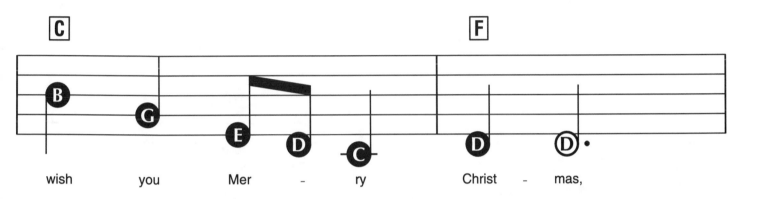

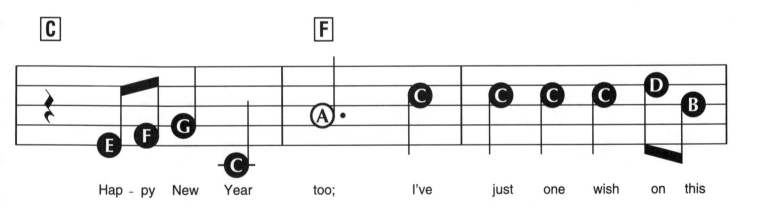

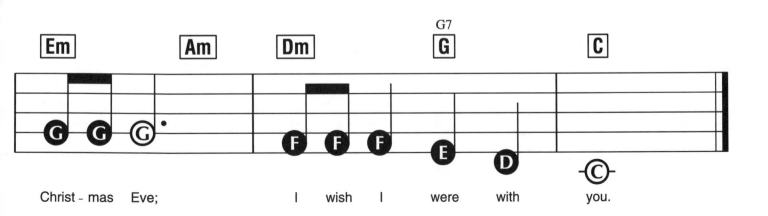

Let It Snow! Let It Snow! Let It Snow!

Registration 2
Rhythm: Fox Trot or Swing

Words by Sammy Cahn
Music by Jule Styne

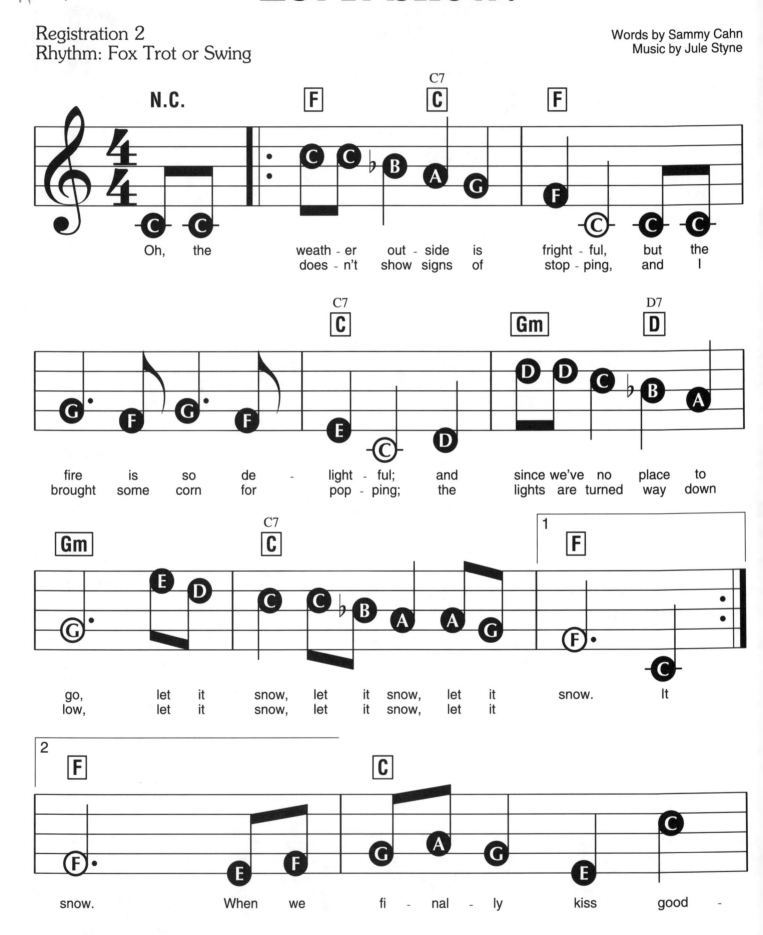

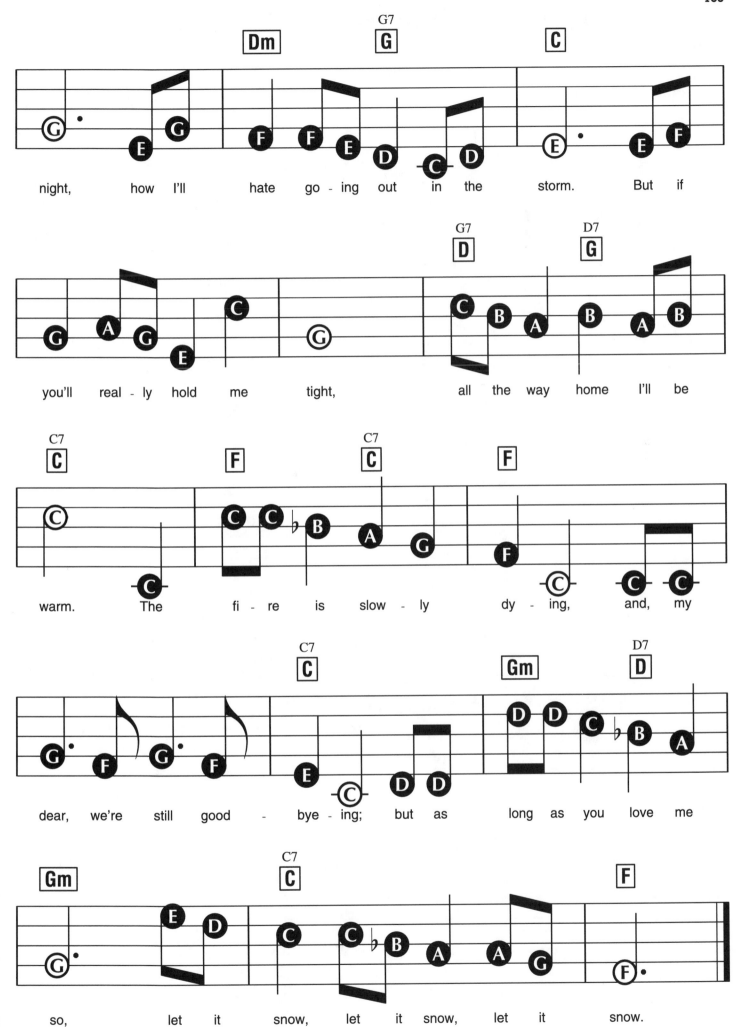

A Marshmallow World

Registration 2
Rhythm: Fox Trot or Swing

Words by Carl Sigman
Music by Peter De Rose

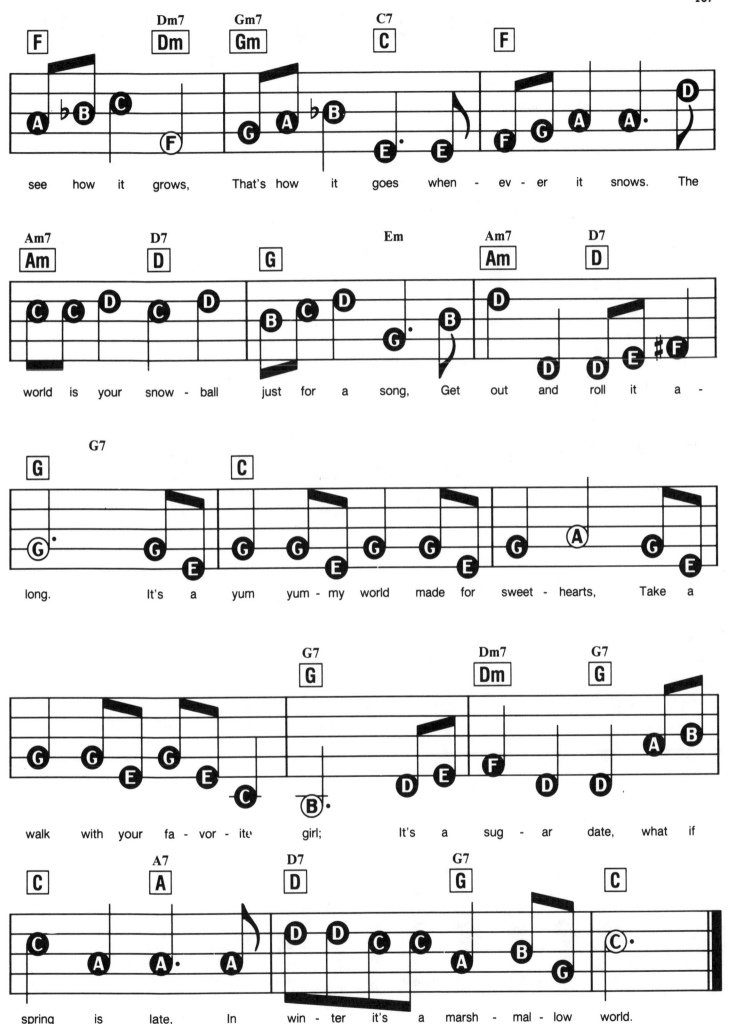

Merry Christmas from the Family

Registration 7
Rhythm: Fox Trot or Swing

Words and Music by
Robert Earl Keen

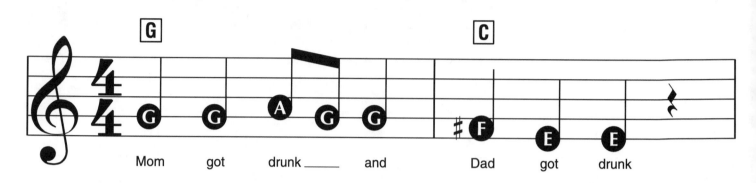

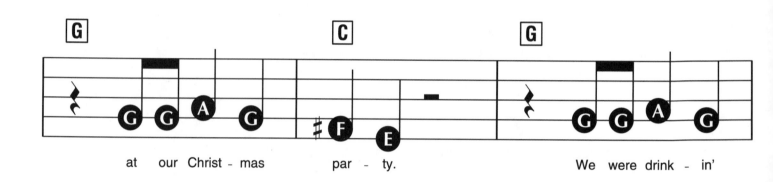

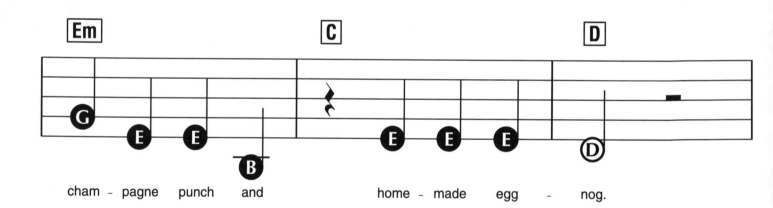

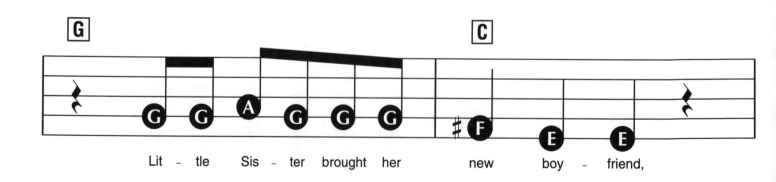

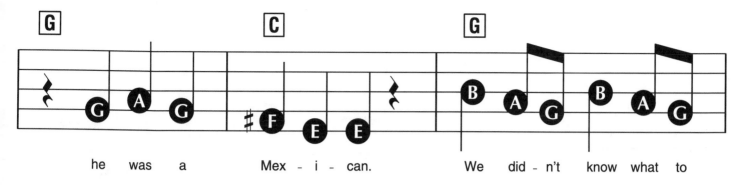

he was a Mex – i – can. We did –n't know what to

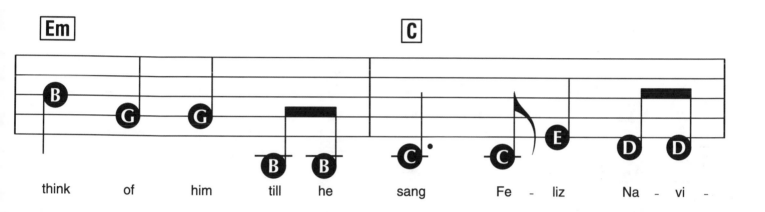

think of him till he sang Fe – liz Na – vi –

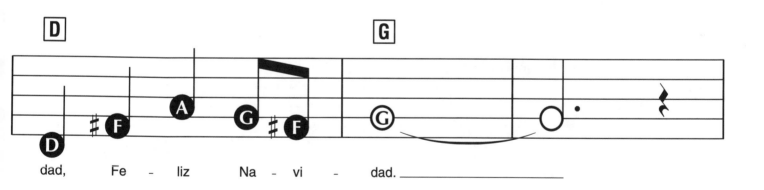

dad, Fe – liz Na – vi – dad. _____

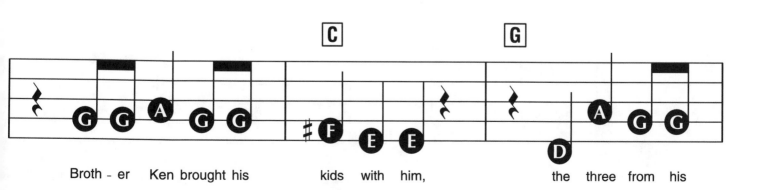

Broth – er Ken brought his kids with him, the three from his

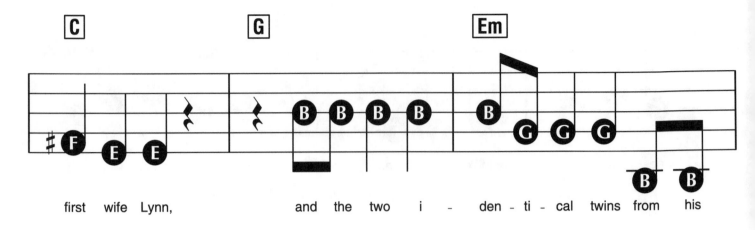

first wife Lynn, and the two i – den – ti – cal twins from his

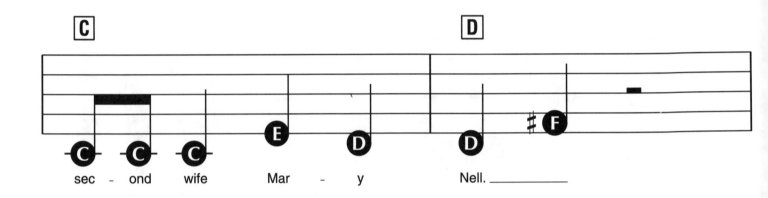

sec – ond wife Mar – y Nell. _____

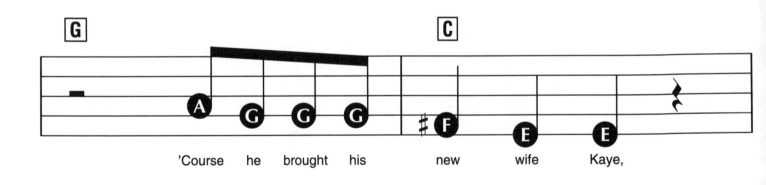

'Course he brought his new wife Kaye,

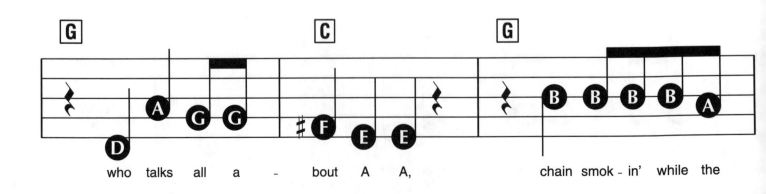

who talks all a – bout A A, chain smok – in' while the

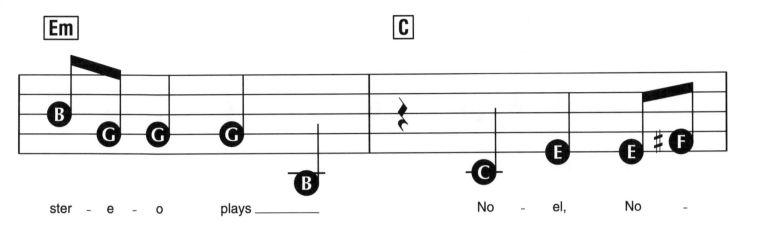

ster - e - o plays _____ No - el, No -

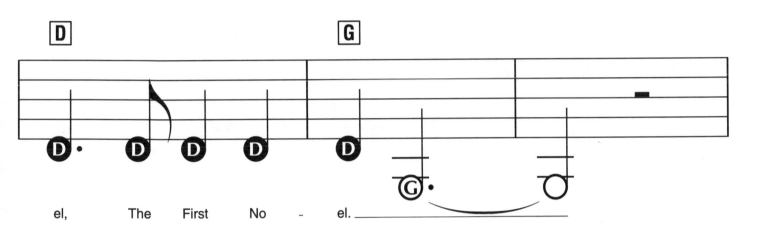

el, The First No - el. _____

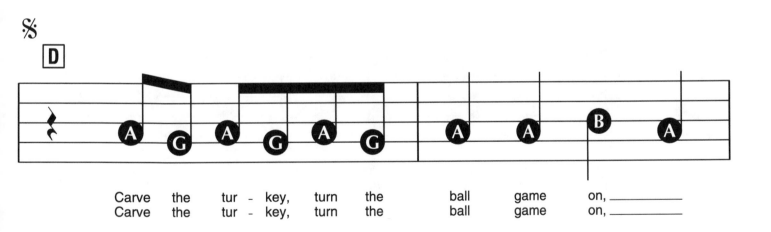

Carve the tur - key, turn the ball game on, _____
Carve the tur - key, turn the ball game on, _____

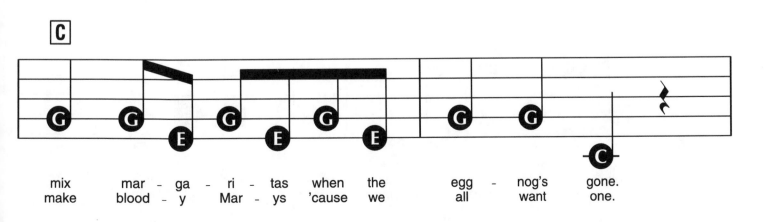

mix mar - ga - ri - tas when the egg - nog's gone.
make blood - y Mar - ys 'cause we all want one.

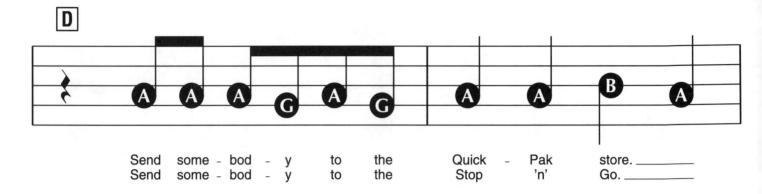

Send some - bod - y to the Quick - Pak store. _____
Send some - bod - y to the Stop 'n' Go. _____

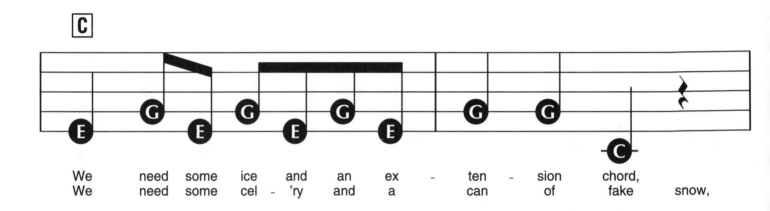

We need some ice and an ex - ten - sion chord,
We need some cel - 'ry and a can of fake snow,

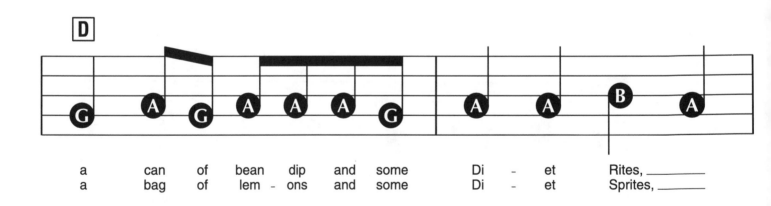

a can of bean dip and some Di - et Rites, _____
a bag of lem - ons and some Di - et Sprites, _____

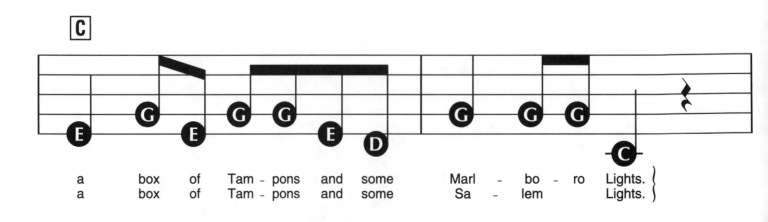

a box of Tam - pons and some Marl - bo - ro Lights. }
a box of Tam - pons and some Sa - lem Lights. }

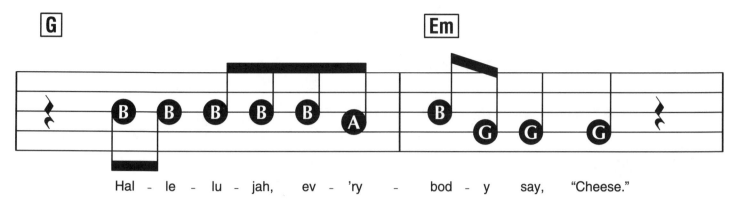

Hal - le - lu - jah, ev - 'ry - bod - y say, "Cheese."

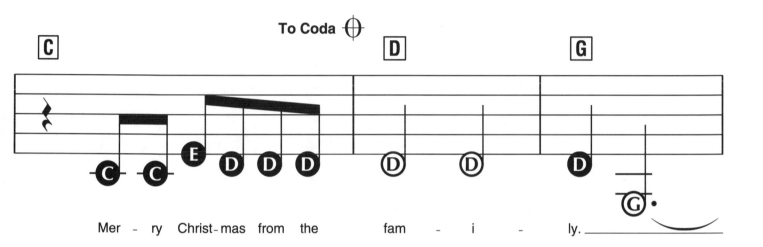

To Coda

Mer - ry Christ - mas from the fam - i - ly. _____

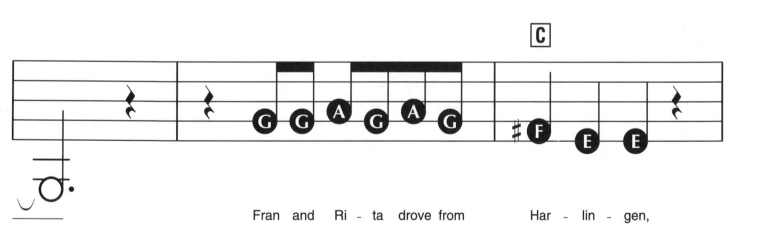

Fran and Ri - ta drove from Har - lin - gen,

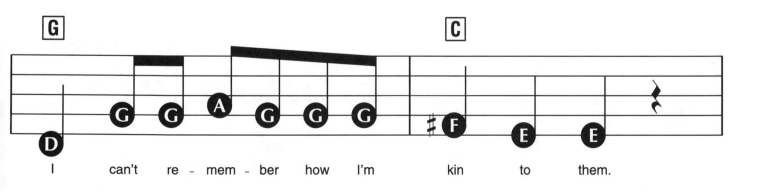

I can't re - mem - ber how I'm kin to them.

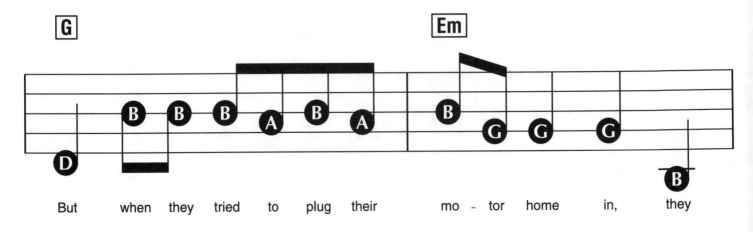

But when they tried to plug their mo - tor home in, they

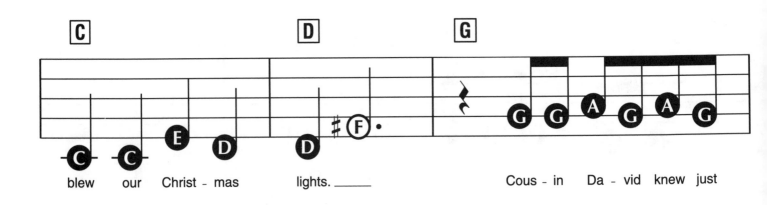

blew our Christ - mas lights. _____ Cous - in Da - vid knew just

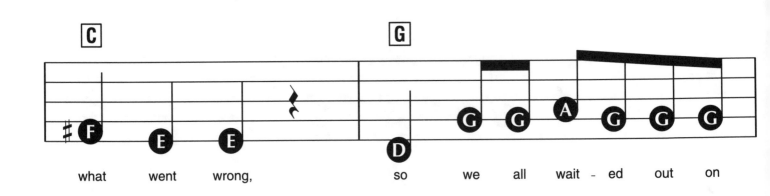

what went wrong, so we all wait - ed out on

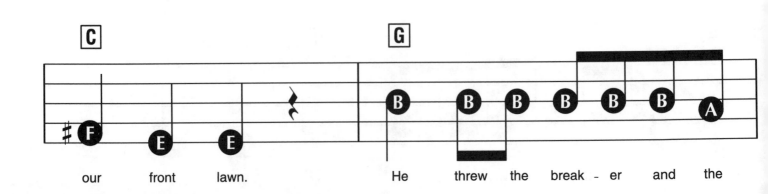

our front lawn. He threw the break - er and the

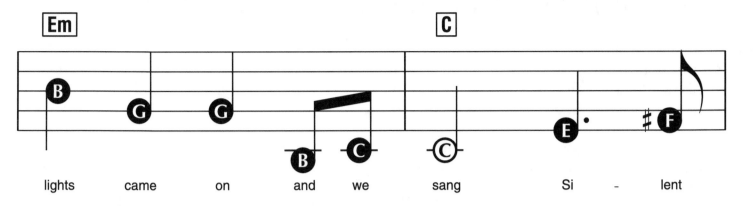

lights came on and we sang Si - lent

D.S. al Coda
(Return to 𝄋
Play to ⊕ and
Skip to Coda)

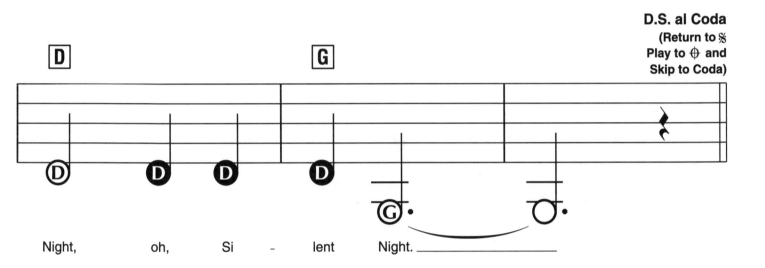

Night, oh, Si - lent Night. _____

CODA

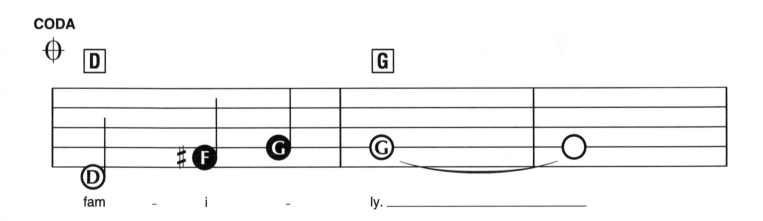

fam - i - ly. _____

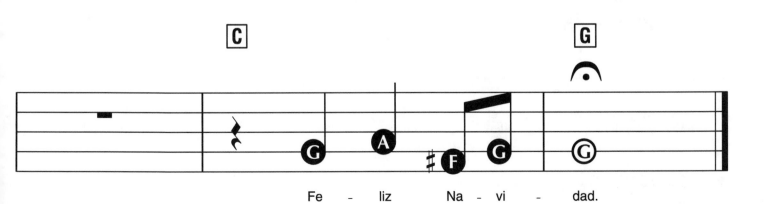

Fe - liz Na - vi - dad.

The Merry Christmas Polka

Registration 9
Rhythm: Polka or March

Words by Paul Francis Webster
Music by Sonny Burke

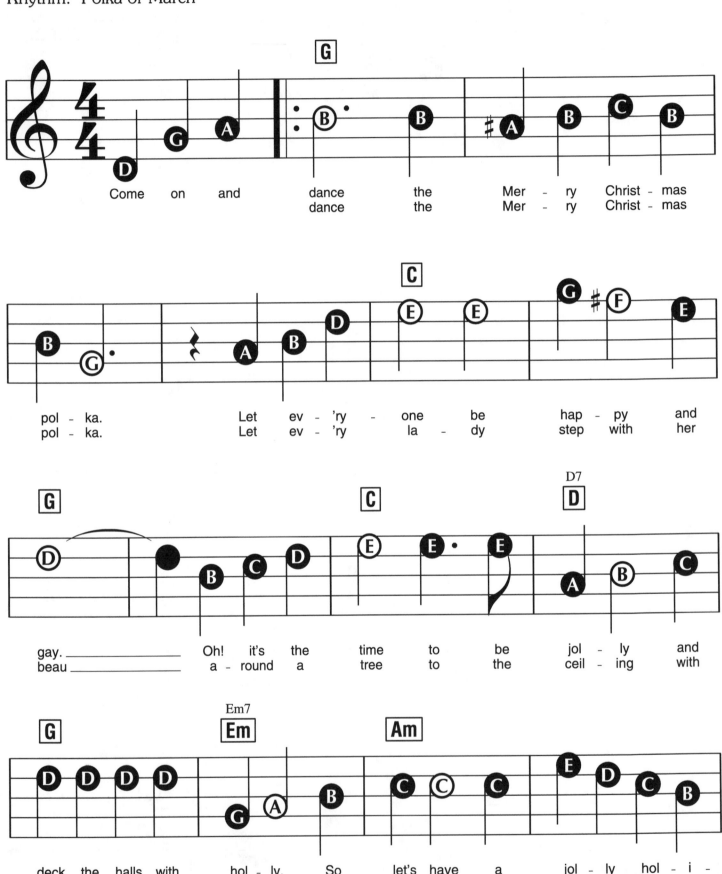

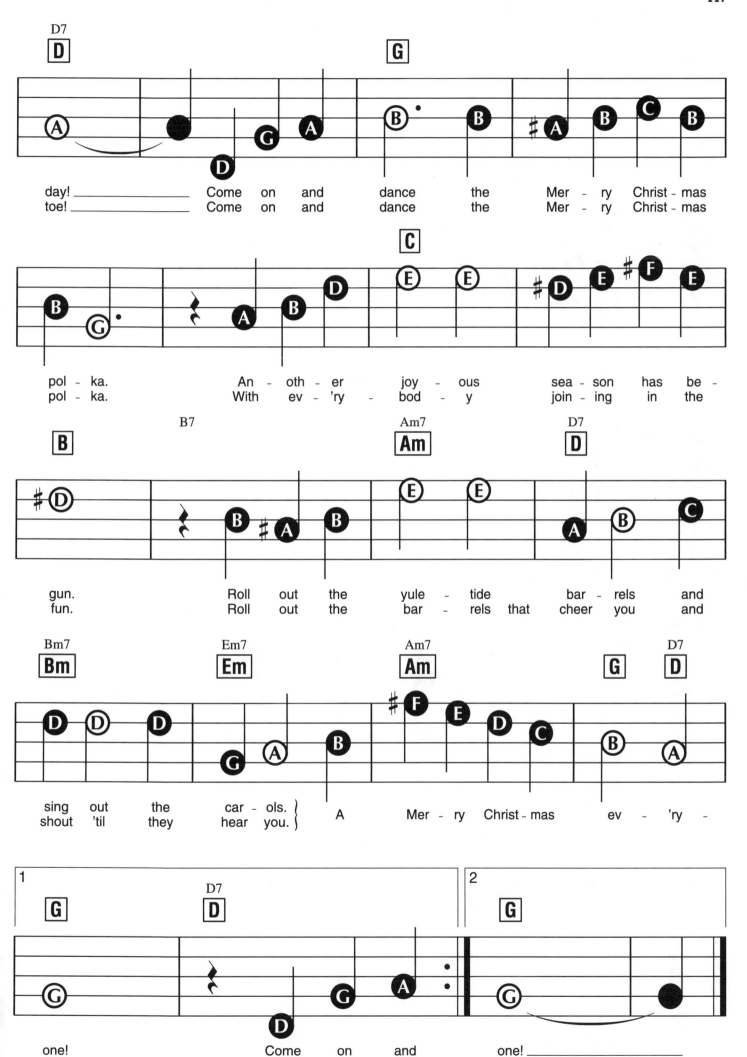

A Merry, Merry Christmas to You

Registration 2
Rhythm: Waltz

Music and Lyrics by
Johnny Marks

Mer - ry, mer - ry, mer - ry, mer - ry, mer - ry Christ - mas to you. _____ May each day be ver - y, ver - y hap - py all the year through. _____ A - round the world you'll see the

Return to ①
Play to ②
Skip to ③

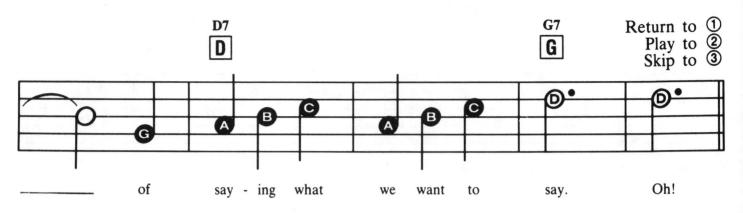

of say - ing what we want to say. Oh!

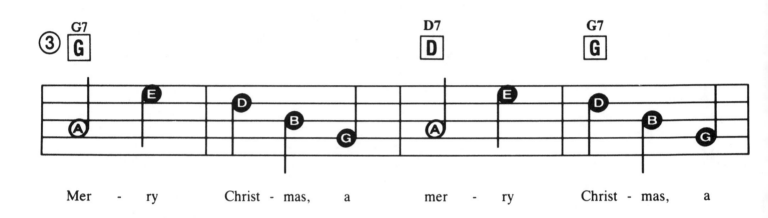

Mer - ry Christ - mas, a mer - ry Christ - mas, a

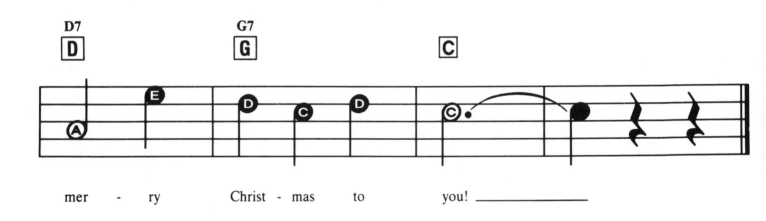

mer - ry Christ - mas to you! _____

The Most Wonderful Day of the Year

Registration 3
Rhythm: Waltz

Music and Lyrics by
Johnny Marks

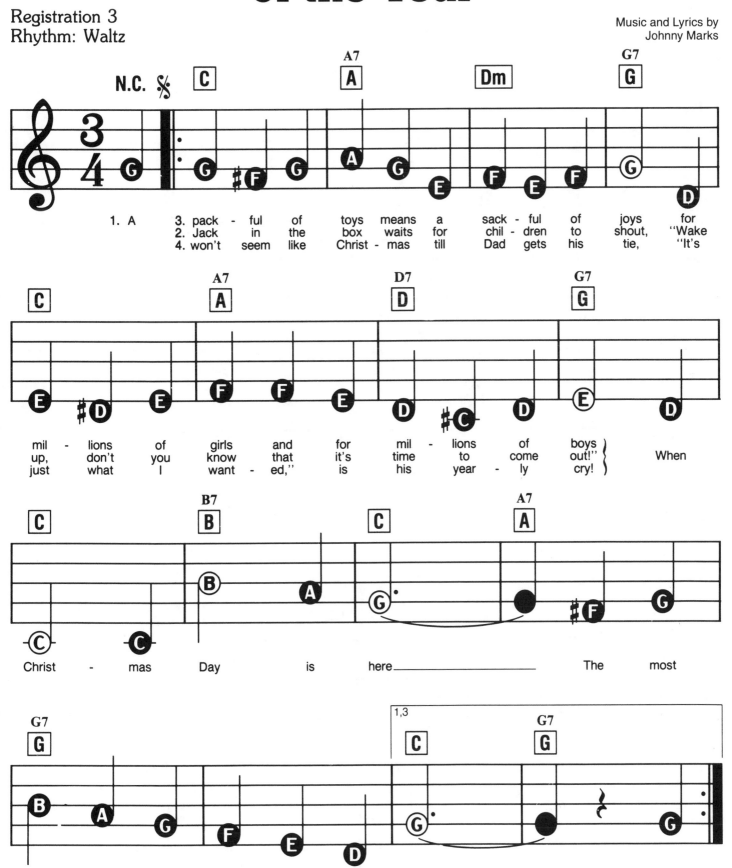

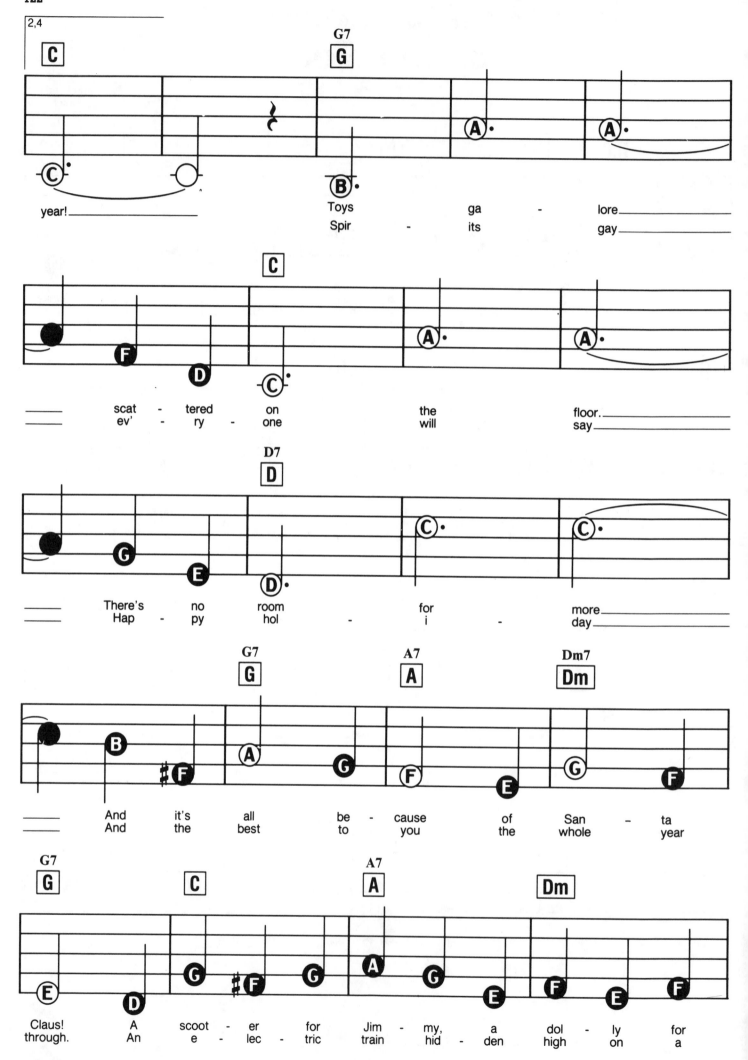

123

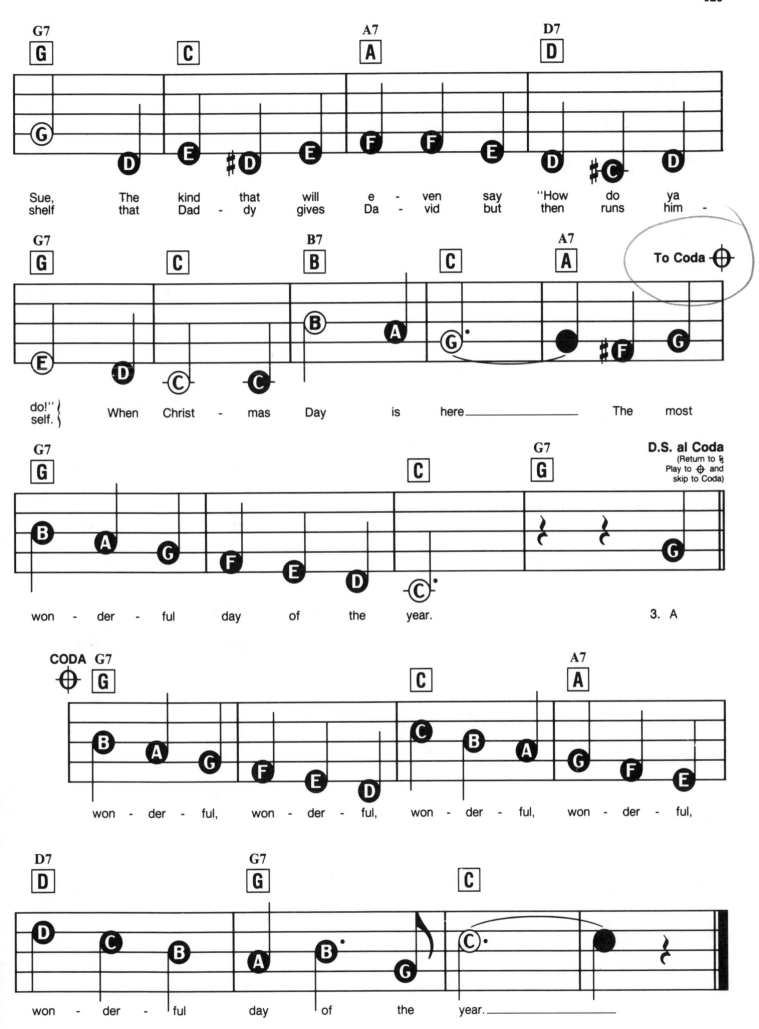

The Night Before Christmas Song

Registration 3
Rhythm: Waltz

Music by Johnny Marks
Lyrics adapted by Johnny Marks from Clement Moore's Poem

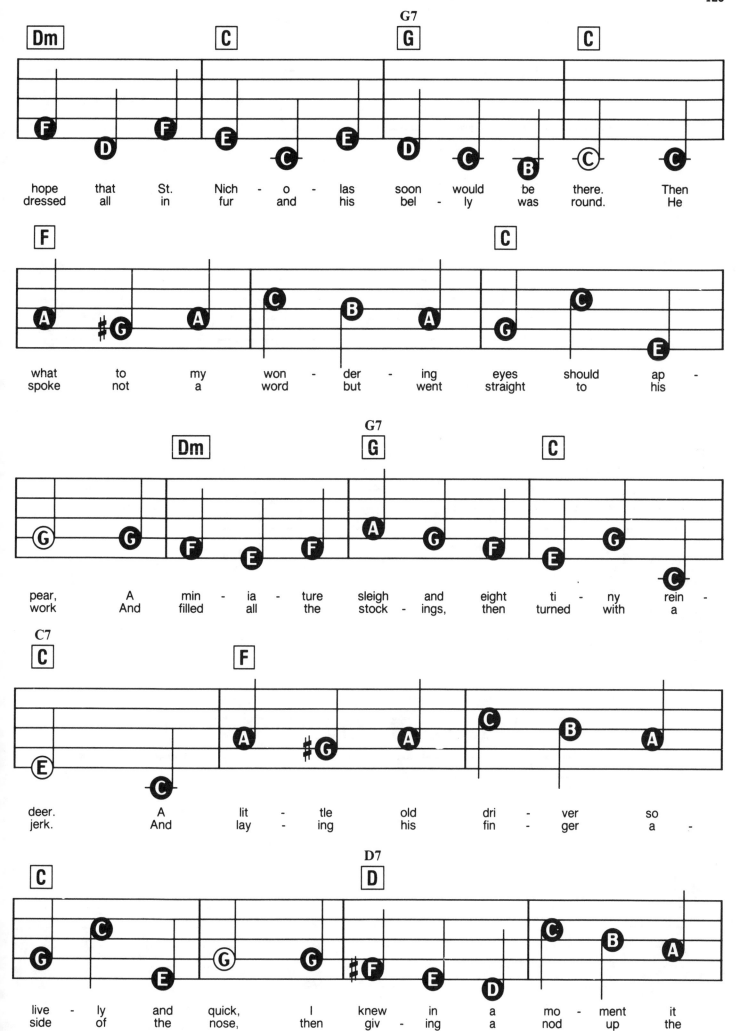

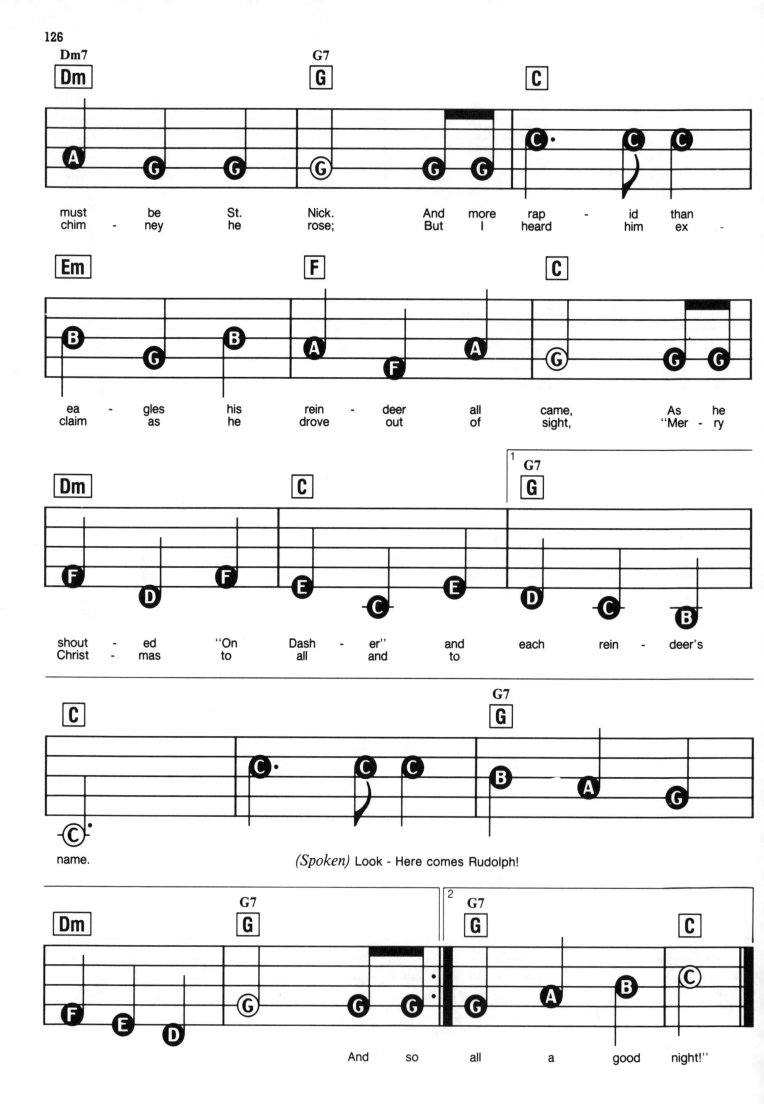

O Christmas Tree

Registration 3
Rhythm: None

Traditional German Carol

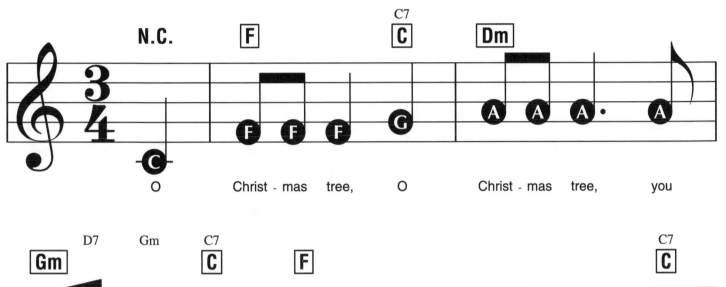

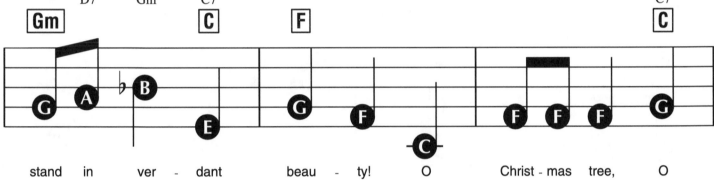

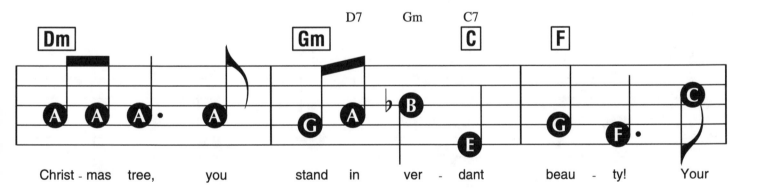

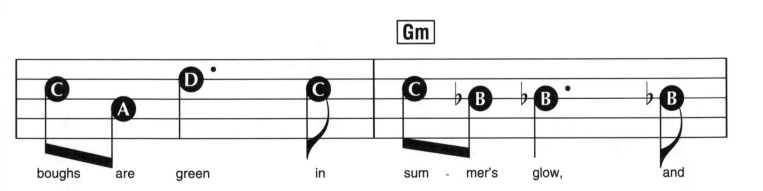

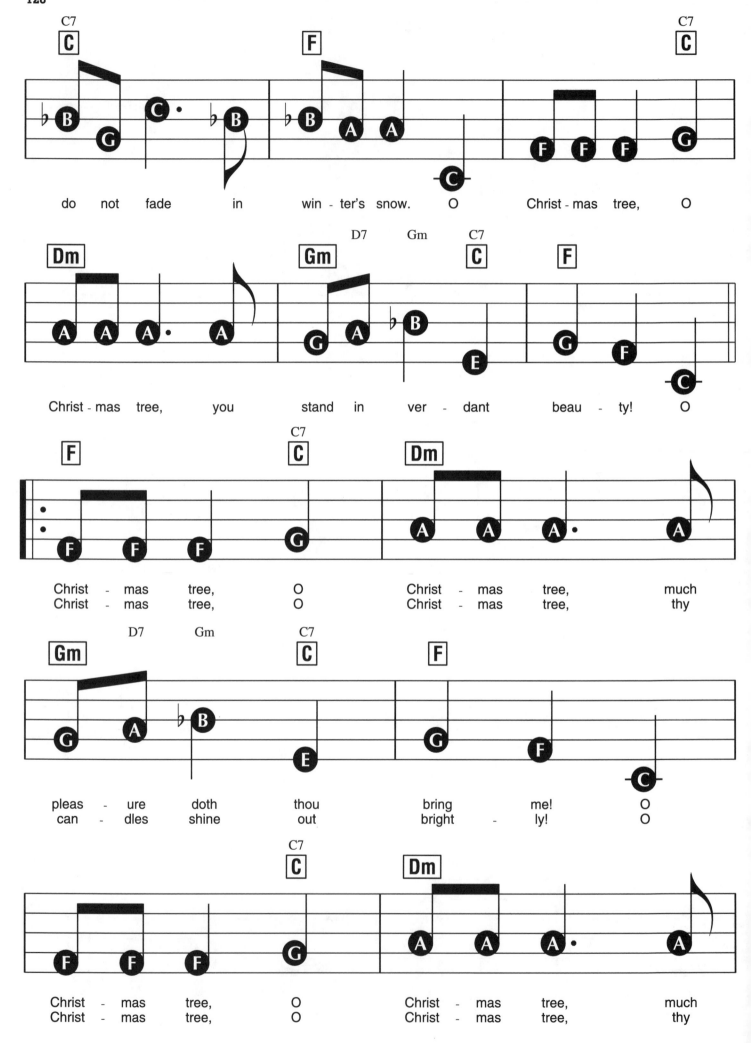

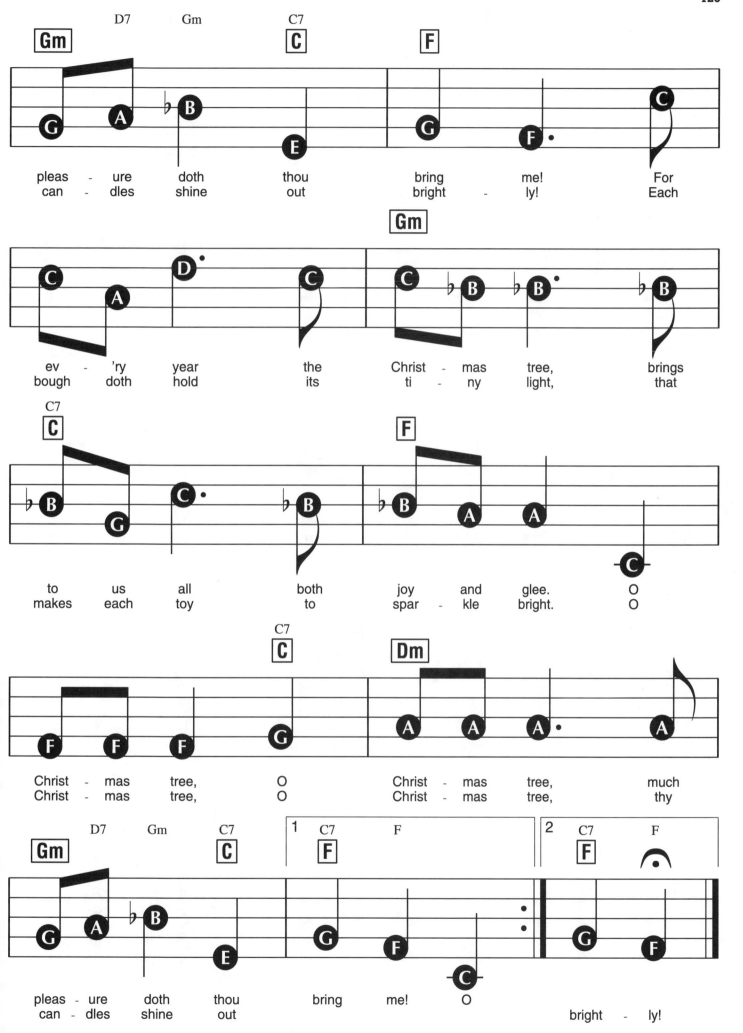

Nuttin' for Christmas

Registration: 2
Rhythm: Fox Trot or Shuffle

Words and Music by Roy Bennett
and Sid Tepper

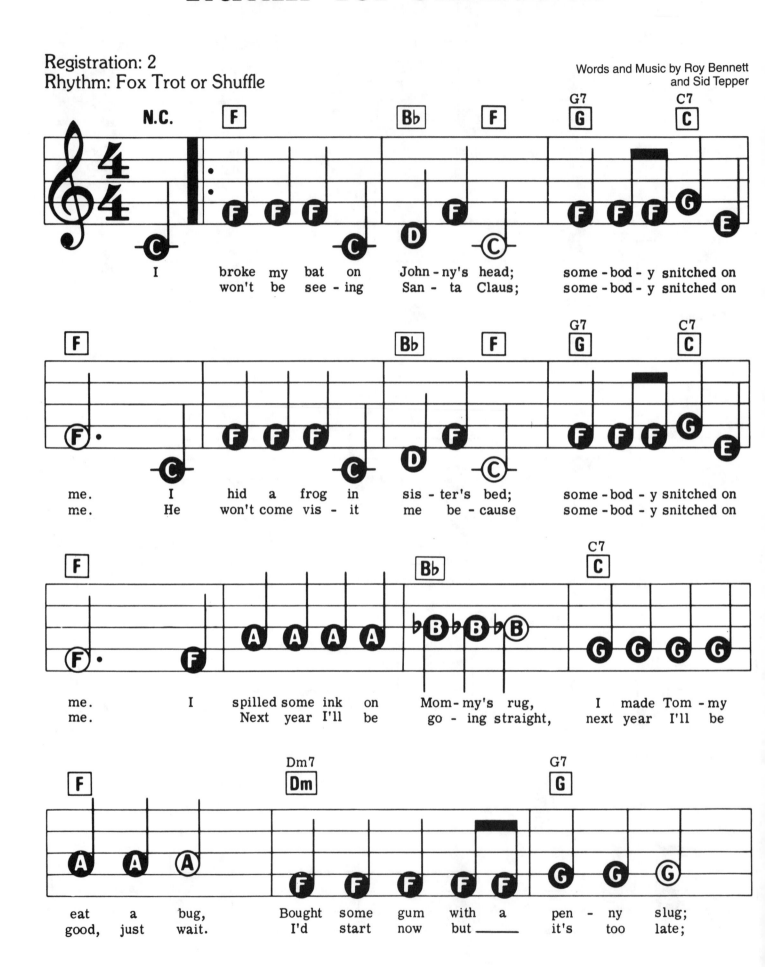

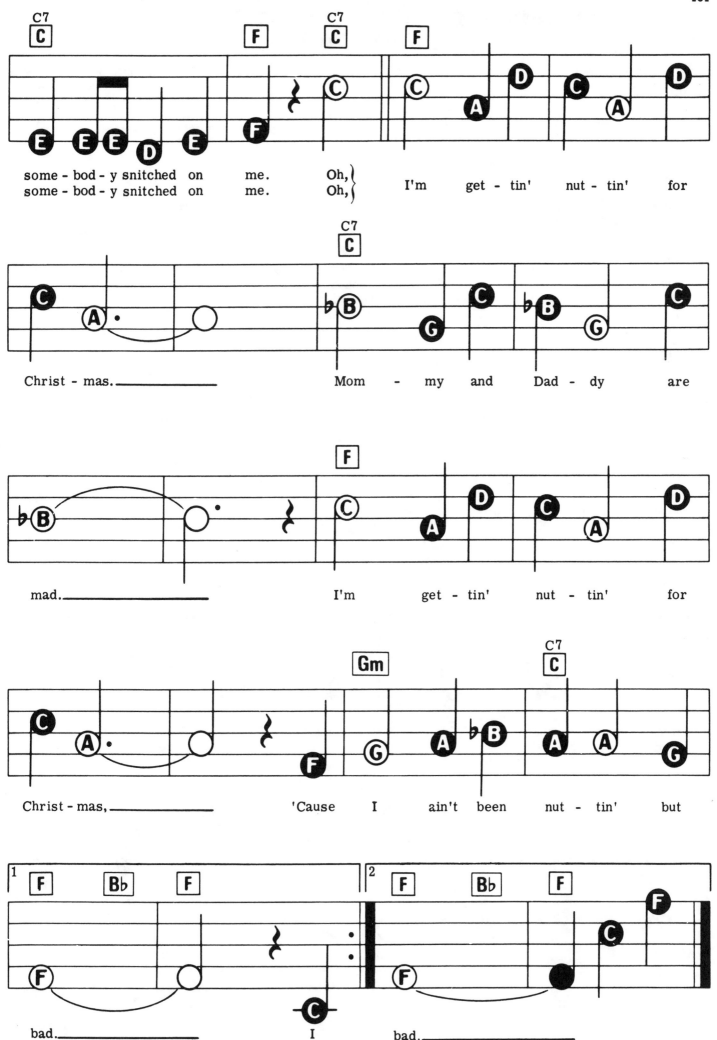

O Come, All Ye Faithful
(Adeste Fideles)

Registration 6
Rhythm: None

Words and Music by John Francis Wade
Latin Words translated by
Frederick Oakeley

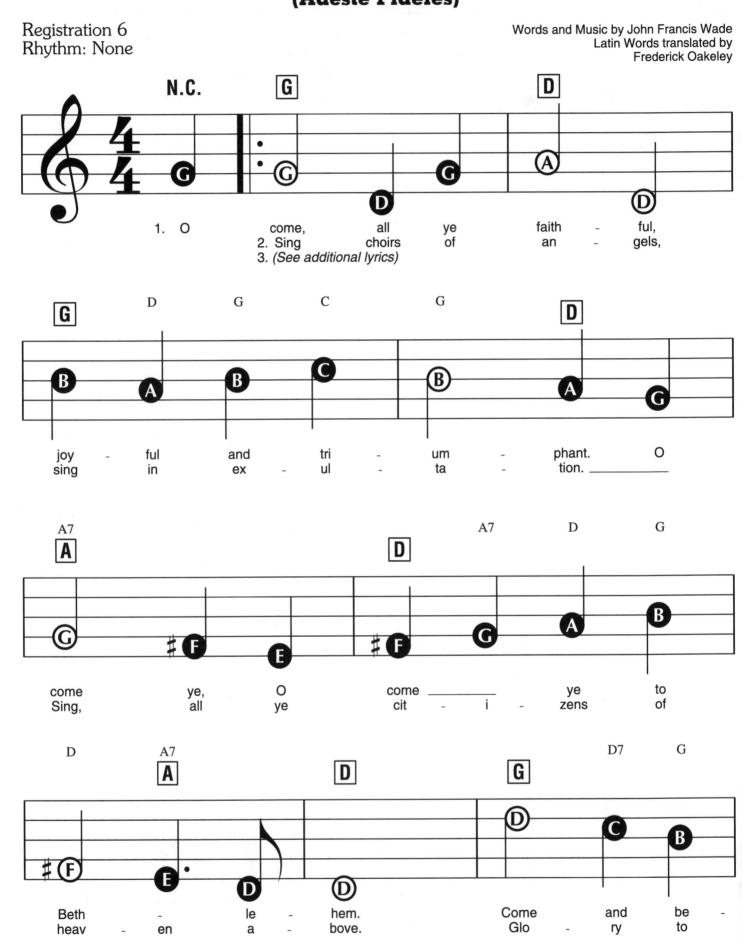

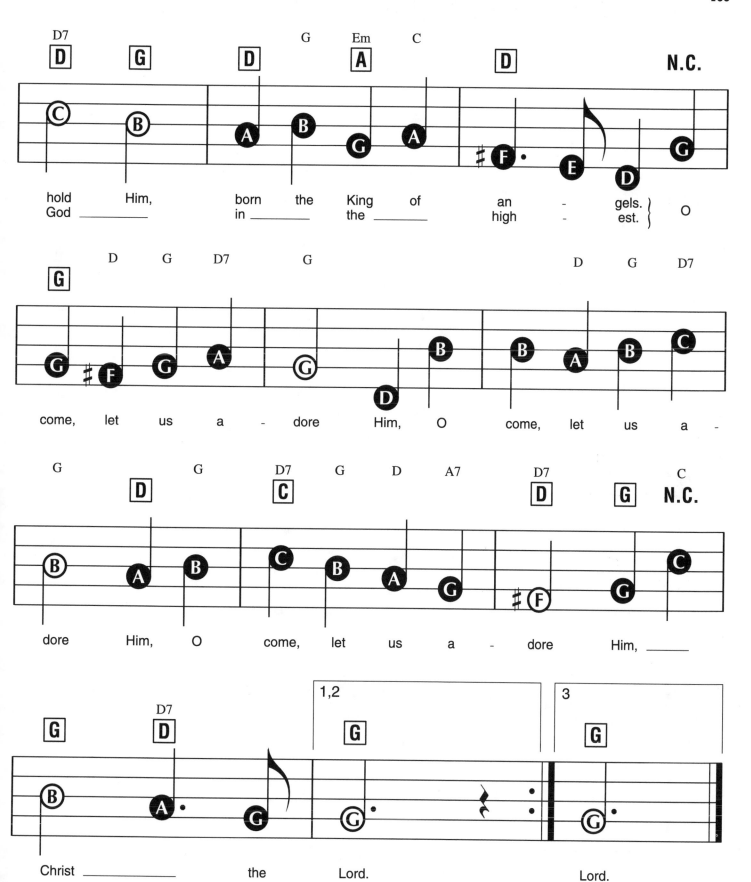

Additional Lyrics

3. Yea, Lord we greet Thee, born this happy morning.
   Jesus, to Thee be glory given.
   Word of the Father, now in flesh appearing.
   O come let us adore Him, O come let us adore Him.
   O come let us adore Him, Christ the Lord.

O Come, O Come Immanuel

Registration 3
Rhythm: None

Plainsong, 13th Century
Words translated by John M. Neale
and Henry S. Coffin

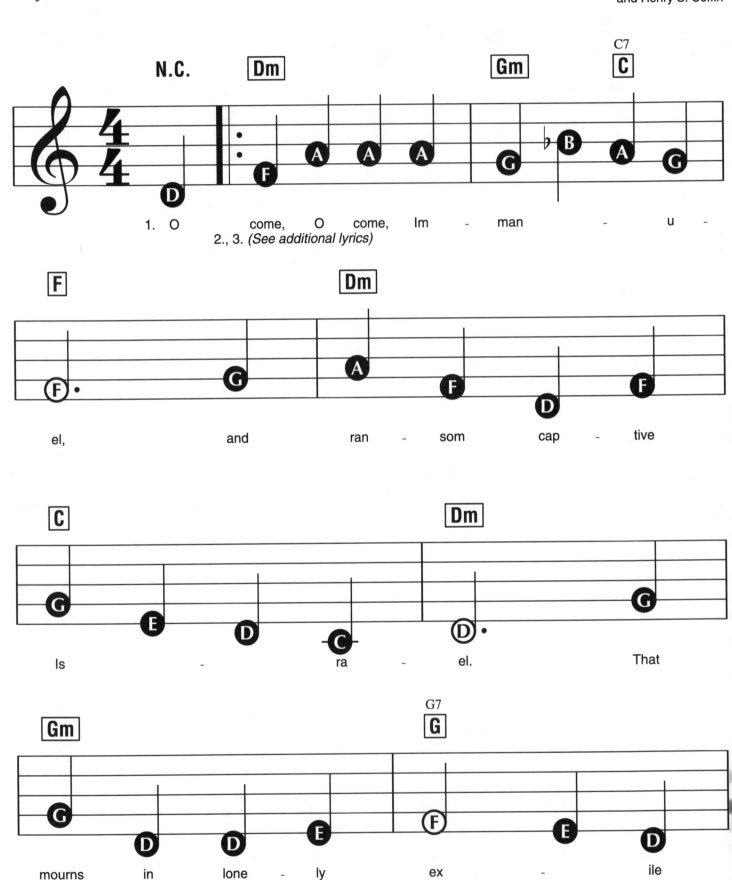

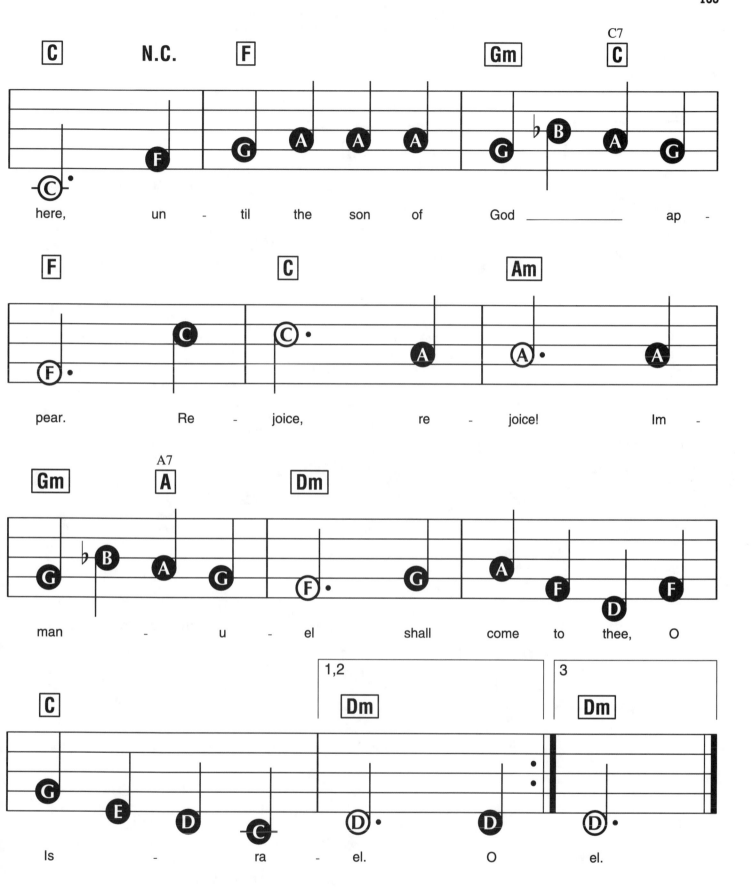

Additional Lyrics

2. O come, Thou Key of David, come,
   and open wide our heav'nly home.
   Make safe the way that leads on high,
   and close the path to misery.

   Rejoice, rejoice! Immanuel
   shall come to thee, O Israel.

3. O come, thou Rod of Jesse, free,
   thine own from Satan's tyranny.
   From depths of hell thy people save,
   and give them victory o'er the grave.

   Rejoice, rejoice! Immanuel
   shall come to thee, O Israel.

O Holy Night

Registration 6
Rhythm: None

French Words by Placide Cappeau
English Words by John S. Dwight
Music by Adolphe Adam

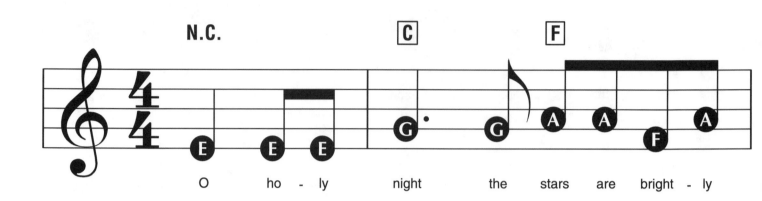

O ho - ly night the stars are bright - ly

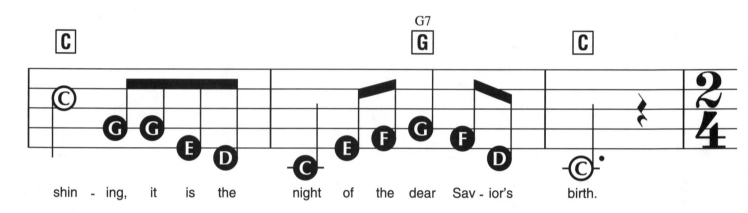

shin - ing, it is the night of the dear Sav - ior's birth.

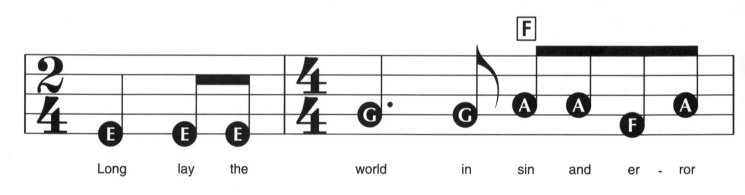

Long lay the world in sin and er - ror

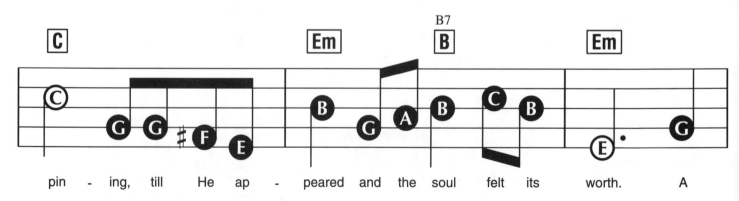

pin - ing, till He ap - peared and the soul felt its worth. A

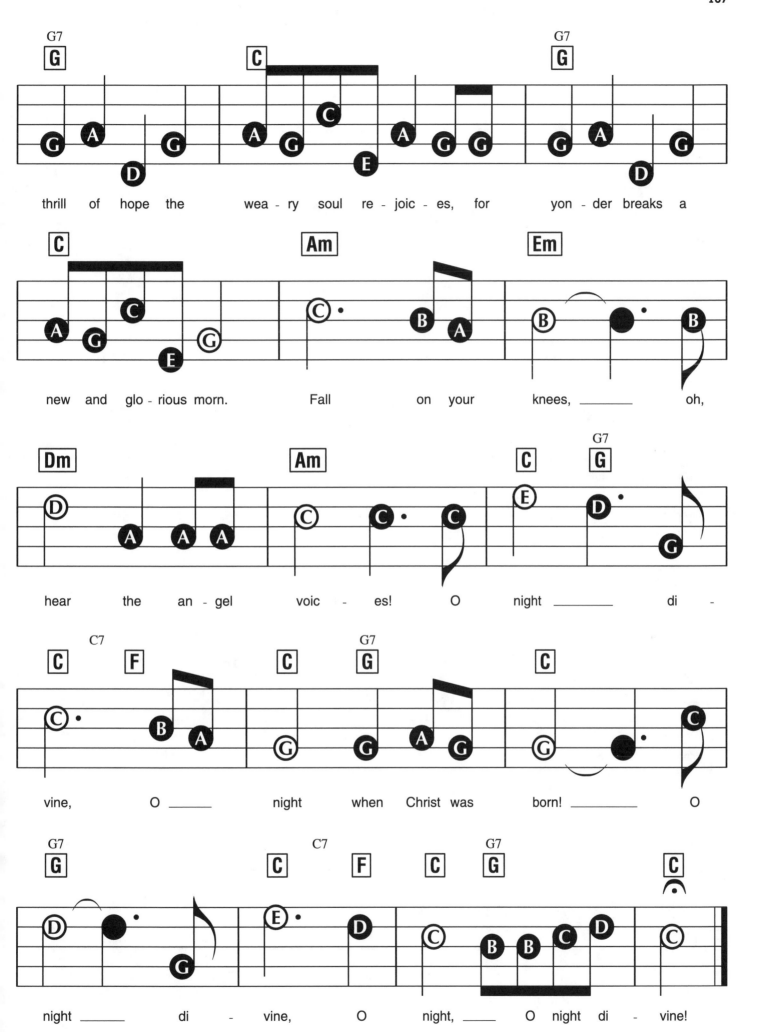

O Little Town of Bethlehem

Registration 1
Rhythm: Fox Trot

Words by Phillips Brooks
Music by Lewis H. Redner

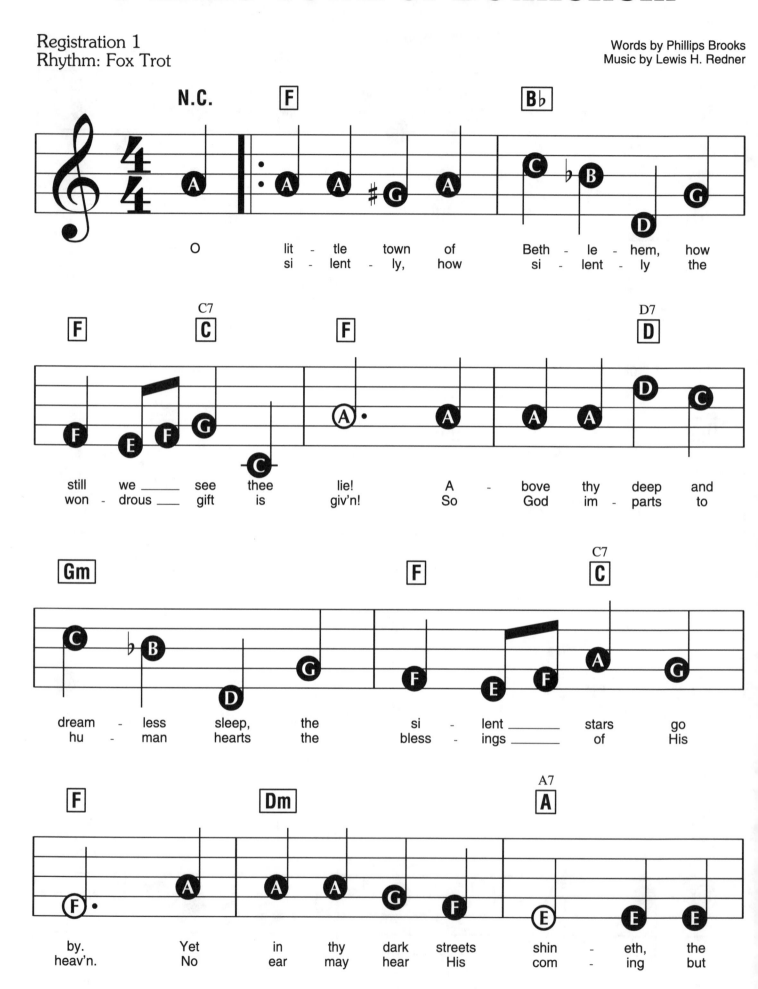

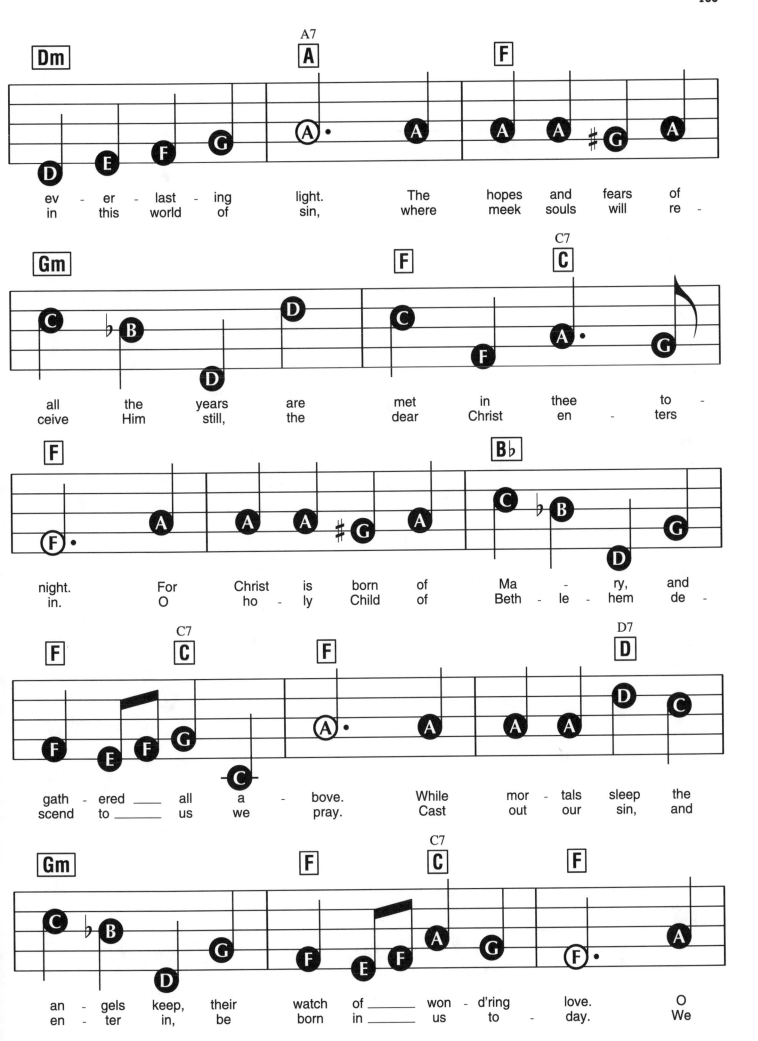

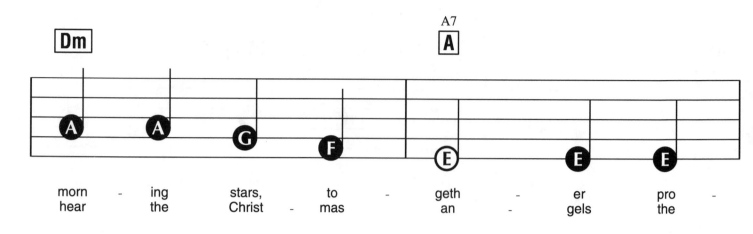

morn - ing stars, to - geth - er pro -
hear the Christ - mas an - gels the

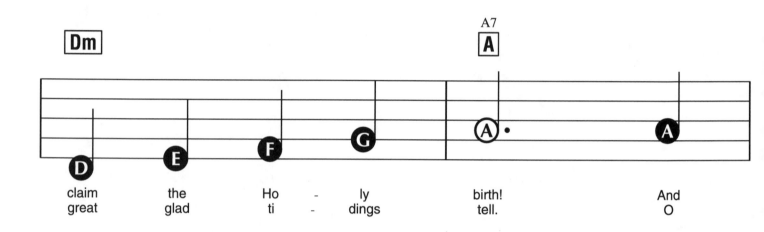

claim the Ho - ly birth! And
great glad ti - dings tell. O

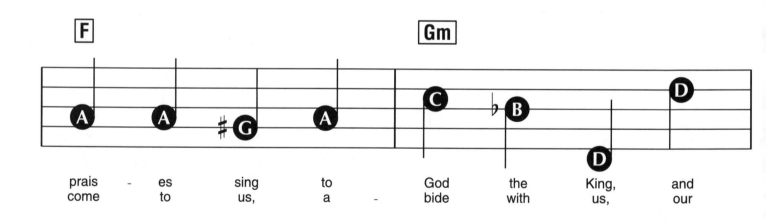

prais - es sing to God the King, and
come to us, a - bide with us, our

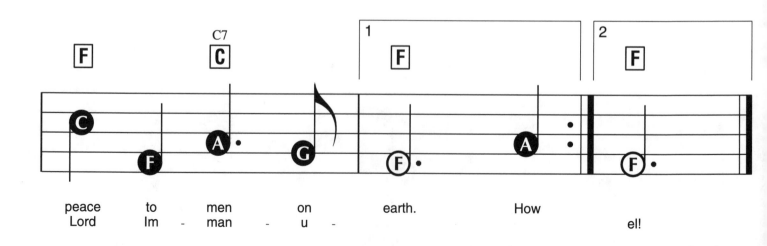

peace to men on earth. How
Lord Im - man - u - el!

Rudolph the Red-Nosed Reindeer

Registration 4
Rhythm: Fox Trot or Swing

Music and Lyrics by
Johnny Marks

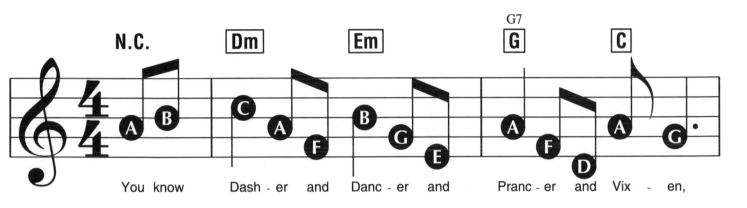

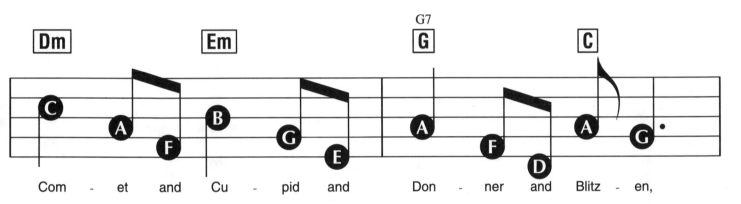

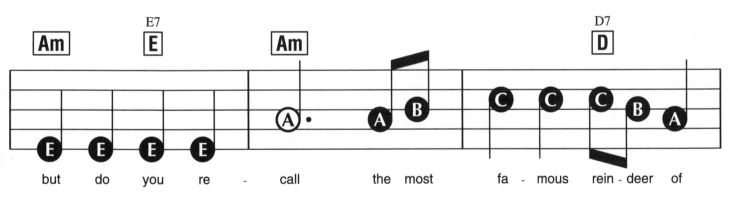

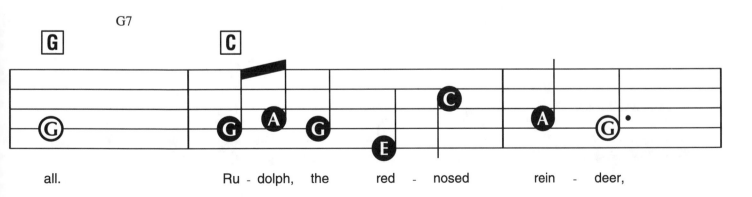

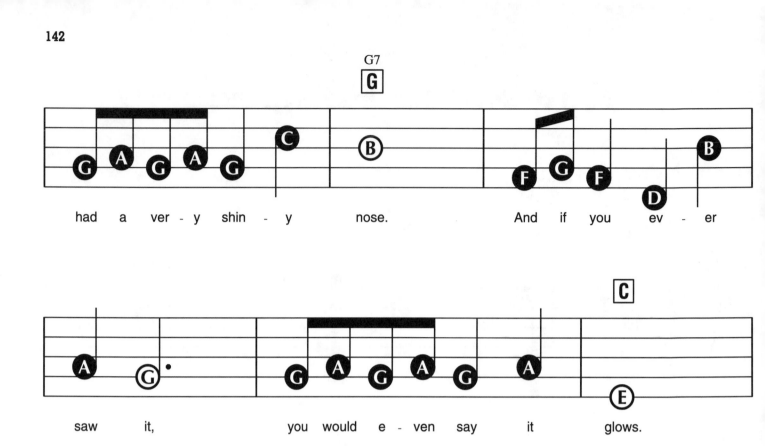

had a ver - y shin - y nose. And if you ev - er

saw it, you would e - ven say it glows.

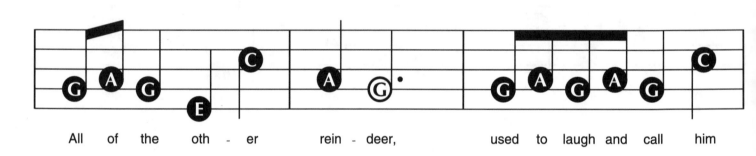

All of the oth - er rein - deer, used to laugh and call him

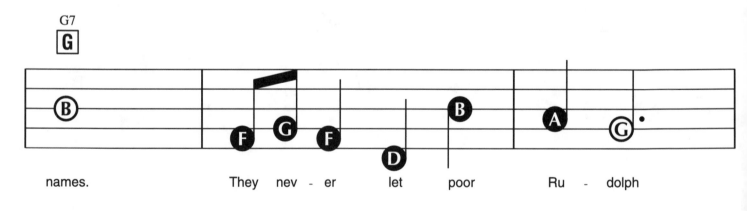

names. They nev - er let poor Ru - dolph

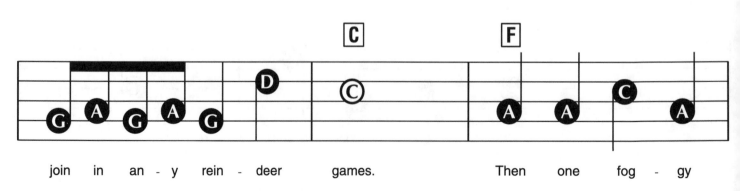

join in an - y rein - deer games. Then one fog - gy

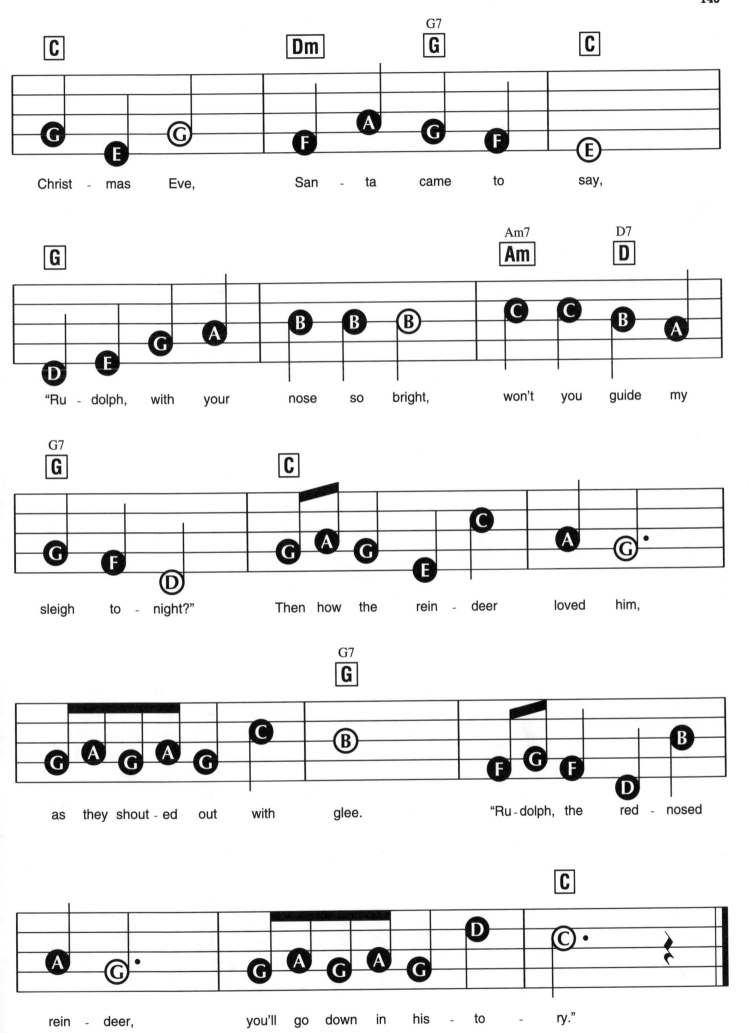

Pretty Paper

Registration 3
Rhythm: Waltz

Words and Music by
Willie Nelson

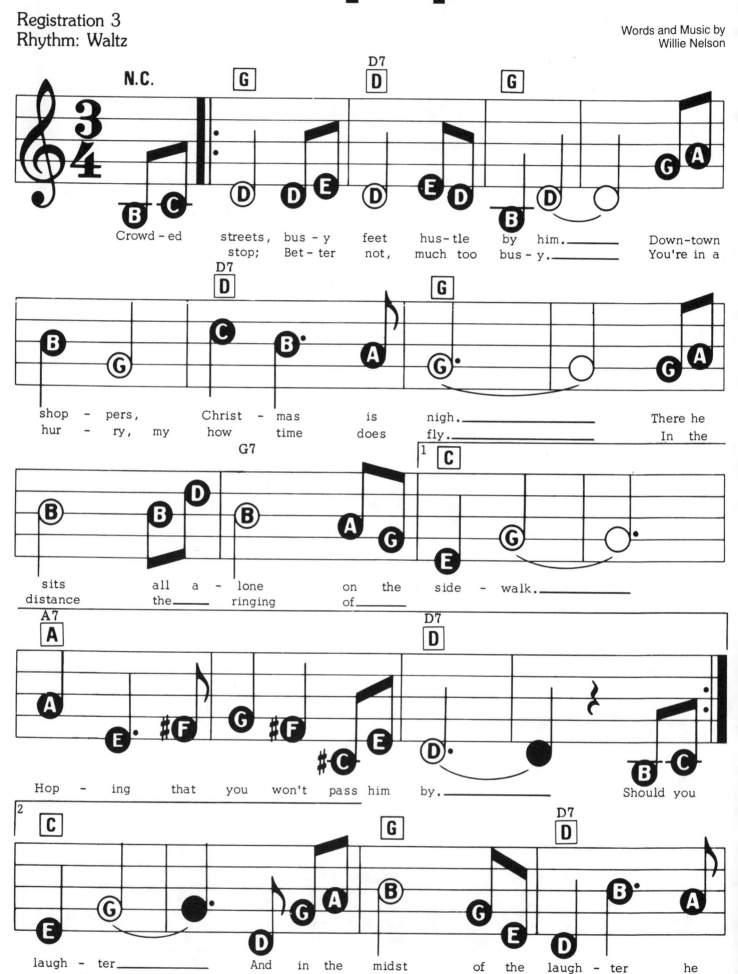

145

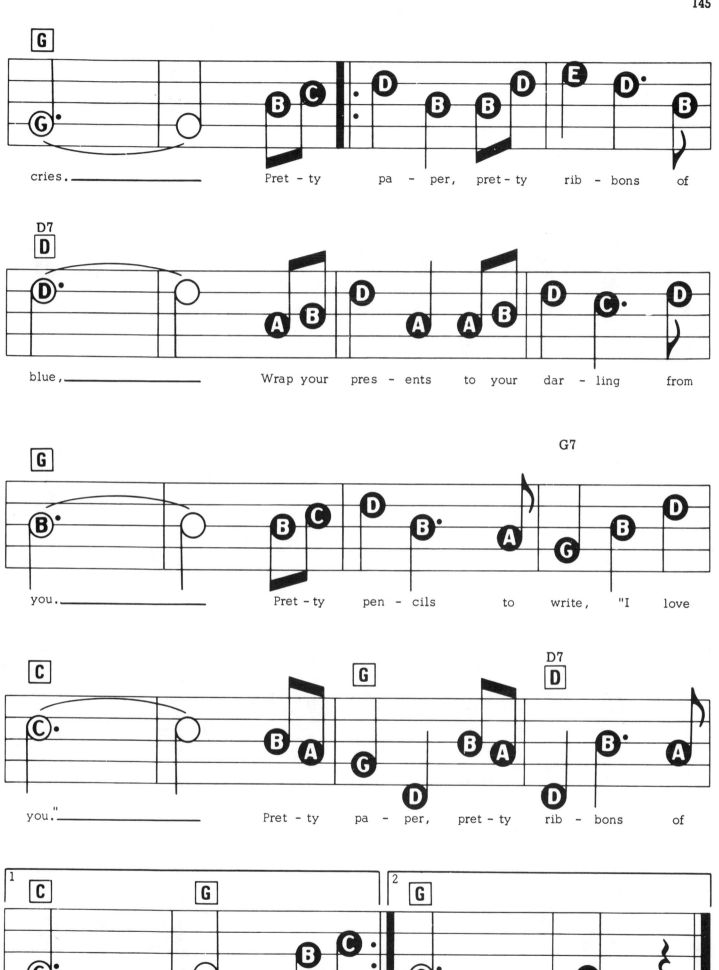

Rockin' Around the Christmas Tree

Registration 2
Rhythm: Swing

Music and Lyrics by
Johnny Marks

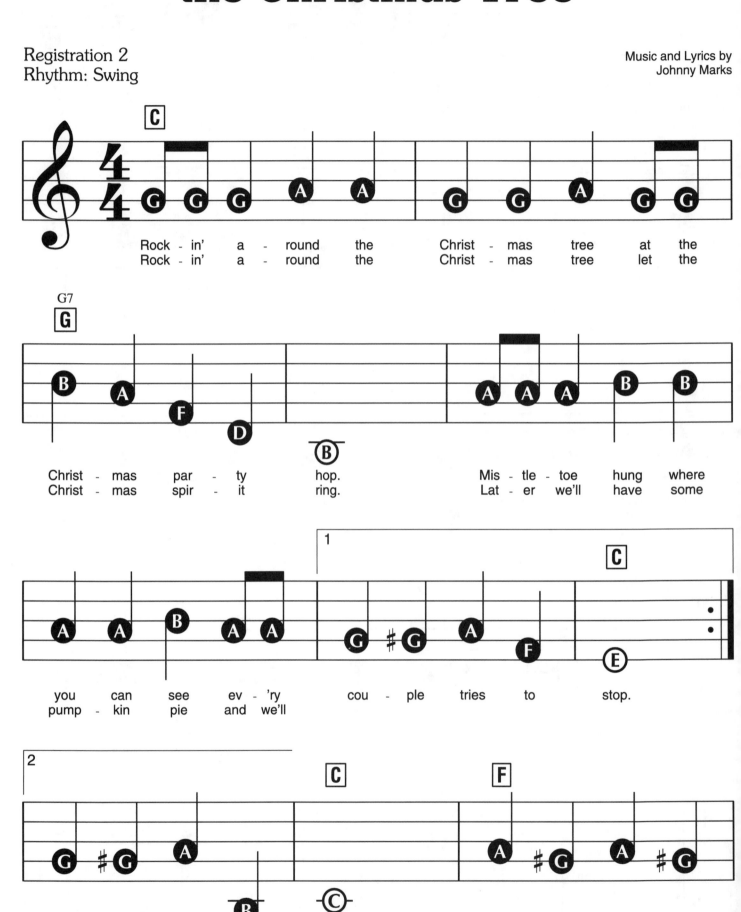

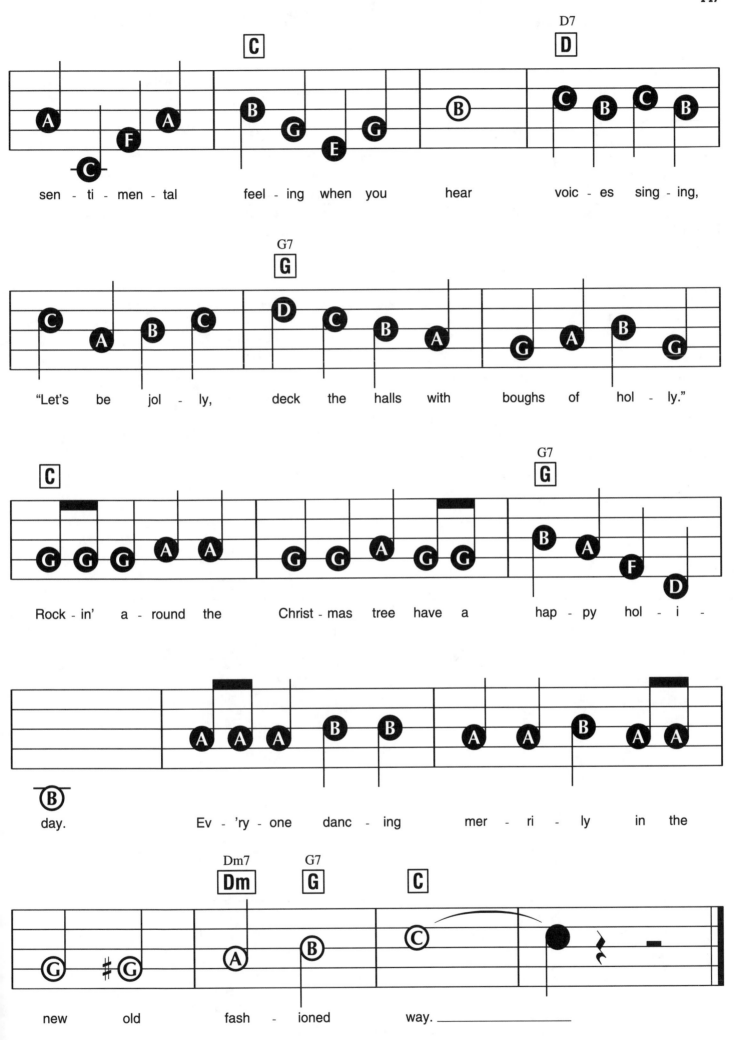

Santa, Bring My Baby Back
(To Me)

Registration 5
Rhythm: March

Words and Music by Claude DeMetruis
and Aaron Schroeder

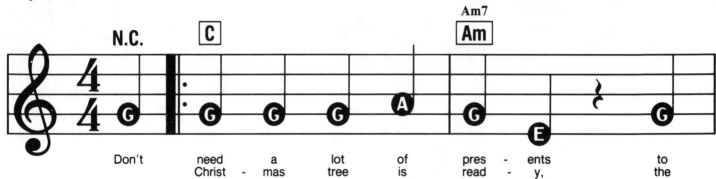

Don't need a lot of pres - ents, to
Christ - mas tree is read - y, to the

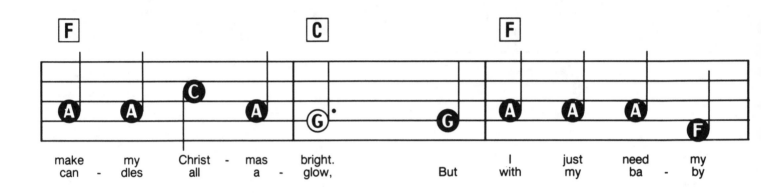

make my Christ - mas bright. But I just need my
can - dles all a - glow, with my ba - by

D7 / C / Eb7

far a - way what good is mis - tle - toe? Oh, San - ta,
ba - by's arms wound a - round me tight.

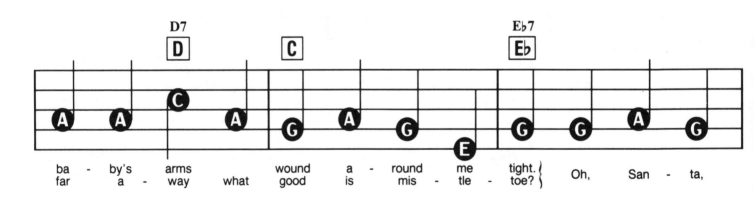

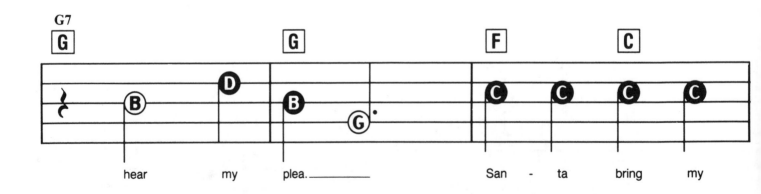

hear my plea._____ San - ta bring my

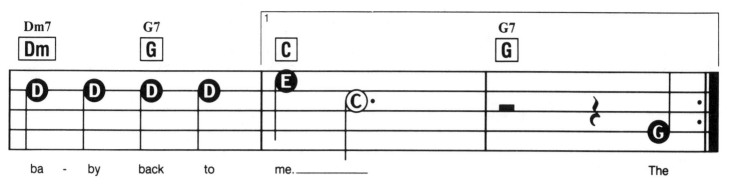

ba - by   back   to   me._____   The

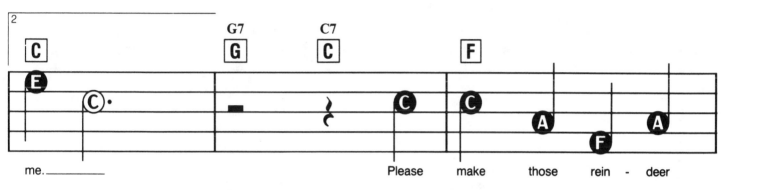

me._____   Please   make   those   rein - deer

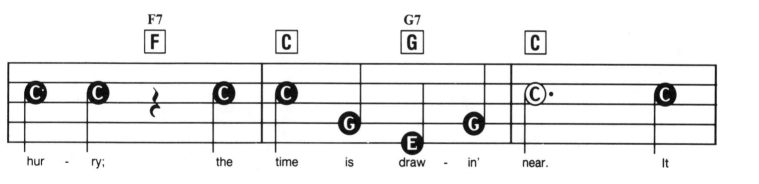

hur - ry;   the   time   is   draw - in'   near.   It

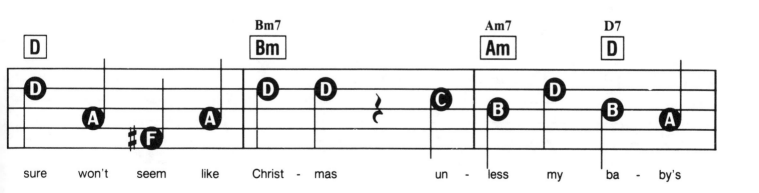

sure   won't   seem   like   Christ - mas   un - less   my   ba - by's

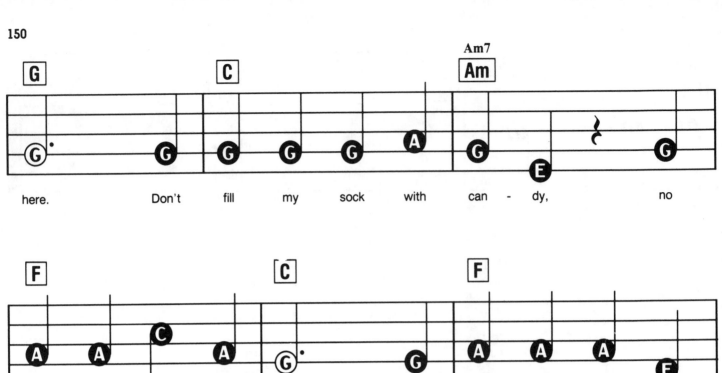

here.   Don't   fill   my   sock   with   can - dy,   no

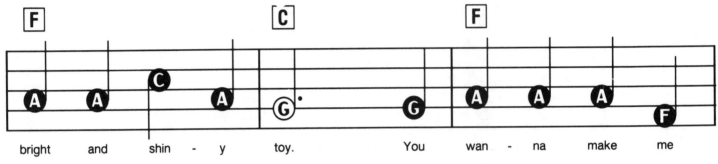

bright   and   shin - y   toy.   You   wan - na   make   me

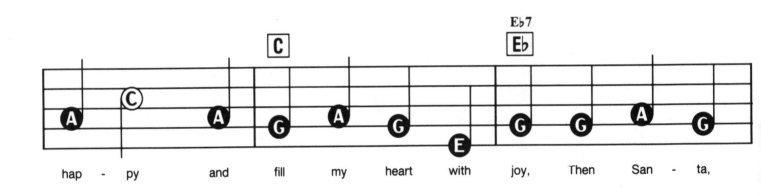

hap - py   and   fill   my   heart   with   joy,   Then   San - ta,

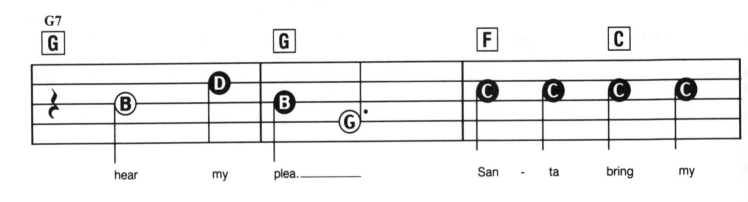

hear   my   plea._____   San - ta   bring   my

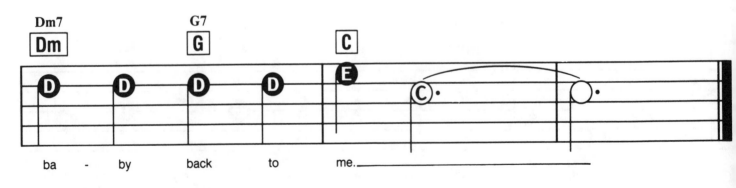

ba - by   back   to   me._____

Shake Me I Rattle
(Squeeze Me I Cry)

Registration 3
Rhythm: Waltz

Words and Music by Hal Hackady
and Charles Naylor

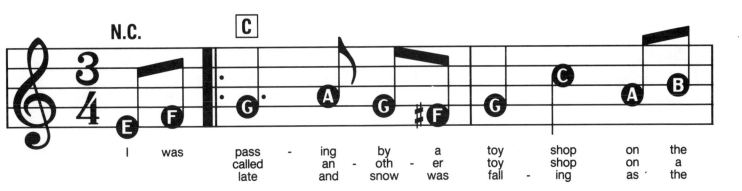

I was pass - ing by a toy shop on the
called an - oth - er toy shop on a
late and snow was fall - ing as the

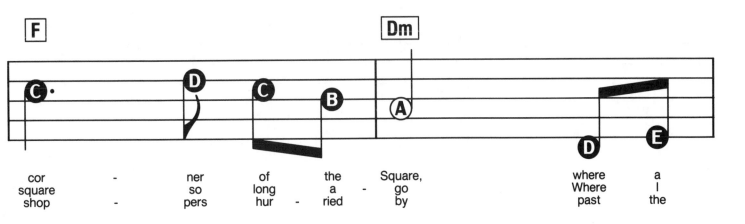

cor - ner of the Square, where a
square so long a - go Where I
shop pers hur - ried by past the

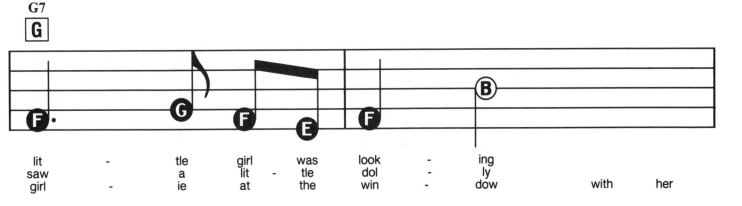

lit - tle girl was look - ing
saw a lit - tle dol - ly
girl - ie at the win - dow with her

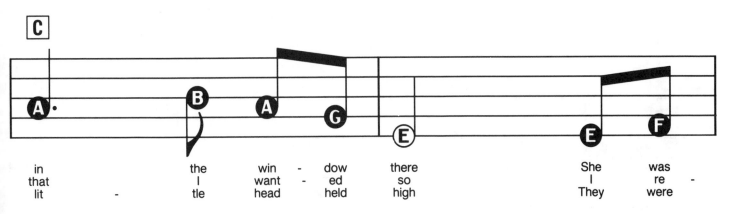

in the win - dow there so She was
that I want - ed I re -
lit - tle head held high They were

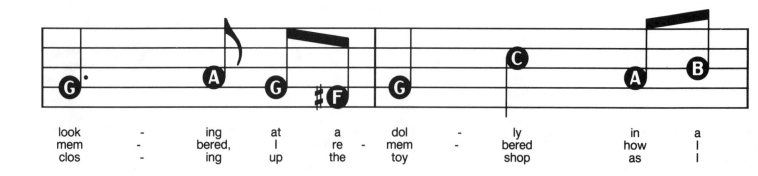

look - ing at a dol - ly in a
mem - bered, I re - mem - bered how all
clos - ing up the toy shop as I

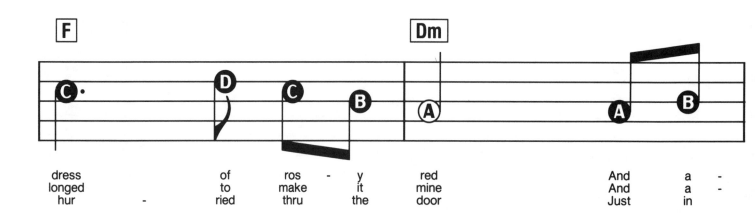

F   **Dm**

dress of ros - y red And a -
longed to make it mine And a -
hur - ried thru the door Just in

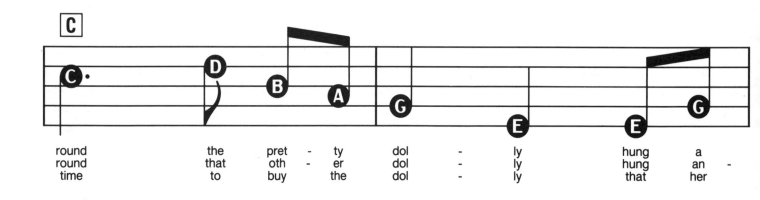

C

round the pret - ty dol - ly hung a
round that oth - er dol - ly hung an -
time to buy the dol - ly that her

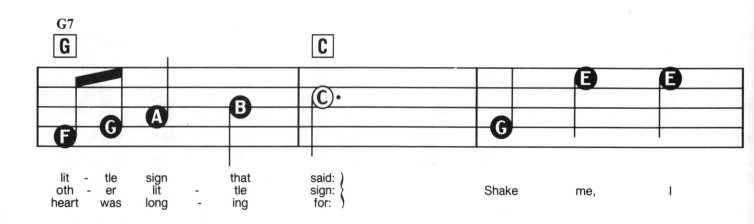

G7

G   **C**

lit - tle sign that said: ⎫
oth - er sign lit - tle sign: ⎬   Shake me, I
heart was long - ing for: ⎭

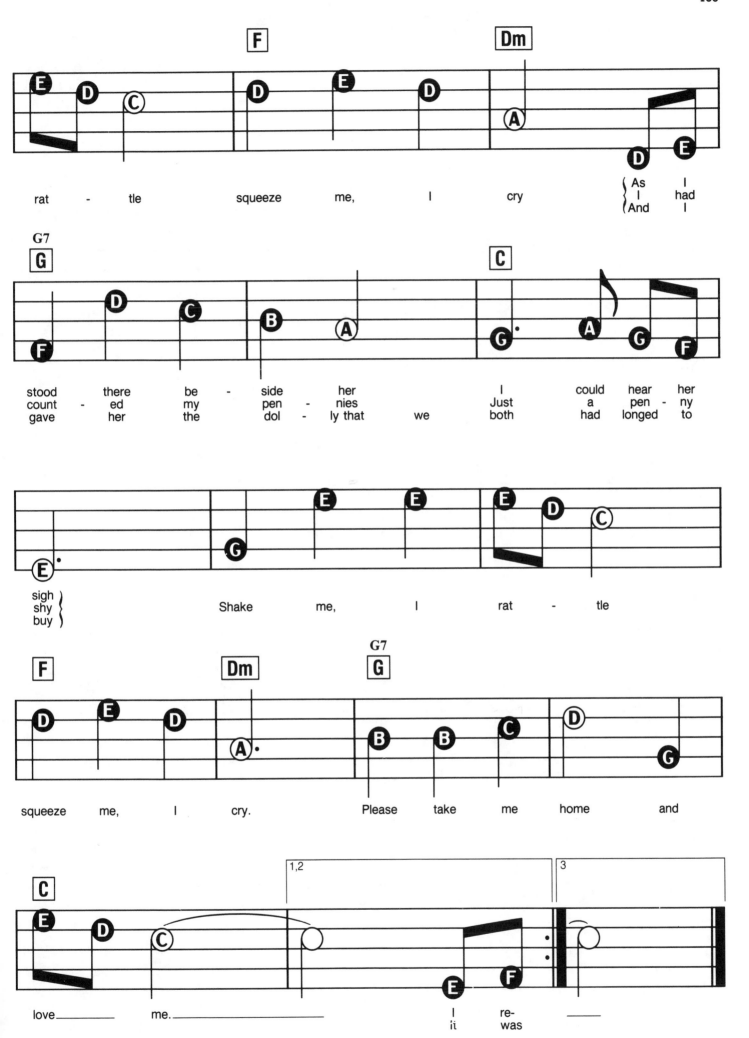

Silent Night

Registration 1
Rhythm: Waltz

Words by Joseph Mohr
Translated by John F. Young
Music by Franz X. Gruber

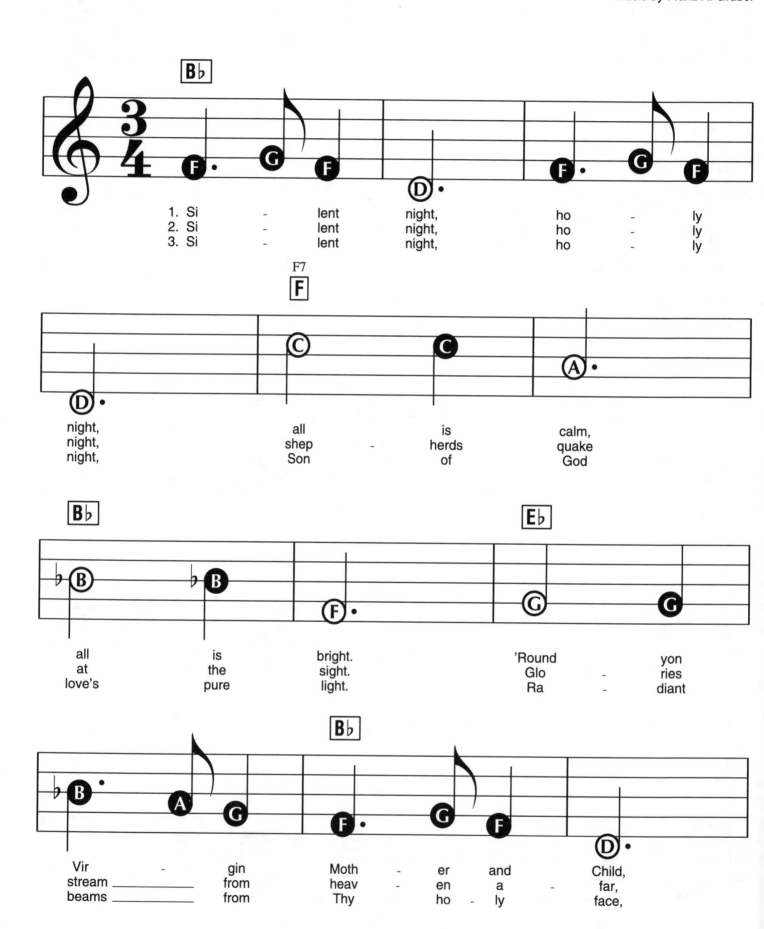

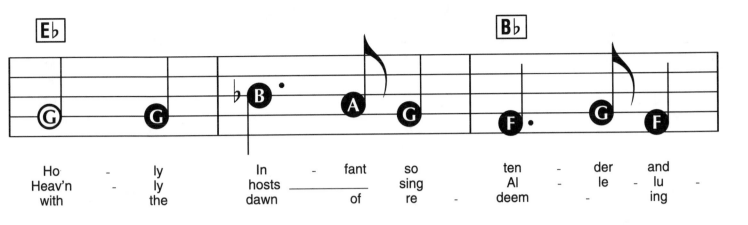

Ho - ly In - fant so ten - der and
Heav'n - ly hosts sing Al - le - lu -
with the dawn of re - deem - ing

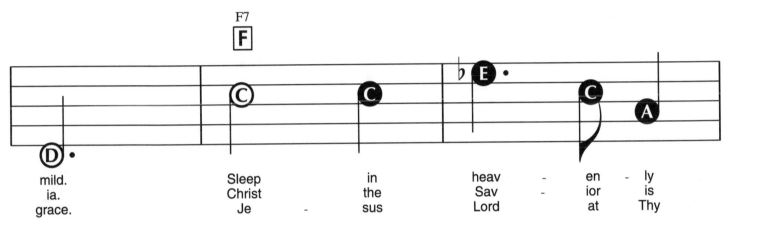

mild. Sleep in heav - en - ly
ia. Christ the Sav - ior is
grace. Je - sus Lord at Thy

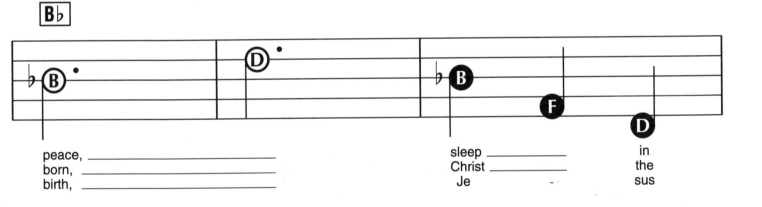

peace, sleep in
born, Christ the
birth, Je - sus

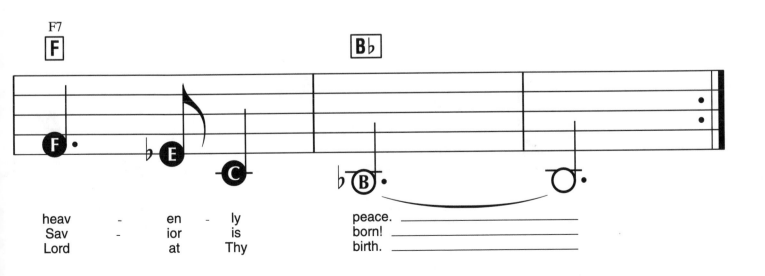

heav - en - ly peace.
Sav - ior is born!
Lord at Thy birth.

V 096

Silver Bells
from the Paramount Picture THE LEMON DROP KID

Registration 7
Rhythm: Waltz

Words and Music by Jay Livingston
and Ray Evans

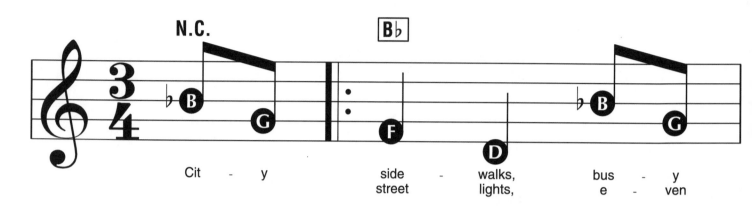

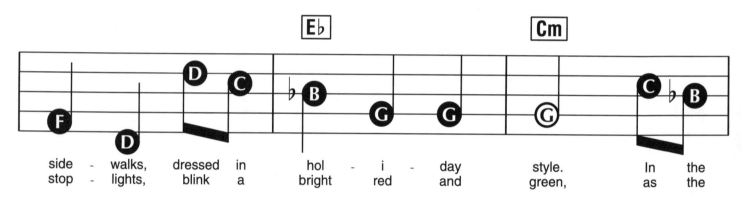

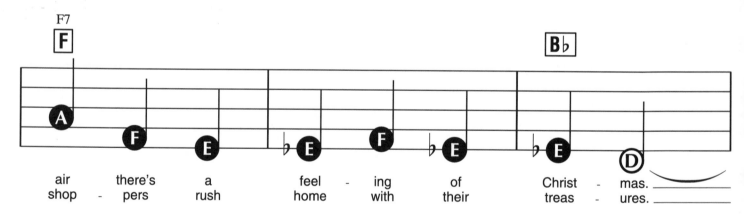

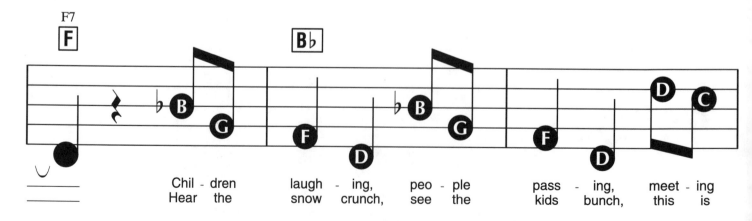

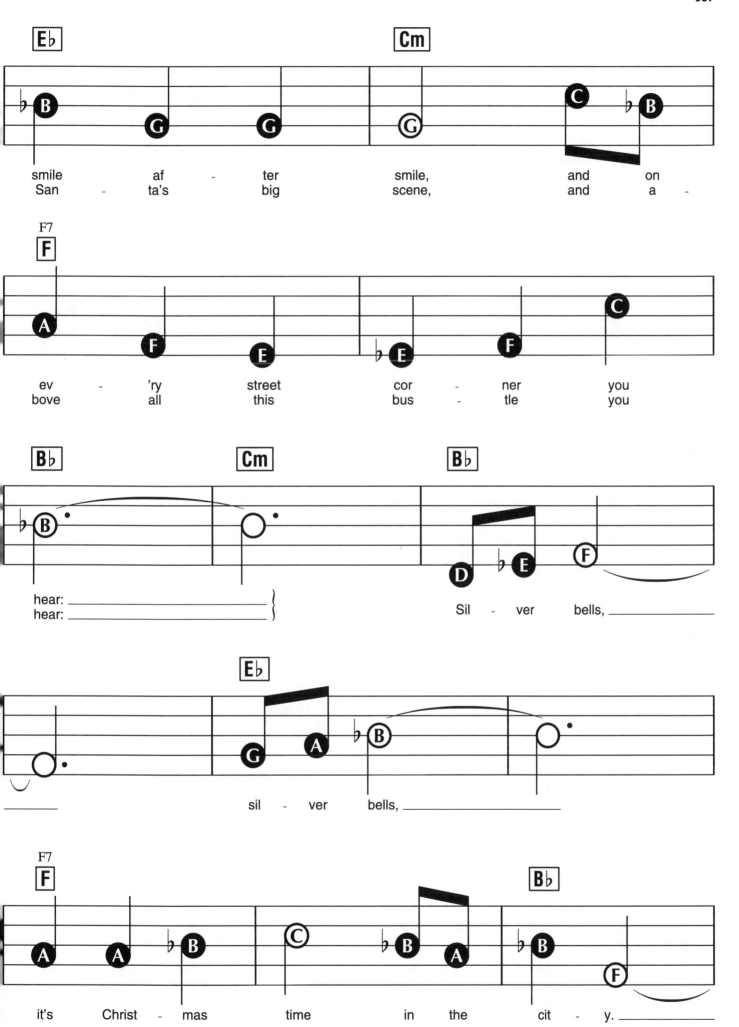

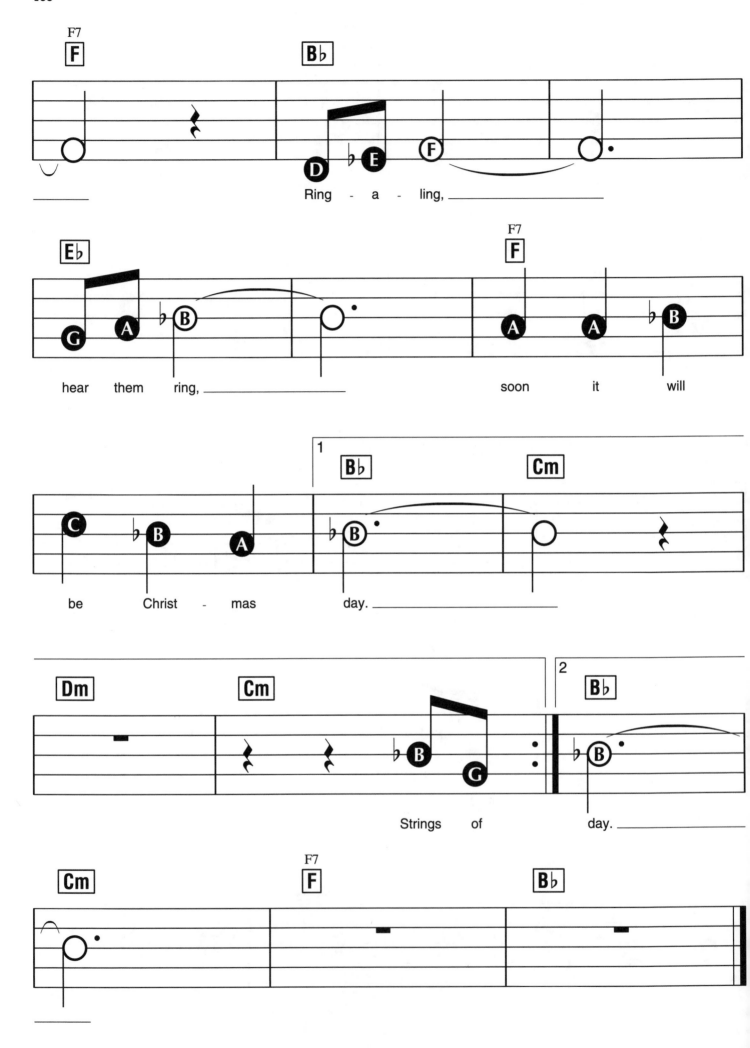

Up on the Housetop

Registration 5
Rhythm: Fox Trot or Swing

Words and Music by
B.R. Handy

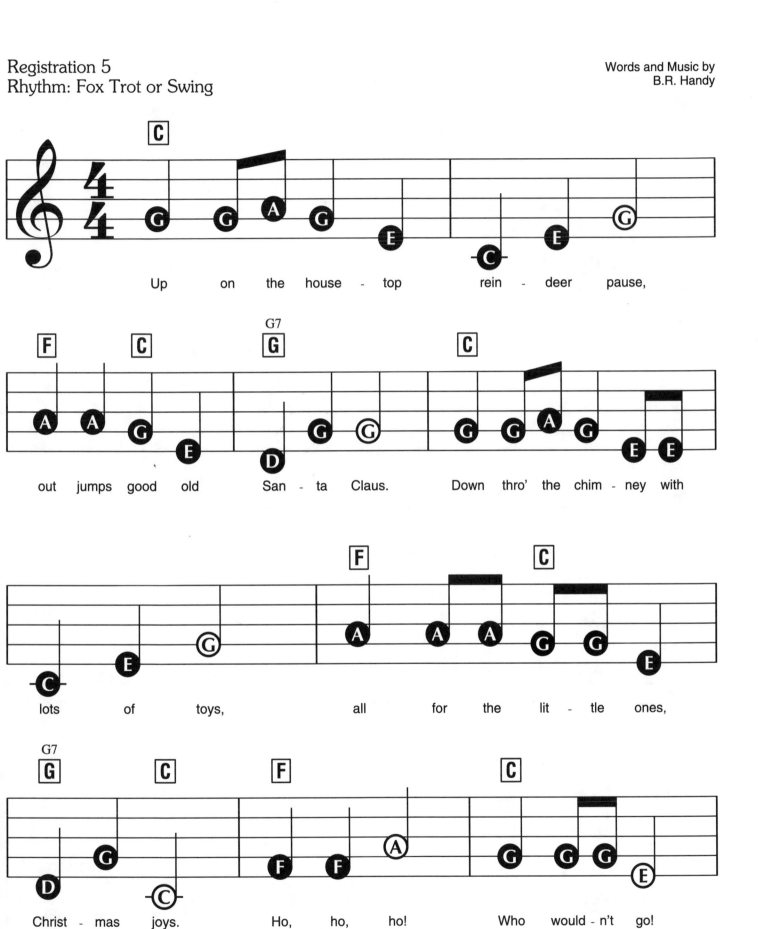

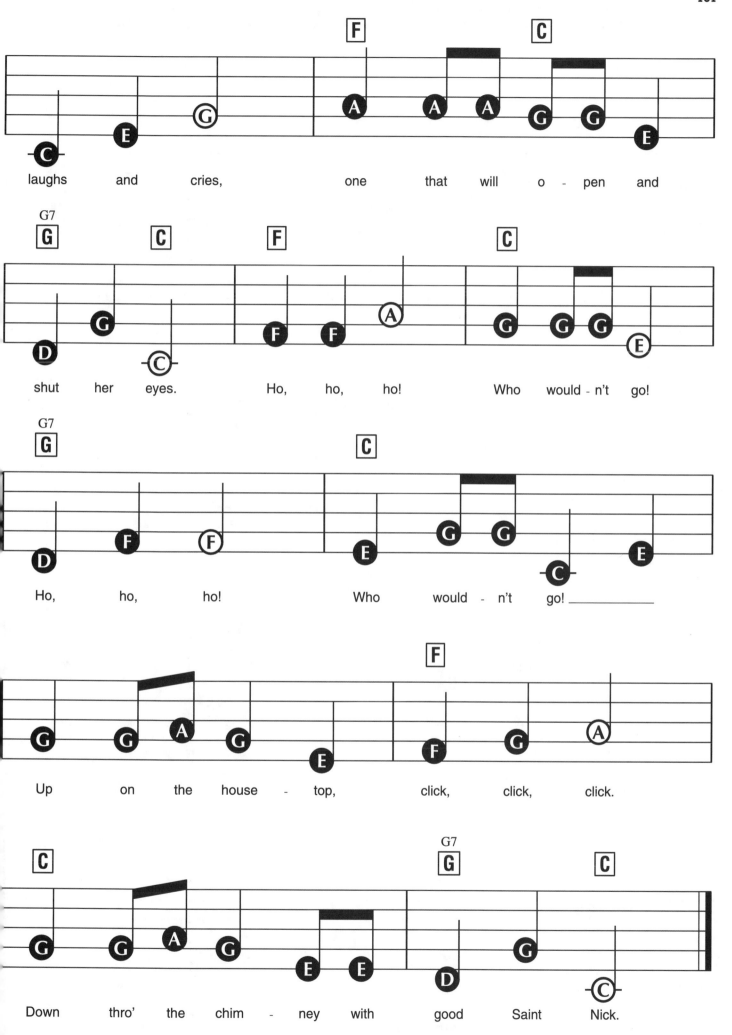

Some Children See Him

Registration 9
Rhythm: None

Lyric by Wihla Hutson
Music by Alfred Burt

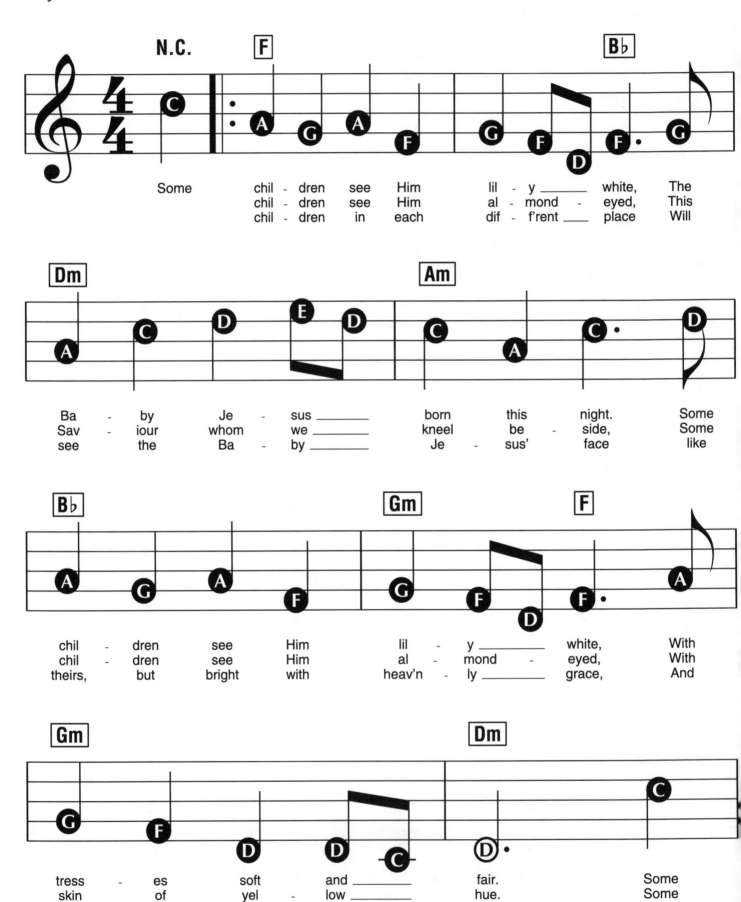

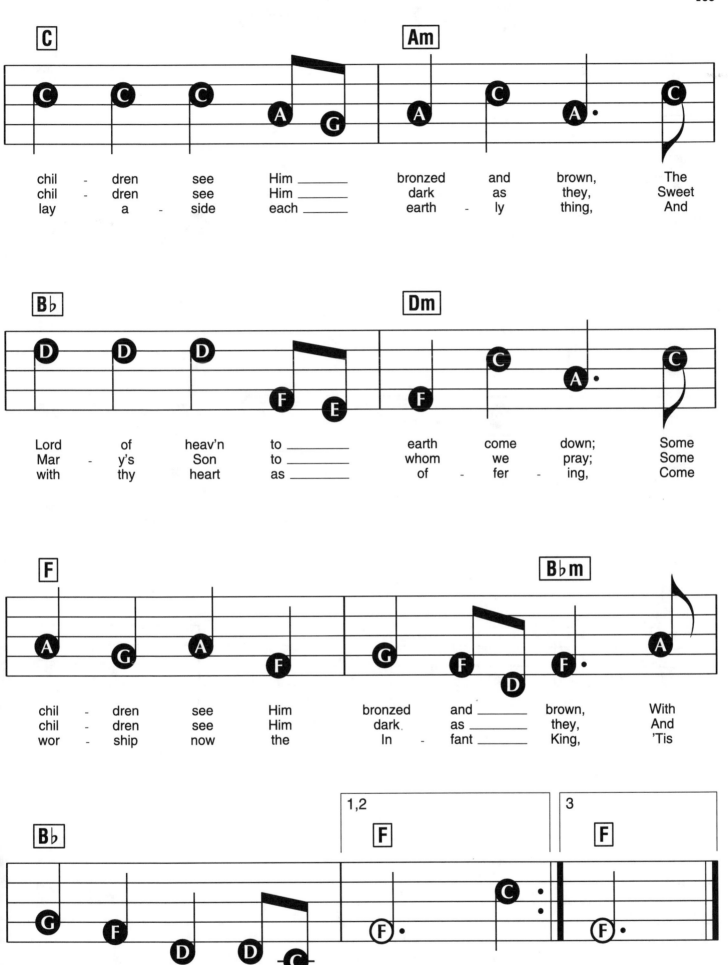

The Star Carol

Registration 3
Rhythm: Waltz

Lyric by Wihla Hutson
Music by Alfred Burt

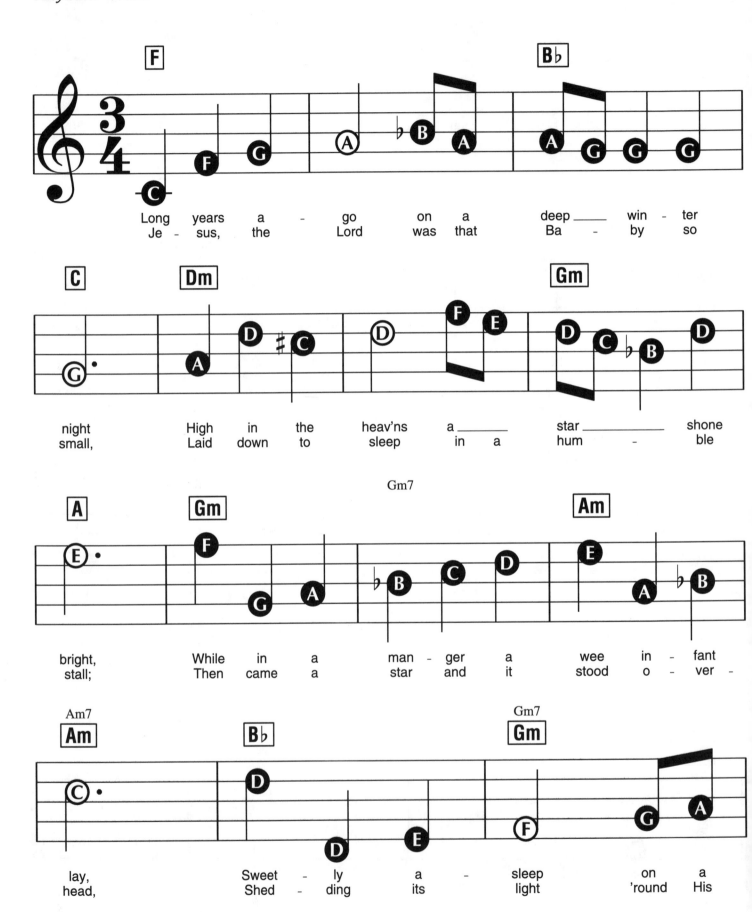

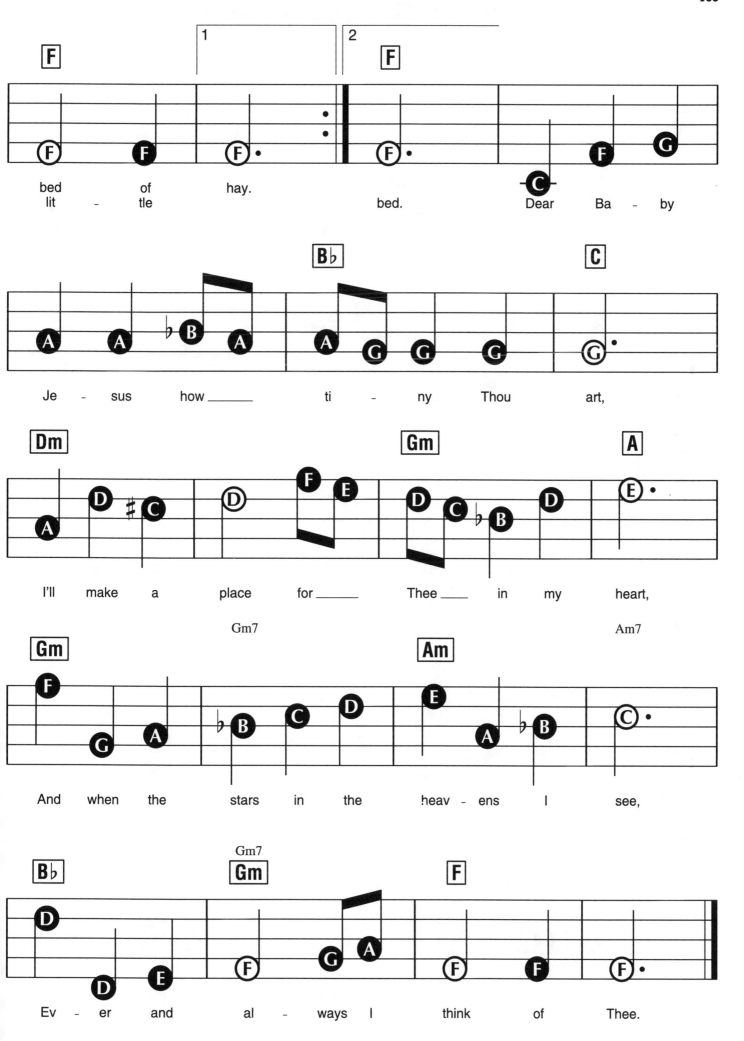

Suzy Snowflake

Registration 2
Rhythm: Fox Trot or Swing

Words and Music by Sid Tepper
and Roy Bennett

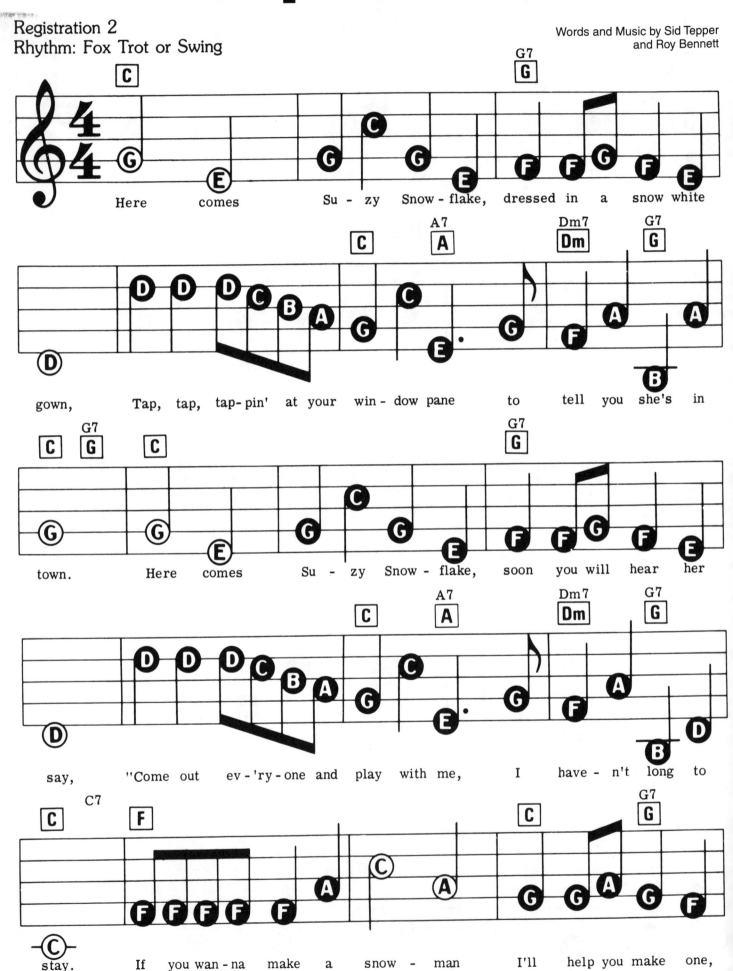

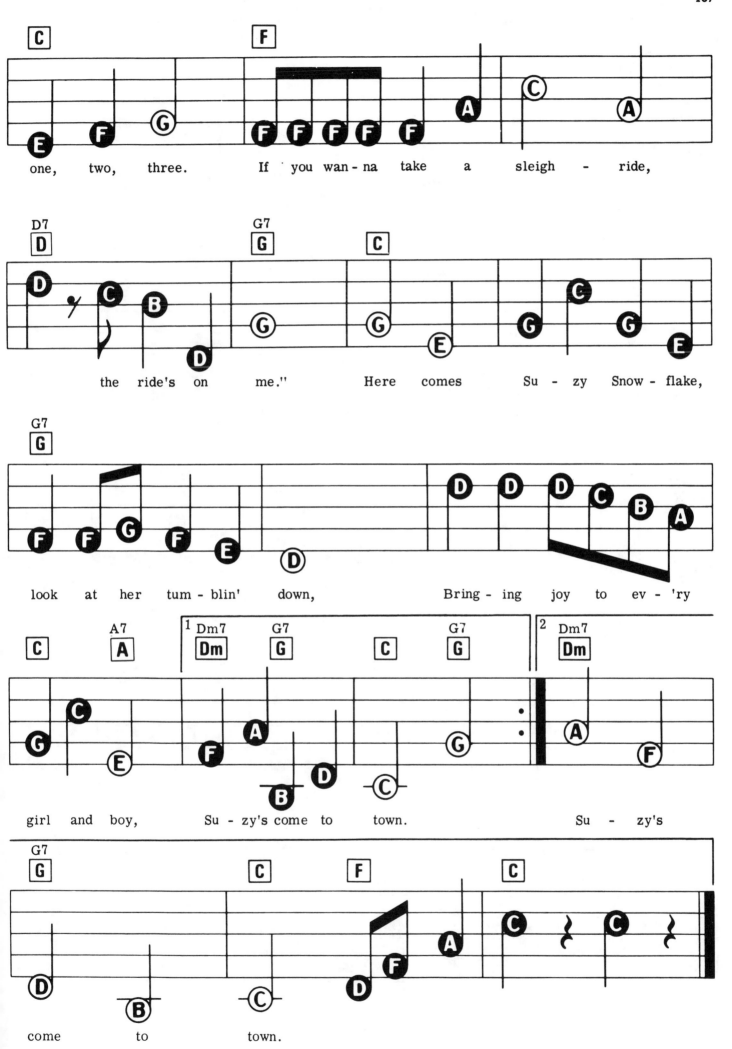

The Twelve Days of Christmas

Registration 5
Rhythm: None

Traditional English Carol

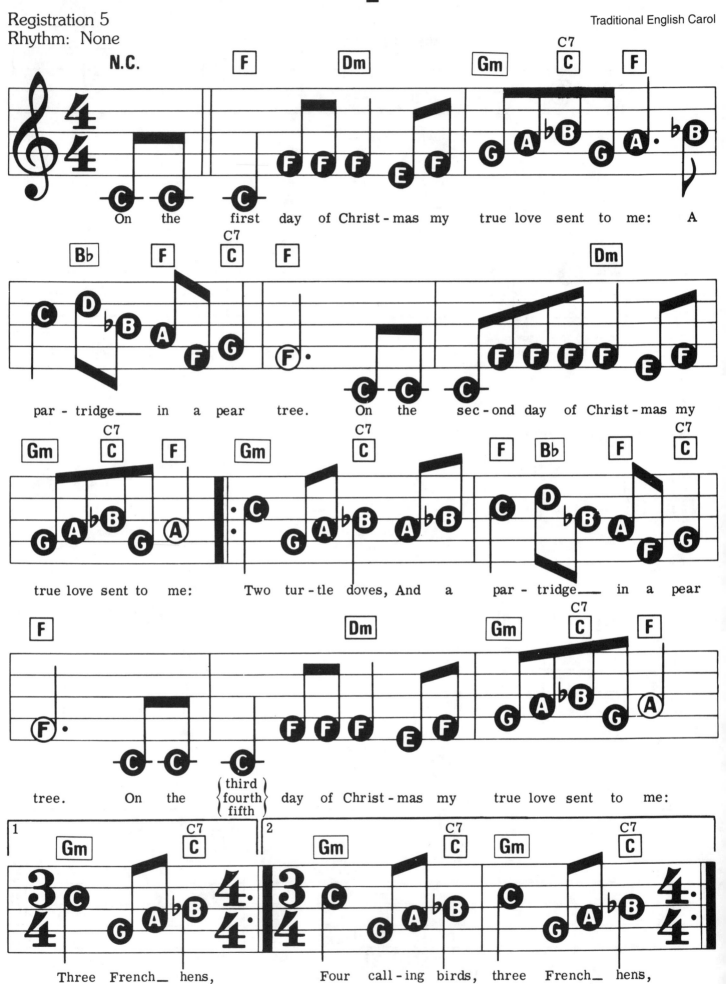

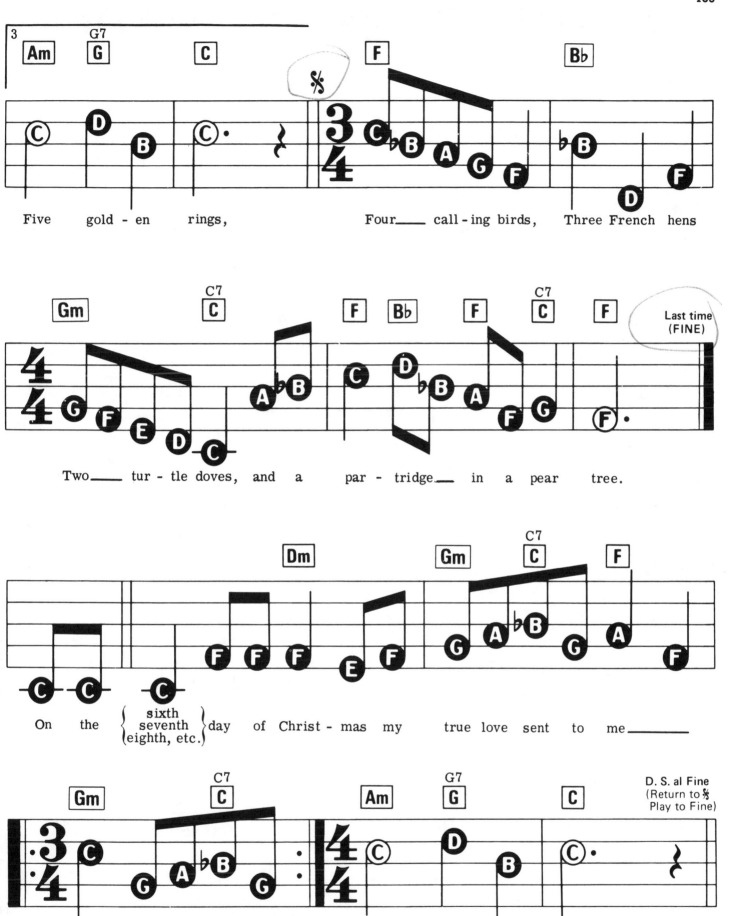

We Three Kings of Orient Are

Registration 9
Rhythm: Waltz

Words and Music by
John H. Hopkins, Jr.

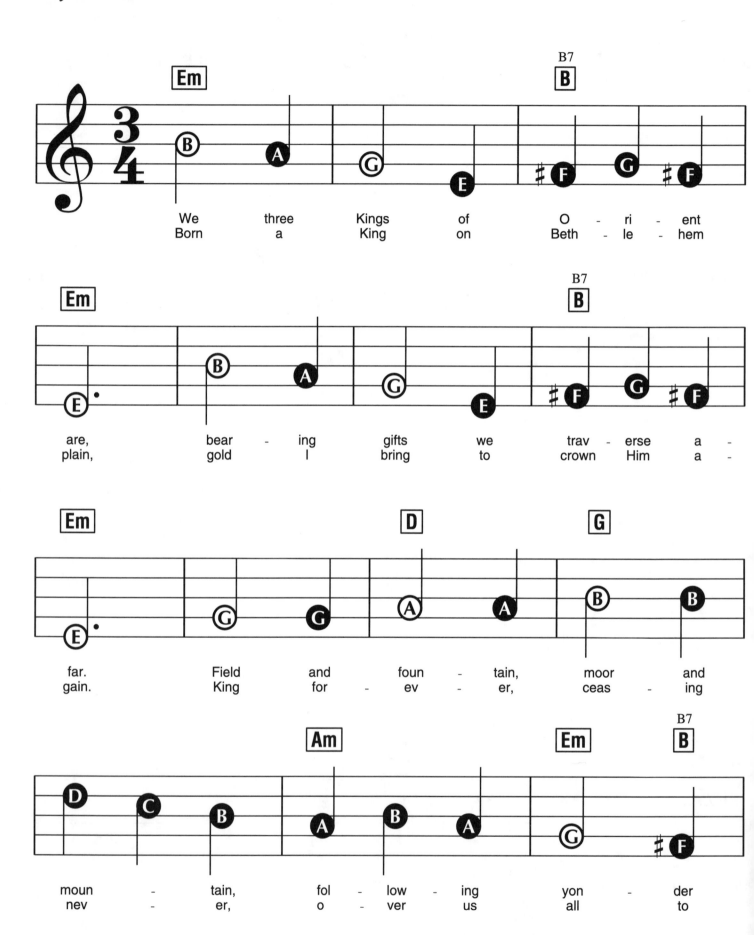

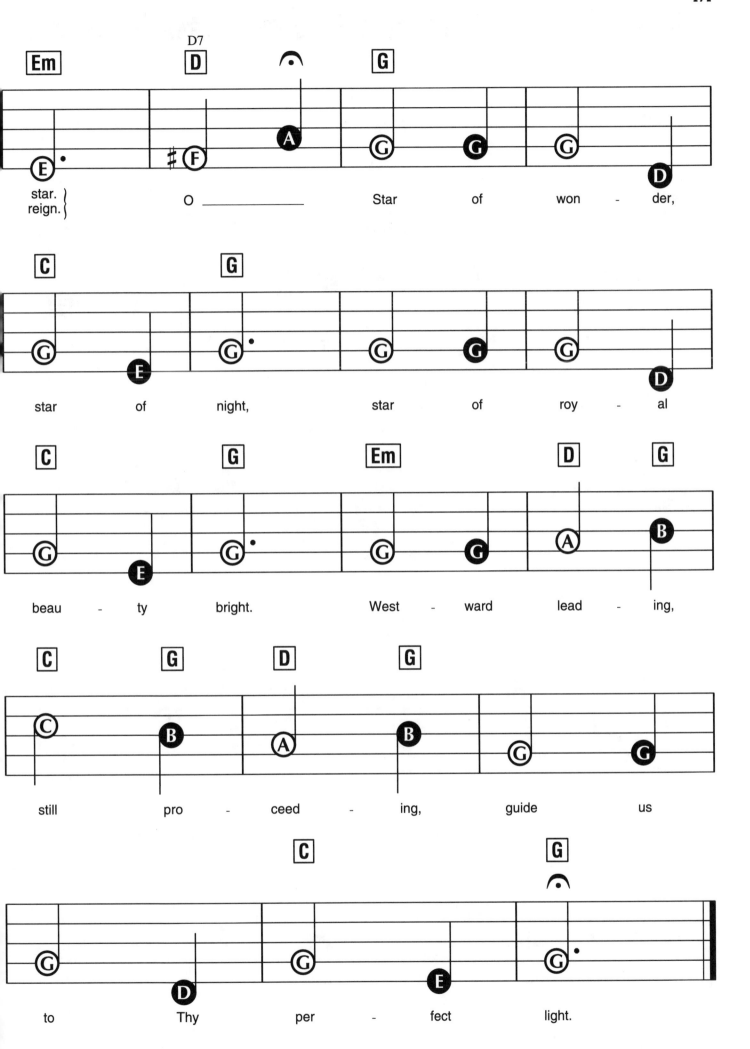

We Wish You a Merry Christmas

Registration 4
Rhythm: None

Traditional English Folksong

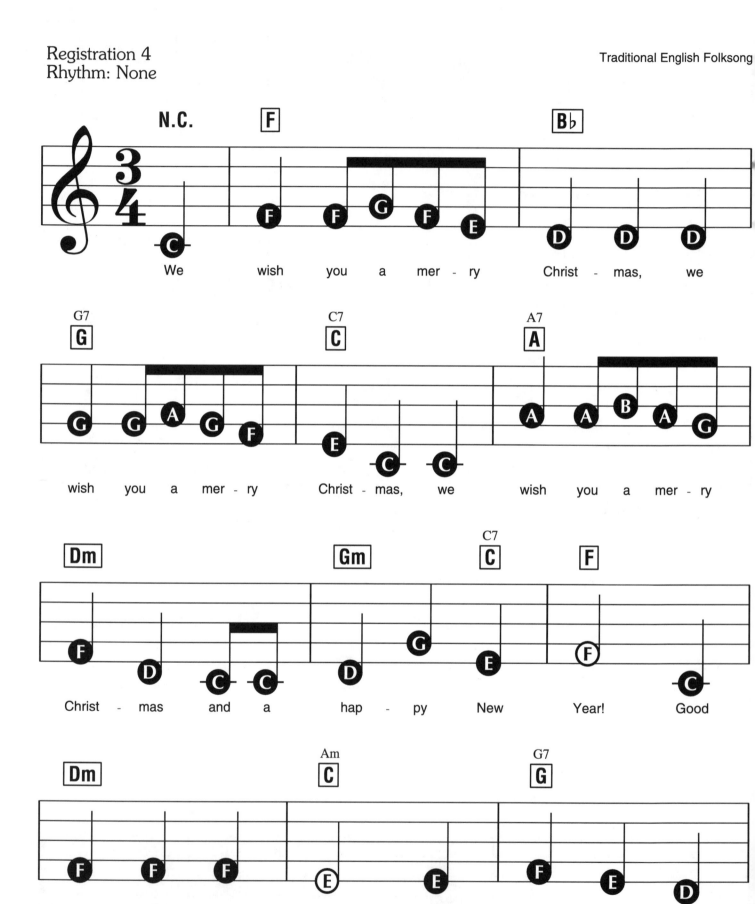

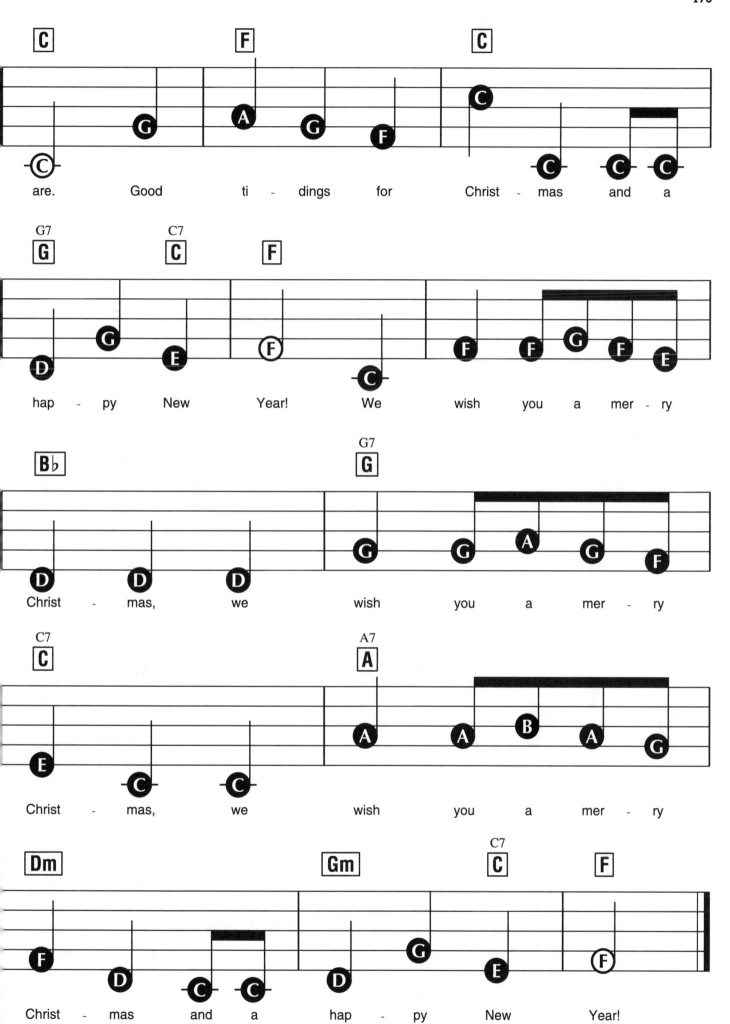

What Child Is This?

Registration 10
Rhythm: Waltz

Words by William C. Dix
16th Century English Melody

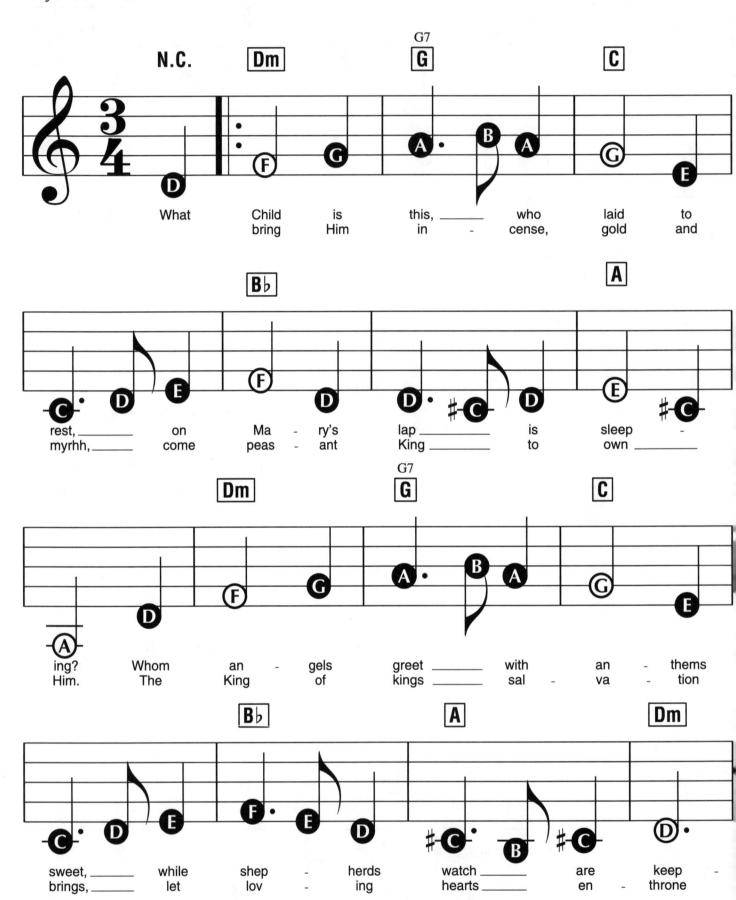

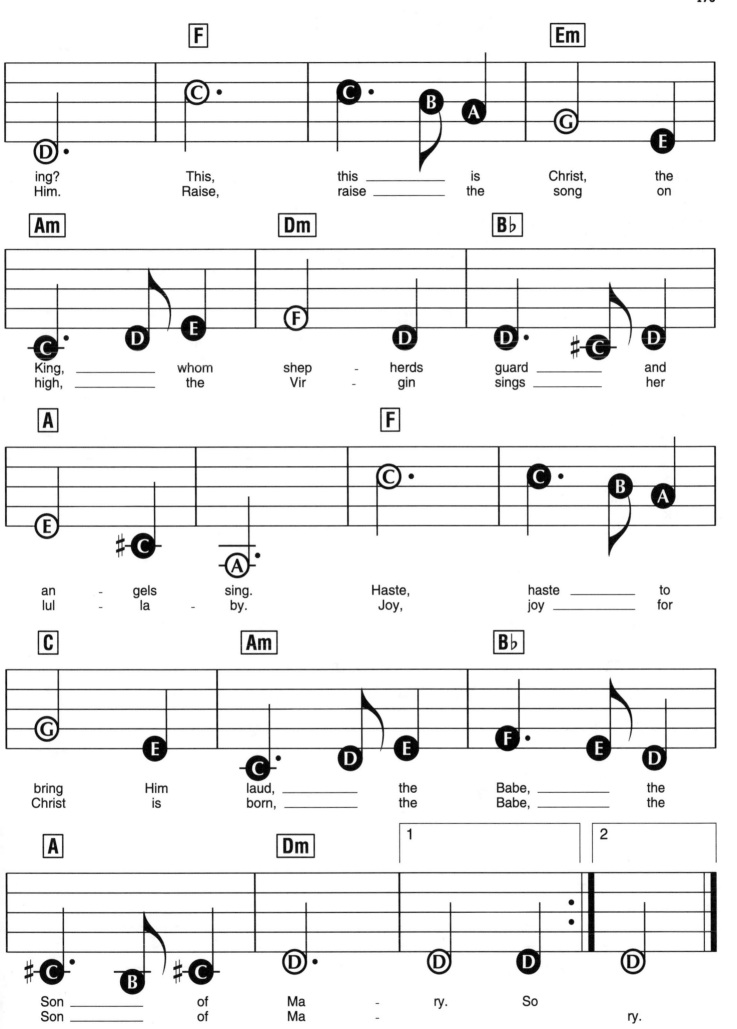

When Santa Claus Gets Your Letter

Registration 9
Rhythm: Swing

Music and Lyrics by
Johnny Marks

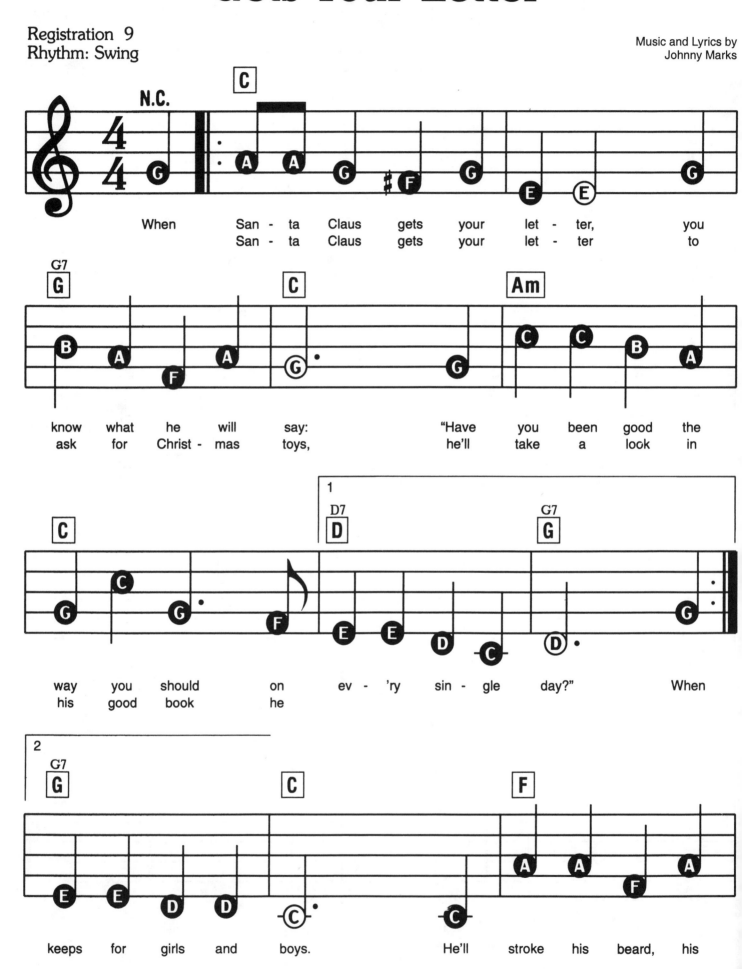

While Shepherds Watched Their Flocks

Registration 1
Rhythm: None

Words by Nahum Tate
Music by George Frideric Handel

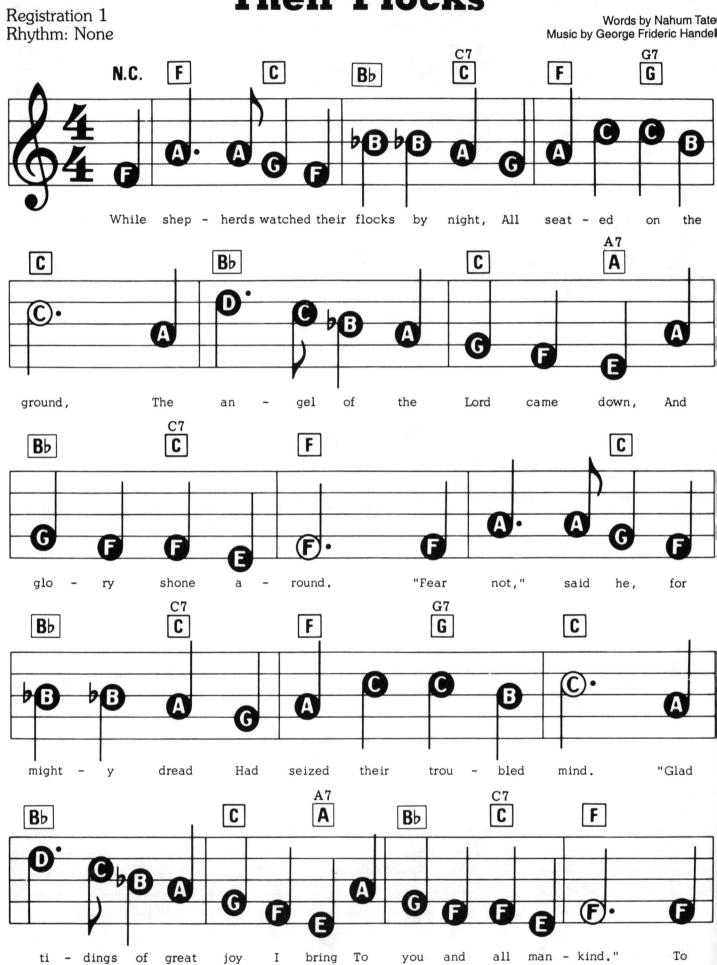

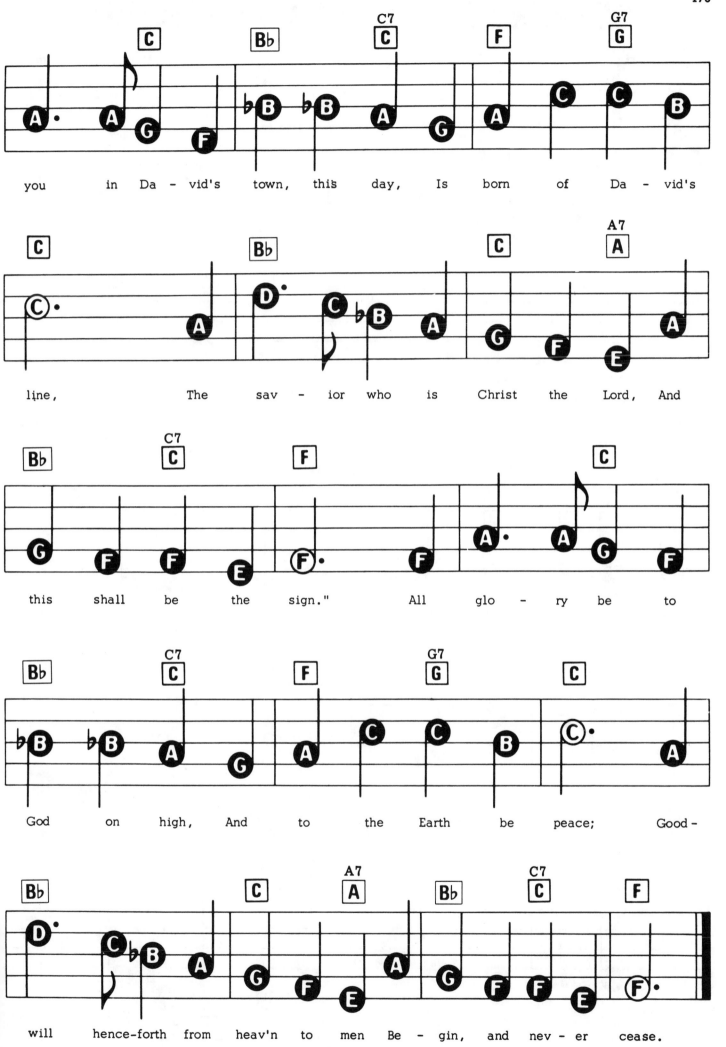

The White World of Winter

Registration 3
Rhythm: Fox Trot or Ballad

Words by Mitchell Parish
Music by Hoagy Carmichael

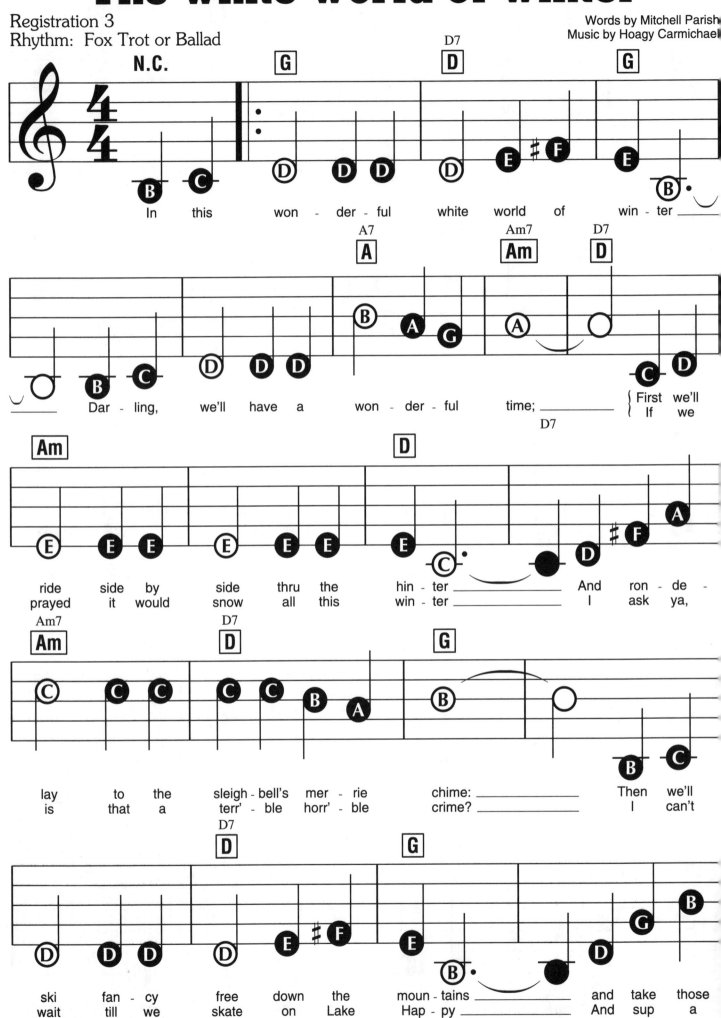

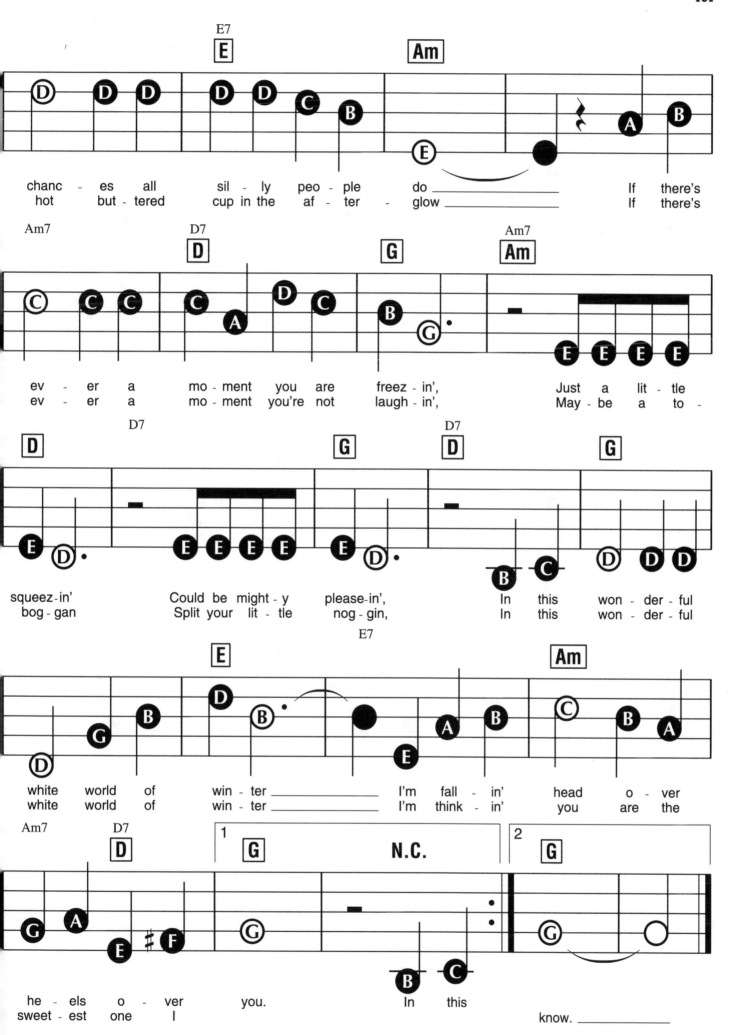

Who Would Imagine a King

from the Touchstone Motion Picture THE PREACHER'S WIFE

Registration 8
Rhythm: Waltz

Words and Music by Mervyn Warren
and Hallerin Hilton Hill

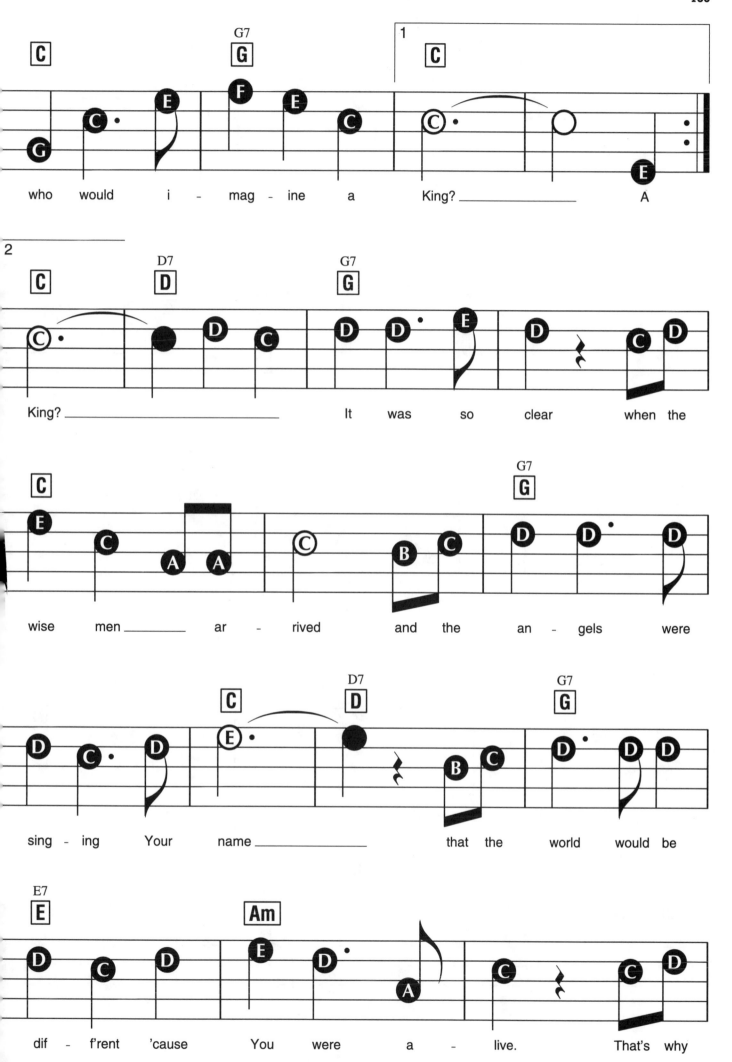

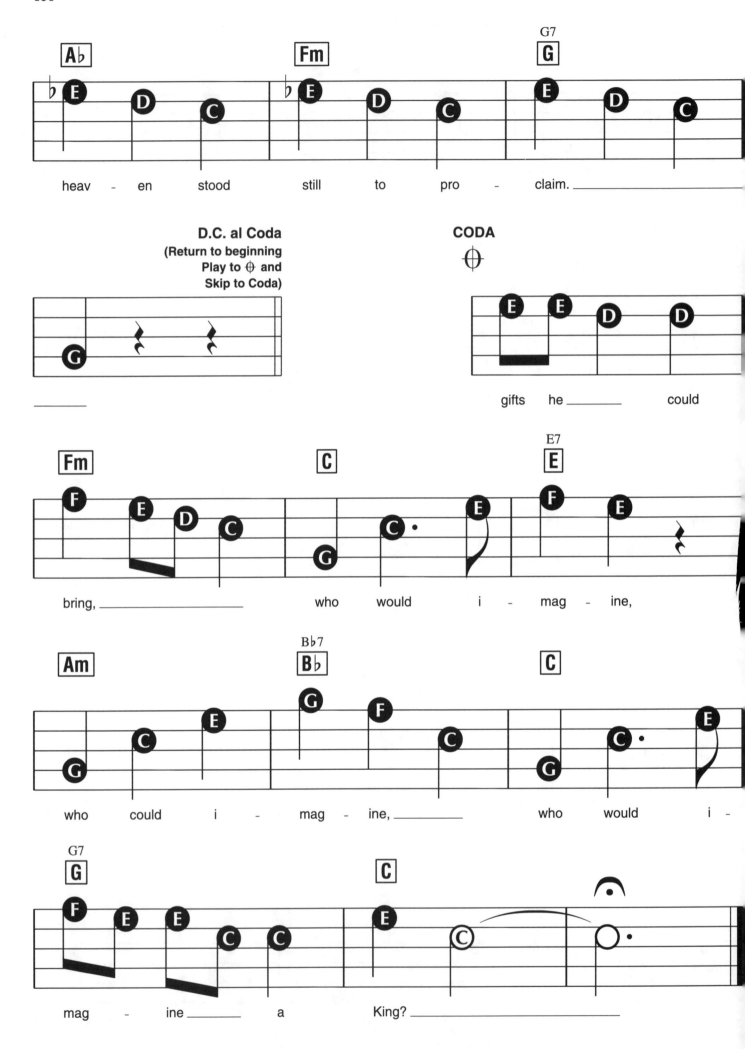

Wonderful Christmastime

Registration 3
Rhythm: Fox Trot

Words and Music by
McCartney

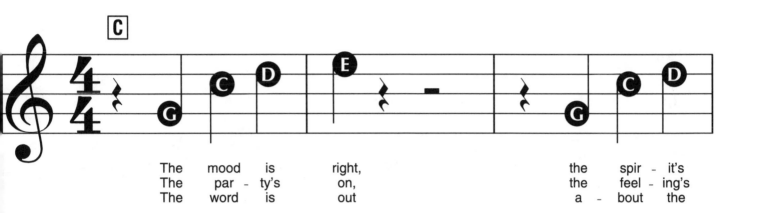

The mood is   right,   the   spir - it's
The   par - ty's   on,   the   feel - ing's
The   word   is   out   a - bout the

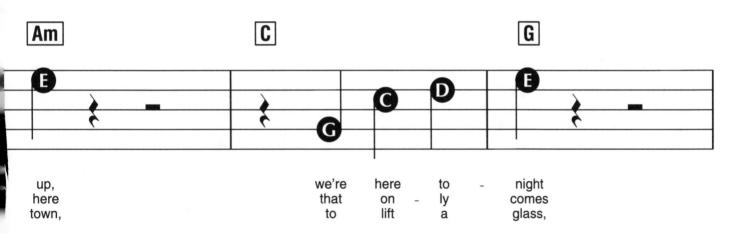

up,   we're here   to - night
here   that   on - ly   comes
town,   to   lift   a   glass,

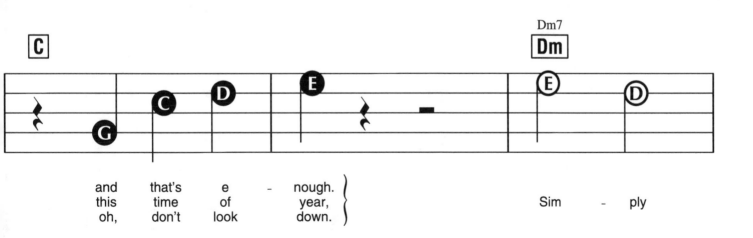

and   that's   e - nough.   Sim - ply
this   time   of   year,
oh,   don't   look   down.

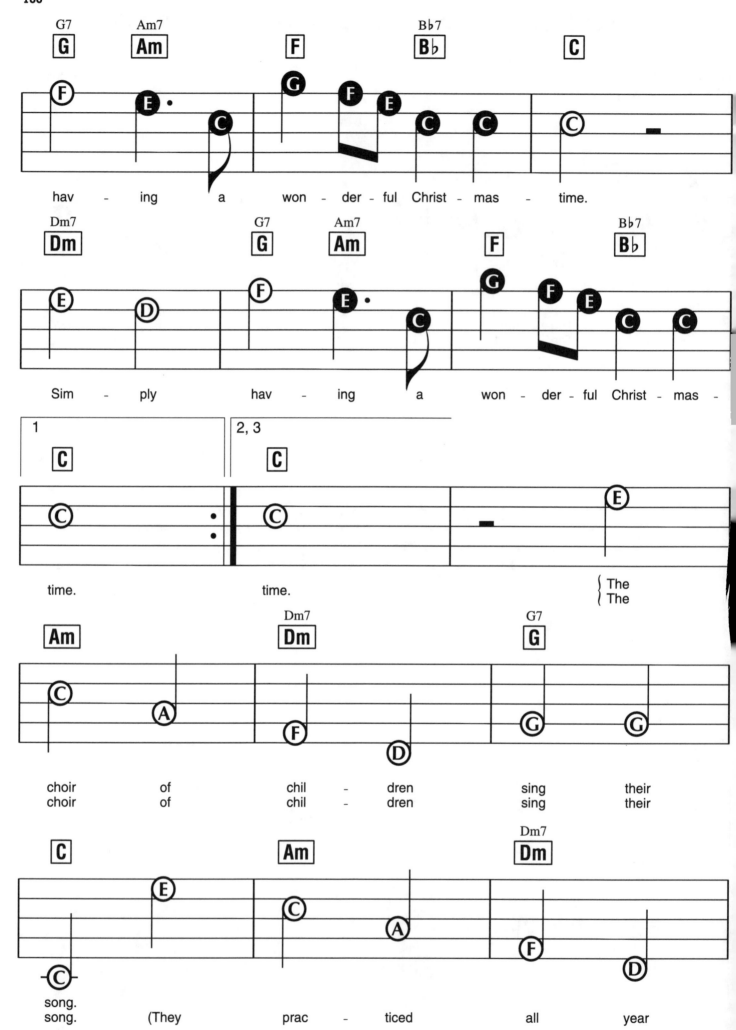

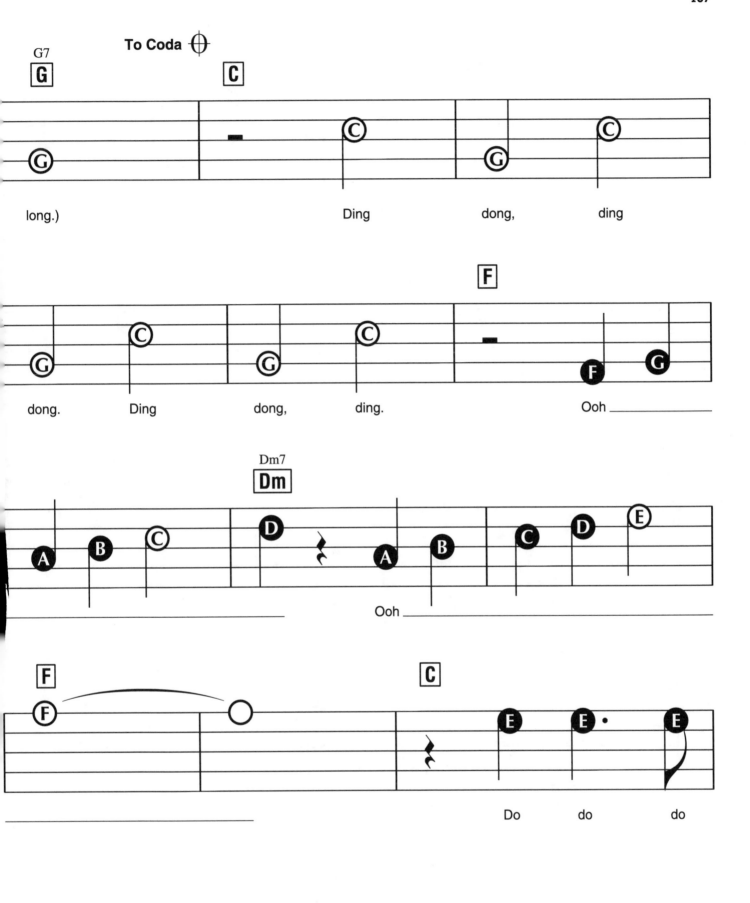

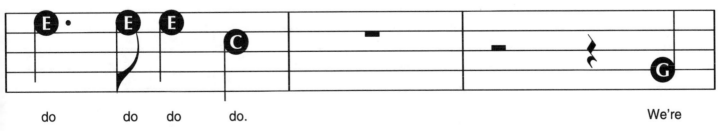

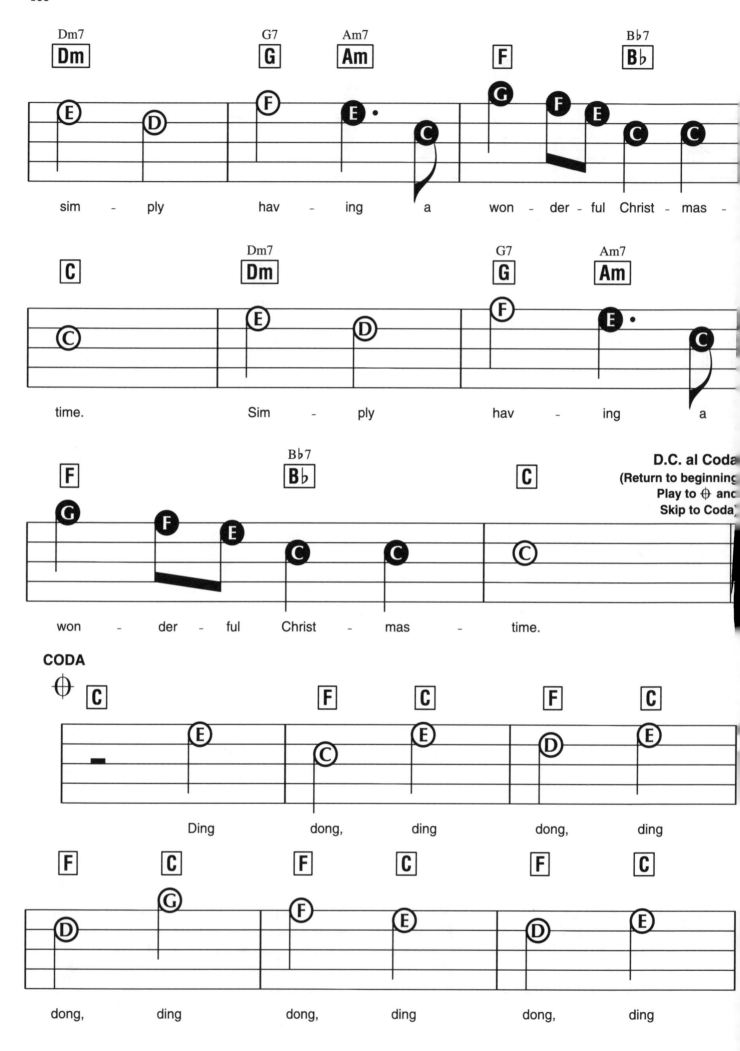

 **Registration Guide**

- Match the Registration number on the song to the corresponding numbered category below. Select and activate an instrumental sound available on your instrument.

- Choose an automatic rhythm appropriate to the mood and style of the song. (Consult your Owner's Guide for proper operation of automatic rhythm features.)

- Adjust the tempo and volume controls to comfortable settings.

Registration

1	Mellow	Flutes, Clarinet, Oboe, Flugel Horn, Trombone, French Horn, Organ Flutes
2	Ensemble	Brass Section, Sax Section, Wind Ensemble, Full Organ, Theater Organ
3	Strings	Violin, Viola, Cello, Fiddle, String Ensemble, Pizzicato, Organ Strings
4	Guitars	Acoustic/Electric Guitars, Banjo, Mandolin, Dulcimer, Ukulele, Hawaiian Guitar
5	Mallets	Vibraphone, Marimba, Xylophone, Steel Drums, Bells, Celesta, Chimes
6	Liturgical	Pipe Organ, Hand Bells, Vocal Ensemble, Choir, Organ Flutes
7	Bright	Saxophones, Trumpet, Mute Trumpet, Synth Leads, Jazz/Gospel Organs
8	Piano	Piano, Electric Piano, Honky Tonk Piano, Harpsichord, Clavi
9	Novelty	Melodic Percussion, Wah Trumpet, Synth, Whistle, Kazoo, Perc. Organ
10	Bellows	Accordion, French Accordion, Mussette, Harmonica, Pump Organ, Bagpipes